THE GENESIS OF INDUSTRIAL AMERICA, 1870–1920

This book offers a bold new interpretation of American business history during the formative years 1870–1920, which mark the dawn of modern big business. It focuses on four major revolutions that ushered in this new era: those in power, transportation, communication, and organization. Using the metaphor of America as an economic hothouse uniquely suited to rapid economic growth during these years, it analyzes the interplay of key factors such as entrepreneurial talent, technology, land, natural resources, law, mass markets, and the rise of cities. It also delineates the process that laid the foundation for the modern era, in which virtually every human activity became a business, and, in most cases, a big business. The book also profiles numerous major entrepreneurs whose careers and activities illustrate broader trends and themes. It utilizes a wide variety of sources, including novels from the period, to produce a lively narrative.

Maury Klein (B.A., Knox College; M.A., Ph.D., Emory University) has been a professor of history at the University of Rhode Island since 1964, receiving a Doctor of Humanities degree and the Distinguished Alumni Award from Knox College in 2001. Klein has been a Newcomen Fellow at Harvard Business School and held a Mellon Fellowship at Hagley Museum and Library. He has published thirteen books, and his numerous articles have appeared in *Forbes*, *City*, the *Wall Street Journal*, the *Washington Post*, *American History Illustrated*, *Sports Illustrated*, and *Civil War Times Illustrated*. Klein has also appeared in documentaries on the BBC and PBS, among other networks.

CAMBRIDGE ESSENTIAL HISTORIES

Editor
Donald T. Critchlow, *St. Louis University*

John Earl Haynes and Harvey Klehr, *Early Cold War Spies: The Espionage Trials That Shaped American Politics*

The Genesis of Industrial America, 1870–1920

MAURY KLEIN

University of Rhode Island

CAMBRIDGE
UNIVERSITY PRESS

CAMBRIDGE UNIVERSITY PRESS
Cambridge, New York, Melbourne, Madrid, Cape Town, Singapore, São Paulo, Delhi

Cambridge University Press
32 Avenue of the Americas, New York, NY 10013-2473, USA

www.cambridge.org
Information on this title: www.cambridge.org/9780521859783

First published 2007

Printed in the United States of America

A catalog record for this publication is available from the British Library.

Library of Congress Cataloging in Publication Data
Klein, Maury, 1939–
The genesis of industrial America, 1870–1920 / Maury Klein.
p.   cm. – (Cambridge essential histories)
Includes bibliographical references and index.
ISBN 978-0-521-85978-3 (hardback) – ISBN 978-0-521-67709-7 (pbk.)
1. United States – Economic conditions – 1865–1918.   2. Industrial revolution – United States –
History – 19th century.   3. Industrial revolution – United States – History – 20th century.
I. Title.   II. Series
HC105.K65   2007
330.973′05–dc22   2007005393

ISBN   978-0-521-85978-3 hardback
ISBN   978-0-521-67709-7 paperback

For Kim and Shannon, with love

Contents

Series Editor's Foreword

In the nineteenth century, the United States underwent a remarkable transformation from an economy based on the production of raw materials and subsistence agriculture to an expanding market economy. In this transformation, handicraft production was replaced by factory production; an elaborate canal system and, later, railroads supplanted a poor transportation system based on rivers and seasonal roads; and rural life began to give way to urban life. By the end of the nineteenth century, the United States had outdistanced England, France, and Germany in the rate of economic growth, per capita wealth, and general prosperity.

These changes were more than just material; they included a shift in mentality. Tried and true patterns of behavior no longer appeared to provide a true compass for responding to this market revolution. Social and cultural life had been reconfigured and continued to undergo startling changes. The only constant seemed to be change itself.

This tremendous growth presents to the student of history important and fascinating questions: How exactly did this happen? What explains American economic success? These questions have intrinsic value for understanding American history. The obvious explanation is that the United States was uniquely blessed with an abundance of natural resources, industrious and innovative people, and a political and legal system that encouraged economic growth, but there is more to the story.

At the center lay American business. Already in the nineteenth century, Europeans and Asians looked at American business for lessons to apply in their own countries. The genesis of the American economic miracle, as historian Maury Klein observes, lay in technological innovation that changed energy sources, transportation, and communication. These changes coincided with an organizational revolution in American business, as giant business firms and organizations revolutionized existing relationships in all aspects of American life – social, economic, cultural, and political. Underlying these profound changes was a more fundamental force: people. Klein presents a remarkable drama that includes a cast of visionaries who sensed the sweep of history, reactionaries who lamented the loss of a seemingly idyllic past, and others caught in the throes of historical transformation.

Donald T. Crithchlow
General Editor, Cambridge Essential Histories

Introduction

THE BUSINESS OF AMERICA

In democracies, nothing is more great or more brilliant than commerce; it attracts the attention of the public, and fills the imagination of the multitude; all energetic passions are directed towards it.

– Alexis de Tocqueville

Anyone who doubts the importance of business history should keep in mind this salient fact: It concerns not merely the history of business in the United States but even more the process by which business came to dominate every aspect of American life. Business is not simply an important element of American life; like it or not, it has become the dominant force in American culture. Try to think of a single human activity that has not been organized into a business of some kind, and in most cases a very large business.

This book is not a comprehensive history of American business. It is rather an interpretation of the most seminal period of that history and seeks to explain how business came to occupy the center stage of American life. The story begins with the most revolutionary process that the world has experienced. Industrialization remains the great divide in human history, separating past from present cultures, transforming values as well as life styles, leaving a monumental imprint on the environment, and setting in motion forces that drove its impact inexorably onward. It transcended ideologies, defied political strictures, ignored moral dictums, overturned social orders, and unraveled the fabric of tradition. In the process American industrialization created the infrastructure for what became the richest and most influential material civilization in history.

1

Industrialization occurred at a time and place ideally suited for rapid economic development. The United States after the Civil War was a hothouse for economic growth, one large enough to spawn giants and to absorb the excesses and aberrations that flowed from their creation. From this fertile seedbed grew three primary paths of innovation in the areas of power, transportation, and communication. These in turn nurtured the growth of large enterprises that forged complex industrial systems within a remarkably short time. It took only half a century for the United States to emerge as the largest and most dominant industrial society on the planet.

The industrial revolution made modern America, and the power revolution made industrialization possible. After 1800 new sources of fuel, most notably coal, gas, and oil, ushered in a new age of machines that created striking advances in the fundamental areas of transportation, production, communication, heating, and lighting. Their impact did more to change the material conditions of human life than had occurred in all prior human history. New technologies developed by an unprecedented generation of inventors and entrepreneurs drove this creation of the world's most advanced material civilization. "Historians looking back," wrote historian Thomas P. Hughes, "may well decide that the century of technological enthusiasm was the most characteristic and impressively achieving century in the nation's history, an era comparable to the Renaissance in Italian history, the era of Louis XIV in France, or the Victorian period in British history. During the century after 1870, Americans created the modern technological nation; this was the American genesis."

The steam engine launched the power revolution by liberating people from the ancient restraints of wind, wood, water, and muscle. From its development flowed the steamboat, the railroad, and a host of machines capable of performing work and producing goods on an unprecedented scale. The harnessing of electric power elevated this revolution to dizzying new heights, creating the most indispensable technology of the twentieth century. At the same time, the transportation revolution performed the seemingly impossible feat of opening up a vast continent rich in resources that were too remote to reach. The railroad became not only the engine of economic development but also the prototype for big business in all its many facets. Similarly, the communication revolution tied together the distant extremes of an enormous nation and expedited the flow of information just as the railroad had the flow of goods and people. More than that, the telegraph and the telephone redefined the meaning of time and space.

Together these three revolutions filled the American landscape with new cities, new enterprises, new peoples, and eventually a new kind of society. They also gave birth to a fourth primary force: the organizational revolution. The industrial economy came to be dominated increasingly by giant firms that threw all existing relationships with the government, the public, and their own workers out of balance. Indeed, their very existence confounded law and tradition alike with the lack of useful precedents for integrating them with other institutions. Viewed at first as anomalies, giant corporations became the harbingers of what evolved into a corporate society that was far more formalized, organized, and integrated than its predecessor.

The giant corporations did much more than reshape the business arena. Their presence spurred the growth of cities, widening the traditional gap between urban and rural life and shifting the balance of population toward the former. They fostered a social credo that came ever more to regard material goods as the primary source of happiness. From this economic hothouse that produced so dynamic a capital-goods economy there gradually emerged a second and more potent phase of growth: the consumer-goods economy with its dependence on mass production, marketing, advertising, and emphasis on defining status in terms of possessions. Lavishly decorated department stores became the most conspicuous temples of consumption, although the more modest chain stores and mail-order houses did far more business.

Not all Americans welcomed the growing legion of giant firms. Many shared the view of humorist Ambrose Bierce, who defined a corporation as "An ingenious device for obtaining individual profit without individual responsibility." Their presence and proliferation generated a national debate on the virtues and vices of bigness. From this clash arose a new and unsettled relationship between government and business, one filled with ambiguities and complexities that reflected the public's own mixed feelings about the new economic and social orders. Amid changing conditions businessmen were alternately elevated to the status of social heroes and cast out as pariahs. However, like it or not, the corporate economy and the organizational society had come to stay. So far reaching was the business ethos that by the end of the twentieth century it had permeated every corner of American life.

When Calvin Coolidge declared that the business of America was business, he uttered the fundamental truth of twentieth-century history. The broadest and most profound movement of the past century has been the irresistible tendency to transform every aspect of American life first into a business and then into a larger business. This metamorphosis began with the coming of industrialization and the rise of big business, which is the story this little book seeks to tell in brief. It departs from conventional business history in seeking to show the pervasive role of business in the broader society and culture. One example of this approach can be seen in the discussion of city bosses in Chapter 7. They offer one example of how politics, like everything else, became a business. In this sense business history serves as a primary doorway to understanding American civilization.

Prologue

A HOTHOUSE FOR ECONOMIC GROWTH

Americans are constantly driven to engage in commerce and industry. Their origin, their social condition, their political institutions, and even the region they inhabit urge them irresistibly in this direction. Their present condition, then, is that of an almost exclusively manufacturing and commercial association, placed in the midst of a new and boundless continent, which their principal object is to explore for purposes of profit. This is the characteristic that most distinguishes the American people from all others at the present time.

– Alexis de Tocqueville

THIS OBSERVATION, MADE DURING THE 1830S BY ONE OF THE most astute foreign observers of American life, could not have been more accurate. Since the founding of the Republic in 1789 the business of Americans has always been business, though for most people in those early years that task amounted to little more than scratching a living from the soil. Yet even the earliest settlers, despite all the hardships they had to endure, grasped the potential and sheer bounty of the new world that had become their home. It was in every respect a land of abundance, and one major American historian, David M. Potter, argued persuasively that economic abundance has been the dominant characteristic of American life. Thomas Dale, the governor of Virginia, observed in 1611 what would become a common theme when he said of his colony, "Take foure of the best kindgomes in Christendome and put them all together, they may no way compare with this countrie either for commodities or goodness of soil."

The United States always possessed the potential to become an enormous hothouse for economic growth. But resources alone were not enough; it took human enterprise and ingenuity to turn them into usable goods.

A host of factors during the nineteenth century transformed the potential of nature's abundance into a reality that would have astonished earlier generations. By century's end the nation, having survived the horrors and disruptions of civil war, managed to create the largest, most productive economy on the planet. In the process it also changed the way people lived in ways that forever separated them from all the generations that had come before.

One way to grasp this change is to think of the United States in the nineteenth century as an economic hothouse. A hothouse is an artificial environment in which plants can be grown under ideal conditions. The American economy, or at least its potential, had always been robust even in its natural state. It offered newcomers staggering amounts of land teeming with resources ranging from thick forests to ample quantities of game and fish to mineral ores. Nature provided a plentiful supply of water, fertile soil, and a variety of climates for growing crops. Hard work and dogged perseverance was required to wrest a living from this strange and often hostile world, but the resources for success were always there. Without them no amount of diligence and ambition could have transformed the wilderness into an economic powerhouse. Without diligence and ambition little would have been done with the most abundant supply of resources.

When the American nation was born, it consisted overwhelmingly of family farms. More than 72 percent of all workers toiled on farms, and only about 5 percent of Americans lived in towns or villages of more than 2,500 people. Most goods were made at home for family use. Artisans did most of the modest manufacturing outside the home along with workers at shipyards and ropewalks, candle makers, and rum distillers. Industry scarcely existed. Virginia had the only working coal mines, and their output scarcely reached a thousand tons a year. Some iron was produced, largely on special plantations, but other metals had to be imported. The general merchant remained the dominant business figure in the economy, serving as financier, distributor, arranger of transportation, and, in league with his fellow merchants, insurer of ships and cargos. In the few cities a sprinkling of shopkeepers emerged. Most of them bought their goods from the general merchants, who sold at both wholesale and retail.

These early generations of Americans reshaped the wilderness into their own vision of civilization. By 1800 their world had come a long way from the first primitive settlements in the early seventeenth century. Forests, their supply of game depleted, had been converted into tidy fields or large plantations, the native Americans subdued or alienated, the imported black people fastened into the chains of slavery, and the population of European immigrants and their descendents growing steadily. Two tiny settlements had mushroomed into thirteen states, and restless pioneers poured across the Appalachian Mountains into the back country, planting the seeds for national expansion by repeating the scenario of converting wilderness into civilization.

As the nation grew larger, problems of transportation and communication grew greater. As the population increased, so did the demand for goods and materials. As the economy expanded, it became more specialized. Growth created political strains as well. If the Constitution created a new American nation in place of a weak Confederation, Thomas Jefferson's purchase of Louisiana in 1803 gave that nation a future it had scarcely dreamed of: the potential to occupy the entire continent. Embracing 529 million acres of land, the purchase more than doubled the size of the United States. Some people doubted whether one government could effectively represent or control even its existing amount of territory, let alone this enormous addition.

The United States had been created a mere fourteen years earlier by a document that gained approval only by sweeping several key issues such as slavery and secession under the rug. Influential people in New England and elsewhere still harbored separatist ambitions. The political and economic desires of New England often clashed with those of the southern states led by Virginia. The region west of the Appalachian Mountains amounted to a wild card in the nation's destiny, perpetually upsetting the balance of power between the original northern and southern states. As settlers poured into its lands, many easterners doubted the ability of the new government to organize or rule the area effectively. They also saw in the rise of new western states a dilution of their own political influence. Their fears were compounded by the presence of foreign powers on every side: the British in Canada, the Spanish in Louisiana (before Napoleon returned it to French control) and Florida, and the French in the Caribbean.

Surprisingly, the Louisiana Purchase did not sate the American appetite for growth even though its huge expanse took decades to digest. Rather it unleashed in Americans a comparable lust for expansion and empire that continued unabated through the nineteenth century. This pattern of rapid growth, fed by a buoyant ideology that came to be popularly known as "Manifest Destiny," bred conflict and soon exposed a glaring clash between American ideals and ambitions, one that gnawed deeply at Jefferson's soul from the beginning. It demonstrated that to many if not most Americans, expansion and acquisition, for all the agonizing and hand wringing that accompanied it, mattered more than anything else.

Among other things the Louisiana transaction compelled Jefferson to go against his own deeply held belief as to the limits of federal power under the Constitution. At a time when the infant nation was struggling to turn its new founding framework into a working system, the purchase provoked a constitutional crisis by undermining the position of those who advocated a strict construction of the document. That a president who had always been a strict constructionist reversed his position so blatantly in the case of the purchase made the effect even more telling. The precedent of this broader approach to interpreting the Constitution proved crucial in the nation's future growth and development. It also opened the door to later expansion of executive power.

Nor was that all. The Louisiana Purchase also sowed the seeds for an expansion of slavery and with it the rise of secessionist theory that ultimately brought to an explosive head the differences between North and South already evident at the dawn of the century. It helped deliver much of the prime land of the South into the hands of planters rather than yeoman farmers, thereby fastening the institution of slavery onto the region. The fragility of American nationalism, so painfully apparent at the time of the purchase, mutated into an even greater and more potent schism during that next half century. With the purchase began a pattern in which expansion inflamed differences between the sections and often provoked political crises ranging from the Missouri controversy of 1819 to the debate over slavery in the territories that followed the Mexican War. It also accelerated the pressure to remove those Indian tribes that occupied land coveted by settlers and planters.

The Louisiana Purchase had still another long-term consequence. Unwittingly it fashioned a precedent for the creation of a republic that embraced diversity with all its strains and dangers. The acquisition of New Orleans with its Creole, French-speaking, Catholic population brought into the United States a culture unlike any other. Whatever diversity already existed in American culture paled in comparison with this new addition to the national mix. During the nineteenth century this pattern of adding new cultures continued at an ever accelerating pace but with a significant difference. Immigrants to the United States brought their strange customs, languages, and values into an unfamiliar setting; Louisiana's residents brought to the Union the place or source of their exotica as well, as did the Southwest territories wrested from Mexico later in the century.

But all these developments lay in the future. At bottom the Louisiana Purchase revealed yet again the willingness of Americans to embrace economic opportunity in the short term regardless of what long-term consequences might ensue. Opportunity was the magic word. As early as the 1770s Hector St. John de Crèvecoeur, a transplanted Frenchman living in Orange County, New York, articulated the essence of what became known as the American Dream:

> There is room for everybody in America: has he any particular talent, or industry? he exerts it in order to produce a livelihood, and it succeeds. Is he a merchant? the avenues of trade are infinite; is he eminent in any respect? he will be employed and respected. Does he love a country life? pleasant farms present themselves; he may purchase what he wants, and thereby become an American farmer. Is he a labourer, sober and industrious? he need not go many miles . . . before he will be hired, well fed at the table of his employer, and paid four or five times more than he can get in Europe. Does he want uncultivated lands? thousands of acres present themselves, which he may purchase cheap.

Nor was Crèvecoeur alone in this view. In 1815 Hezekiah Niles, proprietor of the influential *Niles Weekly Register*, noted the "almost *universal ambition to get forward*" among his countrymen. How different this was, he thought, from the Englishman, where "once a journeyman weaver always a journeyman weaver." In the United States, Niles reported, "one half of our wealthy men, over 45 years of age, were once common day laborers or journeymen, or otherwise very humble in their circumstances when they began." More than a decade later Tocqueville noticed the same characteristic. Americans, he declared, were "haunted by visions of what will be." To that end they were willing to take up any calling or work. "Americans therefore change their means of gaining a livelihood very readily," added

Tocqueville, "and they suit their occupations to the exigencies of the moment. . . . No natural boundary seems to be set to the efforts of man; and in his eyes what is not yet done is only what he has not attempted to do."

From the very first this desire to make a new life, to get ahead, lay at the core of American values. Freedom and liberty mattered greatly, but freedom to do what, if not to better one's material lot in life? To worship the god of one's choice counted for much, but even those fleeing religious persecution were eager to improve their social and material standing as well. No one ever accused the Puritans of a lack of ambition or acquisitiveness. In their rush to get ahead, only a few Americans cared or even thought about what effects their actions of today might have on tomorrow or the next day. And the American environment encouraged this way of doing things. If farmers exhausted the soil or chopped down a forest, they need only move farther west to find fresh soil or new forests. In this manner they depleted the resources of whole regions in a remarkably short time.

Slavery offered a prime example of this pattern. It did not arrive in America full-blown but rather evolved gradually into an institution designed to serve immediate economic needs. As it became clear that certain crops, most notably cotton, tobacco, and rice, could be grown profitably in large quantities, planters organized plantations to produce on scale. However, plantations or even smaller farms required a reliable labor force. Indentured servants, whose lot was not far removed from slavery, proved inadequate to the need. Their term of service expired at some point, and many ran away before that time to start their own life in some distant place. White indentured servants simply vanished into the population, but black servants could not. Eventually the status of black servants mutated by law into the institution of slavery in those states where captive labor was needed even though the arrangement ran counter to the most basic American principles. Other states abolished slavery (but not their prejudice against black people), thereby setting the stage for the worst and most enduring conflict in American history.

Put another way, slavery began as a solution to a short-term labor problem and escalated into a rigid, archaic institution grounded in racial as well as economic issues. Few early Americans imagined even remotely the nightmare it would become. Slavery also became widespread because of another crucial element in the creation of the American economic hothouse: technology. The invention of the cotton gin by Eli Whitney made it possible to grow short-stem cotton profitably on a grand scale. Short-stem cotton had a shorter growing season than long-stem cotton and thus could be grown in many more areas of the South. However, it had to be cleaned of seed and lint. By hand it took a worker an entire day to clean one pound of cotton; a gin increased that output to fifty pounds a day. Within a short time cotton came to dominate the southern economy. From a crop of two million pounds in 1791 the supply of cotton ballooned to nearly a billion pounds by 1860. Between 1815 and 1860 cotton made up more than half the total value of all American exports, leading some southerners to boast that "Cotton is king."

The role of technology in creating the cotton kingdom went far beyond the cotton gin. Where the gin dramatically increased the supply of cotton, new machinery for spinning and weaving cotton revolutionized the production of cloth and generated an enormous demand for cotton to feed the growing number of textile mills in Great Britain and the United States. Powered at first by water, the looms came gradually to employ newly devised steam engines. This process in turn gave rise to large factories in which cloth could be manufactured in unheard of quantities. Farm machinery and a host of new inventions gave rise to a similar expansion of food crops, and sawmills powered by steam engines proliferated at a rapid rate to reduce whole forests to lumber. The steam engine also transformed transportation through its use in the locomotive and the steamboat.

Technology thus became an indispensable factor. It was by its very nature a wild card in that neither its products nor its effects could be predicted. New inventions had the ability to send economic development shooting off in unexpected directions, especially when entrepreneurs took hold of them and worked tirelessly to realize their potential. But new technologies and ambitious businessmen required other key elements as well. To flourish, the economic hothouse also needed congenial financial, political, legal, and social environments. These critical components developed at an uneven pace during the first half of the nineteenth century.

The expansion of trade and the growth of business enterprises led (indeed compelled) some merchants to specialize in finance. After 1815 the most powerful financiers in the nation became those merchants who had been most prominent in moving cotton overseas and importing finished goods from abroad. To expedite their work, a banking network gradually emerged. The first bank to receive a charter opened in Philadelphia in

1781. In 1815 the nation had 206 chartered banks; by 1860 the number had increased to 1,562. During that same period the number of life insurance companies jumped from four to forty-three. Like the banks, insurance companies provided capital for long-term investments, especially mortgages. Increased production meant that new markets had to be found for the growing flow of goods. To reach new markets, transportation had to be improved, and this required larger sums of money than individual investors could provide. In some cases states funded these projects; otherwise groups of individuals pooled their resources through a device that became one of the most important elements of the economic hothouse: the corporation.

From these efforts emerged striking improvements in moving goods and people. On land better roads and turnpikes, many of them privately built, provided some relief, but their contribution ultimately paled before that offered by a stunning new technology: the railroad. To a lesser extent the steamboat did for water transportation what the railroad brought to land movement, and a series of canals created "water roads" connecting once distant lakes and rivers. The first and most spectacular of these projects, the Erie Canal, became the inspiration for numerous imitators, none of which equaled its success. All these improvements led to the emergence of men and companies who specialized in transporting goods. They also resulted in something new to transportation that later generations would take for granted: the creation of regular schedules.

By the eve of the Civil War these changes had planted the seeds of dramatic economic change, but they had not yet taken deep root. The United States in 1860 had 31.5 million people, including 4.1 million blacks of whom 3.8 million were slaves. Only two cities had populations above 500,000, and only nine exceeded 100,000 people. Of the nation's 10.5 million workers, 6.2 million toiled on farms. The federal government employed only 36,672 people, of whom 27,958 or 76 percent belonged to the military. Slightly over half of American children were enrolled in schools. By 1860 the country possessed 30,626 miles of railroad, but none reached beyond the Missouri River. During that year some 3,676 businesses failed, a rate of 21.7 per thousand firms, and hopeful inventors filed 7,653 applications for patents, of which 4,357 were granted. Southerners produced 1.74 billion pounds of cotton, 1.23 billion of which went to Great Britain.

The American economy remained one dominated overwhelmingly by farms and plantations in the country and shops and mills in cities, towns, and villages. Even people of modest means could afford the relatively cheap start-up costs of farming. Most businesses were managed directly by their owner, who relied on traditional tools such as double-entry bookkeeping to track their activity. Larger firms continued to be partnerships rather than corporations in most cases because they did not yet need the advantages provided by the latter. A few notable exceptions like the Springfield Armory and some larger textile mills developed more advanced organizational innovations that helped create what came to be known as the "American system of manufacturing." As historian David A. Hounshell has observed, this approach combined "the idea of uniformity or interchangeability of parts . . . with the notion that machines could make things as good and as fast as man's hands, or even better." It also developed new methods of internal accounting, inventory, and quality control.

Mechanization came gradually to the production of firearms, machine tools, metalworking machinery, axes, shovels, and sewing machines. The first reapers appeared early in the 1830s; during the next three decades other farm implements such as the first threshers, the steel plow, disk harrow, binder, and twine knotter helped expand the output of farmers. Railroads continued to extend lines throughout the nation although their tracks often did not connect to each other's roads. None of the six lines reaching Richmond, Virginia, for example, touched each other. When Abraham Lincoln reached Baltimore on his way to Washington for the inauguration, his railroad car had to be hauled by horse from the President Street depot of the Philadelphia, Wilmington & Baltimore Railroad to the Camden Street station of the Baltimore & Ohio Railroad. In many areas of business and economic life Americans could point with pride to clear signs of progress, but many obstacles still slowed the pace of economic growth, especially in the political and legal realms.

The Civil War became the catalyst that unleashed the full potential of the economic hothouse. For thirty years Americans had locked horns over slavery, expansion, the tariff, internal improvements, and other issues. This interminable wrangling created deep pools of bitterness and resentment that alienated northerners from southerners. The war swept away these political embroilments that had absorbed so much attention and energy for so long. As historian Louis M. Hacker put it, "the war freed men of the obsessive involvement in politics; the war, in fact, cleared the air everywhere." Above all, it destroyed the power of the southern planter class and elevated the Republican party to undisputed control of the federal government. The age of Calhoun, Clay, and Webster gave way to that of Carnegie, Gould, and Rockefeller.

Once in power, the Republican party pursued policies conducive to rapid industrialization that southern congressmen had resisted for years. During the war new legislation reformed the national bank system, provided a homestead act, restored the protective tariff, established land-grant colleges, enabled the construction of a transcontinental railroad, and encouraged immigration. The legal system also contributed by narrowing the range of government interference in business, promoting bankruptcy laws favorable to debtors, and generally widening the range of individual activity in the economy. As legal historian J. Willard Hurst wrote, "From about 1800 to 1870 we can see a pattern of surprisingly deliberate and self-conscious policy . . . that law should increase men's liberty by enlarging their practical range of options in the face of limiting circumstances."

The war also created fertile soil for a rising generation of entrepreneurs. Many of the business titans of the late nineteenth century established their business careers during the war and took care to avoid interrupting it with military duty. Instead they profited from the bonanza of opportunities offered by the wartime demand for goods and services. A sampling of those who drew both capital and experience from the business of war includes Philip D. Armour, George F. Baker, Andrew Carnegie, A. J. Cassatt, Michael Cudahy, Charles Deere, William E. Dodge, Marshall Field, Jay Gould, Marcus Hanna, James J. Hill, August Juilliard, J. P. Morgan, Frederick Pabst, Charles A. Pillsbury, George M. Pullman, John D. Rockefeller, H. H. Rogers, Clement Studebaker, Gustavus Swift, John Wanamaker, Frederick Weyerhauser, William C. Whitney, Peter Widener, and Charles T. Yerkes. These and other entrepreneurs were all between the ages of seventeen and thirty in 1861 but disdained military service in favor of business opportunities.

At the war's end, hundreds of thousands of former soldiers were eager to start their careers and willing to roam the continent in search of possibilities. They became the work force for the industrial and agricultural miracles that followed and were soon joined by a rising tide of immigrants. Although reconstruction of the South dragged on until 1877, the nation had long since turned its attention elsewhere. Tired of bloodshed and the sacrifices demanded by war, most Americans eagerly embraced the more personal goal of getting ahead in life. The entire continent seemed to be opening up for exploitation. Completion of the Central Pacific–Union Pacific line in May 1869 enabled people to reach the Great Plains and distant California by rail for the first time. Other transcontinental roads soon followed, bringing with them settlement and development.

By 1870 the economic hothouse was in full flower and expanding its output. Within thirty years it produced an economy and business environment radically different from anything that had existed earlier. Industrialization literally changed the face, the nature, the society, and the values of America. This process of change involved ten primary factors constantly interacting with one another:

1. Power-driven machinery replaced human and animal muscle as a source of energy for doing all kinds of work.
2. Technological innovations infiltrated every area of business and economic activity, greatly increasing productivity and expanding the range of goods.
3. Production increased in scale by moving from scattered homes and shops to factories or other centrally located facilities.
4. A transportation revolution regularized and speeded up the flow of goods and people.
5. A communications revolution regularized and speeded up the flow of information, enabling firms to do business across the nation while maintaining a centrally located headquarters.
6. A full-blown market economy emerged and extended its reach beyond the local level to regional and national levels.
7. An organizational revolution restructured American business enterprise, enabling it to reach unprecedented size and scale of operation.
8. Specialization came to characterize nearly every aspect of economic activity.
9. Population increased at unprecedented rates.
10. The number of cities and towns increased sharply, as did the proportion of Americans living in them.

Together these factors, coupled with the sweeping changes in the political, social, and legal landscape, brought the American hothouse to full bloom, though at a cost that proved far greater than anyone had imagined. The toll taken by spectacular economic growth ranged from environmental devastation to resource depletion, corrosion of basic American values, dehumanization of the workplace, and a peculiar warping of the American Dream itself. Early in the century Tocqueville caught a glimpse of this last process already eating its way into the American character:

> It is strange to see with what feverish ardor the Americans pursue their own welfare, and to watch the vague dread that constantly torments them lest they should not have chosen the shortest path which may lead to it. A native of the United States clings to this world's goods as if he were certain never to die; and he is so hasty in grasping at all within his reach that one would suppose he was constantly afraid of not living long enough to enjoy them. . . . At first sight there is something surprising in this strange unrest of so many happy men, restless in the midst of abundance.

1

The Marvel of Men and Machines

The life of America is not the life it was twenty years ago. It is not the life it was ten years ago. We have changed our economic conditions from top to bottom, and with our economic conditions has changed also the organization of our life.

– Woodrow Wilson

TWO CRUCIAL ELEMENTS COMBINED TO FOSTER THE RAPID expansion of industrialization: an army of freshly minted entrepreneurs and a stunning array of new technologies that literally changed the face of America. The two were inseparable and indispensable to each other. For alert entrepreneurs, new technologies became not only the key to whatever industry they entered but also the source of a multiplier effect that increased both the scale of their operation and the size of their fortunes. However, technologies could develop only when entrepreneurs sensed their potential, took hold of them, and employed them in ways that ultimately embedded them as the foundation of the American way of production. This mutual dependence proved a potent catalyst for rapid economic expansion.

This interaction between men and machines also produced a profound change in the way people looked at the world around them. Machines do not suddenly knock at society's door and ask to be put to work; nor can they be ordered to their tasks like obedient servants. Their presence in growing numbers, and their increasing productivity and sophistication, required dramatic changes in the structure of the economic system, and these in turn wrought unexpected changes in society itself. By the turn of the century the impact of machines had penetrated every corner of American life. From this new relationship between people and machines

17

emerged a new way of looking at the world, one that embodied the deeper implications of technology. It involved a growing, ultimately overriding concern with technique as well as technology.

Philosopher Robert K. Merton viewed technique as "any complex of standardized means for attaining a predetermined result. Thus, it converts spontaneous and unreflective behavior into behavior that is deliberate and rationalized.... The Technical Man is ... committed to the never-ending search for 'the one best way' to achieve any designated objective."

To some extent the advent of machinery compelled this sort of thinking by forcing people to rearrange their economic system around the capacities of each mechanical marvel, and to accept the likelihood that each new wonder would soon give way to an even better version or be rendered obsolete by some yet unknown replacement technology. In this sense every new machine could be regarded as an agent of both progress and disruption.

The key to understanding the role of technique lies in the terms "efficiency" and "one best way." Industrialism is at bottom a system of production. To operate profitably it must find the most efficient means (i.e., the one best way) of carrying out every function from the broadest strategy to the smallest operating detail. It should hardly be surprising, then, that the industrial world became engrossed with technique. Indeed, many of the great American businessmen considered it the fountainhead of success. As the industrial era unfolded, this passion for technique and efficiency tended to blur the distinction between ends and means. Technique originated as a means for achieving some end; it was a tool and nothing more. As the industrial system matured, however, technique gradually became an end in itself – a field of study, a specialty to which people devoted great amounts of time and resources.

Over time, in a subtle manner, this attention shifted the emphasis from "why" something should be done to "how" it could best be done. This proved to be a profound shift because a technical or "how to" decision is quantitative; it shirks any broader moral or philosophical questions involved. "Best" comes to be equated with "most efficient" way to perform the task at hand without inquiring into the broader consequences or even whether the task needs to be performed at all. Through this process the emphasis on technique gave rise to what became known as the "engineering mentality." It was no accident that engineers emerged as one of the elite professions in the late nineteenth century, or that the gospel of technique benefited from the growing influence of science in American life. By the late nineteenth century, Americans in virtually every profession proclaimed their intention of making a "science" of the field or taking a "scientific" approach to their work.

The gospel of scientific efficiency found its most persuasive voice in Frederick W. Taylor, whose *Principles of Scientific Management* (1911) became a landmark in the quest for the one best way. "Taylor's fundamental concept and guiding principle," wrote historian Thomas P. Hughes, "was to design a system of production involving both men and machines that would be as efficient as a well-designed, well-oiled machine." For a time Taylorism became the rage among some companies with its emphasis on piecework and detailed analysis of performing every function by breaking it down into simple steps to be done within a specified period of time. Often lampooned for his demands, Taylor actually sought to reorganize not just the production process but the entire factory environment for maximum efficiency. Critics denounced him for removing the human element from the process and trying to turn men into mindless machines. It was a charge that would later be hurled at Henry Ford.

The Men

Economists and economic historians, entangled in their elaborate webs of data and statistics, sometimes forget the critical role of individuals in forging the growth of American business. As often happens, some elements and components, in this case the human side of the growth equation, turn out to be important if not decisive even though their contributions cannot be measured. As Thomas P. Hughes emphasized, "Inventors, industrial scientists, engineers, and system builders have been the makers of modern America. The values of order, system, and control that they embedded in machines, devices, processes, and systems have become the values of modern technological culture." Above all, they implanted in American culture a pattern of constant, accelerating change that became most people's definition of progress. One new machine spawned the creation of a dozen others along with improved versions of itself. The resulting stream of innovations affected every detail of daily life from cooking and other routine chores to reading to bathing.

But Hughes omitted one crucial type from his roster: the entrepreneurs. They were to industrialization what the Founding Fathers were to the creation of the American nation. Without them the inventor would have been hard pressed to develop, produce, or find a market for his creation, and industrial scientists, engineers, and system builders would have had no large corporations to hire their services or fund their work. "The organization of the American economy, since its beginning, has been centered around the contribution of the individual following his own interests and motives," declared economist Jonathan R. T. Hughes. "There are no 'forces of history.' . . . Men make economic change." The late-nineteenth-century entrepreneurs generated more economic change than had occurred in all human history. In the process they also changed the way such change proceeded.

Labeled everything from "Captains of Industry" to "Robber Barons" to "Industrial Statesmen," the entrepreneurs remain controversial because Americans have always been conflicted over whether to admire what these men did more than despise them for how they did it. However, no one disputes their role in shaping and overseeing the transformation of the American economy into a juggernaut of wealth and productivity. They became the primary agents of change in American life. Economist Joseph Schumpeter described the characteristic task of the entrepreneur as consisting "precisely in breaking up old, and creating new, tradition." They built the towering new enterprises that came to dominate the American economic landscape. So well did they perform this task that their efforts changed forever the ground rules by which the game of business was played.

What is an entrepreneur? In recent years the term, like many others, has nearly been stripped of meaning by overuse and misuse. The French originally used it to describe men who led military expeditions and other types of adventurers. Other writers assigned it different meanings. In 1815 Jean Baptiste Say defined an entrepreneur as one who brought the factors of production together. For the next several decades, emerging economic theory focused on the measurable aspects of economic activity and paid little attention to the human element. Since most businesses were small, family-operated firms, they offered outsiders little insight into any entrepreneurial role in their development. After 1870, however, the dramatic growth of large corporations in the United States prompted some American economists to look more closely at the role of the men who created these enterprises. As early as 1882 Frederick B. Hawley singled out risk taking as the distinctive role of the entrepreneur, a point later elaborated by economist John R. Commons. However, it proved to be a

German economist, Joseph A. Schumpeter, who developed the concept and reintroduced his brethren to the part played by actual human beings in economic activity.

In a number of works beginning in 1911, Schumpeter emphasized the role of individual initiative over abstract forces in economic development. "The carrying out of new combinations we call 'enterprise,'" he wrote; "the individuals whose function it is to carry them out we call entrepreneurs." Innovation was the hallmark of an entrepreneur, who either did new things or did old things in a new way. Put another way, entrepreneurship was a function rather than a condition or a profession. "Everyone is an entrepreneur," he said, "only when he actually 'carries out new combinations,' and loses that character as soon as he has built up his business, when he settles down to running it as other people run their businesses." When this transition occurred, the entrepreneur turned into a manager performing an entirely different function.

The entrepreneur performed five kinds of activity. He or she might introduce some new type or quality of goods or some new method of production, open some new market, acquire some new source of raw materials or partly finished manufactured products, or impose some new form of organization on an industry. The key element in each case was innovation, the doing of either something new or something old in a new way. The entrepreneur was neither a manager, a capitalist, nor an inventor. The last created things but became an entrepreneur only if and when he had the ability to produce or market or make a business out of his invention. Thomas A. Edison managed to do this when he not only invented the first commercial incandescent light bulb but turned it into the core of a new industry by developing an entire power system.

This function made the entrepreneur an agent of change, and people did not always welcome change. Most people ground their lives in patterns of habit and routine, which Schumpeter and others saw as the primary obstacle to innovation. "Past economic periods govern the activity of the individual," he wrote in a memorable passage. "All the preceding periods have . . . entangled him in a net of social and economic connections which he cannot easily shake off. They have bequeathed him definite means and methods of production. All these hold him in iron fetters fast in his tracks." Entrepreneurs were a special type because they disturbed people by disrupting the familiar, and their actions often got rewarded with resentment and hostility.

This powerful urge toward routine was an enemy of original thinking or insight because it prevented people from looking at things in a different light. "Everything we think, feel, or do often becomes automatic," Schumpeter observed. Familiarity provided not only comfort but safety as well, shielding an individual from contradiction and criticism. Routine required no new thought or energy, but going beyond it put one in a place without clear rules or data for making decisions. "Carrying out a new plan and acting according to a customary one," declared Schumpeter, "are things as different as making a road and walking along it." In freeing himself and others from the dead weight of the past, the entrepreneur had to show courage and exert leadership of a special kind.

Stepping beyond the conventional wisdom required not only original thinking and new action but also the courage to pursue it in the face of uncertainty. Success depended upon the ability to see things in a way that later proved to be true even though they could not be verified at the moment. It also involved a talent for grasping the essential facts of a situation without understanding how such conclusions were reached. A number of great American entrepreneurs echoed this sentiment long before Schumpeter expressed it. "A man who is liable to rapid thinking very often arrives at conclusions without being able to tell the process," observed Jay Gould, the railroad and telegraph magnate, "and yet he is satisfied the conclusions are correct.... If you undertake to give the evidence by which they are reached you could not tell how it was done."

Gould personified the type described by Schumpeter. His unimpressive, often sickly body contained one of the most incisive and creative intellects in the nation. John D. Rockefeller once called him the greatest businessman in America. During the 1870s and 1880s Gould rearranged the railroad map of the country, not only by what he did but by what his actions forced others to do in response. He understood earlier than anyone else that the future of the railroad industry lay in the creation of large systems. As head of the malnourished Erie Railroad, he compelled the two strongest railroads in the nation, the Pennsylvania and Commodore Vanderbilt's New York Central, to reverse their longstanding policies and expand westward to meet his threat.

Later Gould gained control of the floundering Union Pacific Railroad, expanded it rapidly, and turned it into one of the dominant transcontinental lines. Then he left that road, bought control of the Missouri Pacific, a small road between St. Louis and Kansas City, and built a powerful 7,000-mile system around it. His expansion policies forced every major system to rethink its strategy and policies. At the same time Gould created telegraph companies, sold them to the industry giant, Western Union, and then acquired that company. In his hands Western Union more than doubled its miles of wire. Gould also took charge of New York's elevated railway lines and imposed order on them.

No entrepreneur took greater risks or invested more of his fortune in the work of expansion and development. He was widely acknowledged to be a financial genius, pioneering new techniques and demonstrating an uncanny mastery of them. While carrying out this work with breathtaking speed and daring, he earned a reputation as the most hated man in America. Although personally quiet and unassuming, he could be ruthless, unscrupulous, and astonishingly unorthodox in his methods. Everything about his manner and way of doing business was original.

The courage to leap across defined boundaries required a special type of person. Schumpeter characterized the entrepreneur, like other types of leaders, as one driven "to found a private kingdom, usually, though not necessarily, also a dynasty." He craved both power and independence and often revealed a desire to succeed for the sake of success itself rather than the rewards it might bring. He also possessed a love of work, thrived on meeting challenges with energy and ingenuity, rejoiced in overcoming difficulties, and delighted in changing things. For these reasons the entrepreneur's personality was often a curious blend of ego and rationality. Not surprisingly, many great entrepreneurs possessed unpleasant if not abrasive personalities.

Although the great entrepreneurs were distinctive individuals with widely varying personalities, they did possess some traits in common. Above all else, they were persistent and determined persons who shared a fierce drive to succeed and let no obstacle stand in their way. In addition, they all had some supreme talent as well as a joyous zest for their work and a sheer delight in the doing of it. Along with a powerful desire to succeed, they brought amazing levels of energy to their work. They tended to be strong-willed and competitive people eager to make their mark on the world and on their own terms. Contrary to popular myth, they were not lone wolves but relied heavily on others to help them achieve their goals. They combined some compelling vision with a rage for order. Many if not most of them were perfectionists in their work, never satisfied with anything less than maximum effort and results.

These qualities often led entrepreneurs into failures as well as successes. The very persistence and determination that drove them to realize their visions also worked against them when that vision was flawed. Most entrepreneurs, great or otherwise, paid their dues in life by pursuing ventures that failed. The greater the entrepreneur, the more spectacular tended to be his flops. Their typical pattern, after all, was to throw themselves into some project, turn a deaf ear to those who said it couldn't be done or warned that disaster loomed, and battle relentlessly against all obstacles. For some, failure meant the loss of their company and/or fortune as well; for others it became merely one of many setbacks in their careers. Rare was the person who climbed the ladder of success without an occasional slip.

Entrepreneurs have been an essential ingredient of the American hothouse from the beginning. They were the necessary gardeners who made it develop, and they could not have found a more nurturing environment in which to work. As a new nation the United States had far less dead weight of the past to overcome. It was a work in progress, a unique spawning bed for opportunity and innovation that encouraged American entrepreneurs to think big. The resources for success were abundant, and the restraints on individual action were few. As a people going places in a hurry, Americans valued change more than stability, largely because they assumed that change would bring something better.

The laws of the land promoted individual action in several ways. Unlike Great Britain, where law was grounded in custom, American law was written and thus more dynamic than static. Bankruptcy statutes, for example, were framed to give debtors enough breathing space to survive their downfall and get back into the game. Where other societies shackled debtors so severely that they could scarcely repay their obligations let alone start new careers, American laws of tort were constructed in ways that defined and limited damage awards so as not to penalize risk takers drastically. This proved crucial in the turbulent American business world, where failure came often even to men who ultimately became successful entrepreneurs.

So too with contract law. Between 1800 and 1875 it not only expanded steadily but also lifted restrictions on the transfer of land and smoothed the way for conducting business at a distance. It also created new and simpler means for dealing with credit, agency, employment, leases, and other agreements. Over time the very nature and function of the corporation was redefined as well. From its original purpose as an instrument of mercantile policy it evolved into a potent tool for private development. The courts also moved to protect private enterprises from attempts by the state to regulate their activities.

The unique blend of ingredients within the economic hothouse did much to nurture another breed of American besides the entrepreneur. This was the hustler, a quintessential type found in every village and town, hungry for riches and anxious to find the shortest path to them. As early as the 1830s Alexis de Tocqueville took his measure. "It would be difficult to describe the avidity with which the American rushes forward to secure this immense booty that fortune offers," he wrote. "In the pursuit ... he is goaded onwards by a passion stronger than the love of life. Before him lies a boundless continent, and he urges onward as if time pressed and he was afraid of finding no room for his exertion."

This quest made changelings of Americans, who cheerfully moved from one place and profession to another when circumstances dictated. If one prospect or enterprise didn't pan out, they simply walked away and took up another, often in some other place. If one line of work fell flat, they jumped into another, sometimes several others. In a nation that worshiped success stories it is easy to overlook the fact that failures far outnumbered the fortunate few who clawed their way to success. From the beginning the fecund American landscape was littered with the broken dreams of men whose ideas and ambitions, large and small, never took root. Europe had its long history and monuments; America had its ghost towns crowded with the spirits of failed entrepreneurs and hustlers. Nevertheless, enough men made it big to inspire others into vigorous efforts to follow suit.

Opportunity beckoned like the siren's call for every generation of Americans, but few found fortune to be as favorable or fickle as during the Civil War. Those who marched off to battle often met death or disfigurement as their fate. But war breeds opportunity as well as tragedy, and the roster of men noted earlier, as well as many others, reaped rewards they might never have attained in ordinary times. "It's good fishing in troubled waters," observed Daniel Drew, one of the most lethal financial predators. War bred uncertainty; markets fluctuated with every turn in the tide of battle. The task of financing the war opened giddy realms of speculation. Most of all, the voracious needs of the military for goods and services presented opportunities on an unprecedented scale. Small wonder then that ambitious men shunned the killing fields to seek fabulous opportunities at home that might never come again. Banker Thomas Mellon scolded his son for even thinking of enlisting:

> I had hoped my boy . . . was not such a goose as to be seduced from duty by the declamations of buncombed speeches. It is only greenhorns who enlist. You can learn nothing in the army. . . . In time you will come to understand and believe that a man may be a patriot without risking his own life or sacrificing his health. There are plenty of other lives less valuable or ready to serve for the love of serving.

The war became an ideal breeding ground for entrepreneurs, who turned national tragedy to their advantage in several ways. Some earned fortunes through government contracts for supplies and services. Others grew rich through business coups that exploited wartime uncertainties. Bankers profited from the abnormal financial conditions wrought by the war and the need to underwrite its enormous costs. Finally, all these men gained invaluable business experience by operating in the frenetic, shifting arena of wartime. The lessons learned in this extraordinary classroom prepared them for larger, more ambitious ventures in later years. The peculiar climate of a long and exhausting war forced personal priorities into focus in a manner not possible in peacetime. Emerging in the confused air of the postwar era with the resources of the West waiting to be exploited, this generation of entrepreneurs was fortunate enough to be the right men in the right place at the right time with their newly honed talents.

A new era in American life was truly dawning in 1865, although few people could yet fathom its nature. The American republic was slowly being reshaped into one nation indivisible. Slavery was gone, replaced by something not at all clear. The South would never be the same and would continue to resist change while nursing its bitterness over the Lost Cause. But the North too would never be the same. The war scarred its soul in ways that would stain the next half century. It also unleashed an euphoria of self-interest that sent thousands of ex-soldiers and others streaming west in search of new opportunities. Politics took a back seat to business and personal interests. Industrialization and mechanization, which had been developing since the 1830s, accelerated after the conflict's end. For alert entrepreneurs, this meant nothing less than a proliferation of opportunities in areas that scarcely existed before the war.

For many entrepreneurs in this new postwar milieu, technology became the key to success. The relationship between entrepreneurs and technology should be obvious by now. New machines do not invent themselves or find uses for themselves or variations on themselves. Neither do they proliferate or find markets on their own. However, their development and maturation became magical in the hands of the right inventors and promoters.

The Machines

In 1900 Edward W. Byrn, a Patent Office official, surveyed the progress of technology during the century just closing and was amazed at what he found. "In the field of invention the Nineteenth Century has been unique," he gushed. "It has been . . . a gigantic tidal wave of human ingenuity and resource, so stupendous in its magnitude, so complex in its diversity, so profound in its thought, so fruitful in its wealth, so beneficent in its results, that the mind is strained and embarrassed in its effort to expand to a full appreciation of it." Where the ancients had given civilization enormous monuments built with vast teams of manual laborers toiling for years, the nineteenth century had been "peculiarly an age of ideas and conservation of energy, materialized in practical embodiment as labor-saving inventions, often the product of a single mind, and partaking of the sacred quality of creation."

For all his hyperbole, Byrn hardly exaggerated the significance of what he cataloged. Nor did he overestimate the impact of invention. Technology was the engine that drove industrialization and the accelerator that steadily quickened its cycles of change. New inventions literally reshaped the world around them, often in ways no one could predict. Although value neutral in itself, the effects of technology on society were value laden and often devastating. Every new technology threatened some entrenched interest with extinction. Older industries and trades were swept away in the wake of new ones, bringing loss of jobs and identity to some people and gain of both to others. Displacement became a way of life in American society just as mobility had always been.

Technology has been changing human existence since the days of the cave dwellers, but never had it come so far in so short a time. In 1800 the re-volutionary steam engine had barely made its appearance along with the cotton gin and the Franklin printing press. The telescope, the compass, gunpowder, clocks, and a variety of hand tools had been around for ages, but power still depended on wind, water, wood, and muscle. The candle and the torch provided the only relief from darkness, and no message traveled faster than the person or beast carrying it. Nearly all work consisted of hard, unending manual labor. An inefficient open hearth gave a home its heat and cooking. To keep the fire burning required chopping down more than an acre of trees every year. Water had to be carried by hand from a stream or well. Food had to be killed, caught, or grown, then made from scratch and eaten mostly in season. Clothing had to be sewn or spun by hand. Homes and furniture had to be constructed laboriously with hand tools.

Farmers worked their fields with a hoe, plow, harrow, and scythe, which limited the amount of land cultivated. By himself a farmer could barely work twenty to thirty acres of crops, and hired hands were hard to come by. Everything that a person needed but could not make for himself had to be bought from an artisan – someone trained in a craft. Most artisans, who made up about 10 percent of the colonial American population, lived in cities or towns. Mills powered by waterwheels or animals performed the arduous task of grinding corn and other grains. Sawmills did the same for lumber and tanning mills for leather. Ironmasters directed the difficult task of producing iron on iron plantations. All areas of American life were labor intensive, and the supply of labor, like that of artisans, was always scarce. For this reason, Americans more than any other people looked to machines to expedite and expand their work.

Inspirations for new devices came in all sizes and shapes. As early as 1834 a Vermont blacksmith named Thomas Davenport applied for a patent for an electric motor to drive streetcars. Lack of a power source kept a practical version of such a motor from being realized for another half century. In 1847 another inventor, Walter Hunt, patented a little gizmo that became popular as the safety pin. The rise of canning technology spurred the invention of the Sprague corn cutter, which could slice enough corn off cobs in one day to fill 15,000 cans, and the Scott and Chisholm pea sheller, which removed as many peas from pods as 600 workers could manage by hand. Dr. R. J. Gatling changed the face of warfare when he received his first patent in 1862 for a ten-barreled killing machine that evolved into the modern machine gun.

By 1900 new technology had transformed nearly every basic area of American life in ways no one could have imagined a century earlier. The steam engine ushered in the first of two power revolutions. "What has not the steam engine done for the Nineteenth Century?" wrote Byrn. "It speeds the locomotive across the continent . . . [and] the mighty steamship on the sea; it grinds our grain; it weaves our cloth; it prints our books; it forges our steel, and in every department of life it is the ubiquitous, tireless, potent agency of civilization." Later in the century steam also powered the dynamo, which made possible the generation of electricity on a large scale. The railroad opened the continent to settlement and regularized the movement of goods and people on land. The steamboat changed river life forever by making it possible for boats to travel upriver. The telegraph conquered distance in communication, as did the Atlantic cable. Late in the century the telephone opened another new era in communication.

Electricity banished the tyranny of darkness and later pioneered a revolution in production as steam had earlier. New printing presses, linotype machines, and other devices made possible the cheap, ubiquitous daily newspaper. The typewriter, tabulator, and other machines revamped office routines, while sewing machines relieved people of the drudgery of sewing by hand. Reapers, mowers, binders, harvesters, and other tools enabled farmers to work larger tracts of land with fewer helpers. Vulcanized rubber found a hundred uses in everything from shoes to rainwear to insulation to bicycle tires. Advances in chemistry produced a host of new products from coal tar such as medicines, perfumes, aniline dyes, benzene, and carbolic acid. They also gave the world glucose syrup, nitroglycerine, cheap aluminum, and fertilizers.

Relatively cheap gas lighting became a staple of city life, and the use of gas soon extended to heating and cooking as well. New machines transformed both woodworking and metal working, to say nothing of whole new generations of machine tools. The ancient art of spinning and weaving gave way to giant factories in which a handful of employees tended machines that could produce more in a day than could have been made in months by hand. Shoes and boots also benefited from new machines that boosted production and lowered prices. Power machinery also made possible affordable carpets, furniture, and other fixtures for homes. The burgeoning food industry began to invade the home with ready-made products like bread and cereal. Indoor plumbing sanitized the disposal of waste and made bathing and household chores like cleaning much easier.

Photography made its debut in 1839, advancing from daguerreotypes and the cumbersome wet-plate process to George Eastman's little Kodak camera that allowed anyone to take pictures anywhere. Where the camera preserved images, the phonograph captured sounds for posterity. The popular graphophone both recorded and played back music or talk. The bicycle became an urban fad, and the automobile made its fateful appearance on the American scene, the harbinger of a revolution that would literally transform the national landscape. The x-ray machine made its debut in the 1890s and soon offered doctors a potent new tool in their diagnoses. The century also brought the discovery of germ theory, use of anesthesia, artificial limbs, antiseptic surgery, and other advances. New telescopes, microscopes, and spectroscopes transformed the field of optics, and the kinetoscope offered the promise of a seductive new form of entertainment in the form of moving pictures.

New or improved machines dramatically increased production in many areas. In 1881 James Bonsack patented a machine that could produce 70,000 cigarettes in ten hours; within a few years an improved version upped that figure to 120,000 at a time when the most skilled worker could turn out about 3,000 a day. That same year also witnessed the birth of a machine capable of producing billions of matches and packing them in boxes. A new mechanical crusher enabled Proctor & Gamble to produce its Ivory soap in enormous quantities. Other machines allowed Henry P. Crowell to put together an integrated mill in 1882 that turned out huge amounts of crushed oats. His Quaker Oats brought a new addition to the breakfast table, packaged cereal. Other manufacturers, including Borden, H. J. Heinz, Campbell Soup, and Libby, adopted continuous-process canning techniques to churn out products that changed the way Americans cooked and ate. The first "automatic-line" canning factory opened in 1883 and could produce 3,000 cans an hour. Increasingly people moved from homemade to store-bought foods as the quality and variety of the latter increased.

Refrigeration technology spurred the rise of giant firms in meat packing, fruits, and vegetables. During the late 1870s and 1880s, refrigerated railroad cars, which utilized ice and heavy insulation, enabled men like Gustavus Swift and Philip D. Armour to ship meat across the nation in competition with local butchers. Their huge factories in Chicago put hogs and steers on assembly – or rather disassembly – lines and extracted not only an impressive range of food products from each animal but also such by-products as lard, bristles for brushes or upholstery stuffing, meat extracts, and fertilizer. By the 1880s whole trains carrying only fruit left California to provide distant areas with their first opportunity to enjoy fruit out of the local growing season. Huge quantities of vegetables moved eastward as well. Milk also moved to cities by the trainload, and the production of bread, butter, and cheese shifted from the farm to the factory.

Europeans had always regarded Americans as barbarians in their eating habits because of their penchant for downing meals as quickly as possible without the slightest hint of amenities. The new technologies creating more food that was cheaper, quicker, and easier than homemade versions only reinforced this image of a people bolting their meals in order to get on with their business. However, if the dining manners of Americans did not improve, their appearance did. By the century's end most men and about half of the nation's women and children wore clothes produced in factories. Although the well-to-do still acquired their clothes from tailors and seamstresses, the styles worn by the wealthy were copied into cheaper versions sold off the rack. Foreign observers marveled at how difficult it was on the street to tell the banker from his clerk or the shop girl from the lady of society.

The home, too, underwent profound changes, especially in urban areas. Central heating and the cooking stove replaced the fireplace. Gas lamps illuminated every room and by 1900 were giving way to electric lights. A whole new industry sprang into being to furnish houses with sinks, bathtubs, and toilets. As the home's newest room, the bathroom became a showplace for new technology. New machines enabled firms not only to produce large quantities of furniture but also to make such adornments as scroll designs for doors and windows a commonplace feature. Ready-mix paints and varnishes gave homes a broader palate of colors and were more easily applied with the newfangled spray gun. The house itself became a factory product as early versions of prefabricated homes reached the market before the century's end.

Cities underwent a striking facelift thanks to new products and construction techniques that made possible the erection of skyscrapers. This triumph of technology, with its skeleton of steel girders, used walls not for support in the traditional manner but simply for decoration and to keep out the weather. Structural steel and new foundation techniques anchored the building firmly. Plate glass kept windows intact higher up, and elevators enabled people to reach the upper floors conveniently. New fireproofing techniques such as hollow tiles for floor arches made the building safer and lighter. The first steel-framed structure, William Le Baron Jenney's Home Insurance Building in Chicago (1885), rose a modest ten stories. By1898 New York already boasted a host of skyscrapers topped by the thirty-two-story Park Row Building. Fifteen years later it would be dwarfed by the Woolworth Building, its fifty-five floors reaching 760 feet into the sky. In 1800 church steeples had dominated the urban skyline; a century later they were rapidly fading from view, especially in the larger cities.

Advances in bridge technology allowed traffic to flow in and out of cities with ease. The best of them became monuments to the age of technology. These included the double-decked suspension bridge over Niagara Falls (1855), the Eads Bridge in St. Louis (1873), which was the first to cross the Mississippi River, and the glorious Brooklyn Bridge (1883). Large cities especially relished another form of monument, the train station, as their gateway to visitors, most of whom arrived by rail. New York took the lead here as elsewhere with two imposing edifices, the magnificent Pennsylvania Station and later the even more splendiferous Grand Central Station. The latter was a marvel of both architecture and engineering with its two distinct levels to separate suburban from interurban traffic, a loop enabling trains to turn around without reverse movement, complete electrification to eliminate smoke, and a system that allowed trains to move in either direction on all four approach tracks.

These developments comprise only the highlights of change that penetrated every corner of American life. New technologies proved instrumental in all of them. Early in the nineteenth century the United States began to develop what might be called a culture of invention. Driven by necessity and/or the desire for profit, tinkerers across the nation strove to build new machines or improve existing ones to solve some problem. One need only look at the mounting flood of patent applications or glance through the columns of any issue of *Scientific American* to appreciate their zeal and the infinite variety of their projects. Most of their devices vanished into the mists of history, but a surprising number survived to exert some influence. The accumulated effort of these zealots created a foundation for future development as well as a tradition of invention. Taken together, they became the giants on whose shoulders later generations of inventors and engineers stood. They changed not only the material world but also the way in which their work proceeded.

Like nearly everything else in American life, technology felt the shaping hand of the organizational revolution. For most of the nineteenth century inventors were often quirky loners toiling in obscurity. The most successful of their number, such as Thomas A. Edison, were lionized as cultural heroes – sometimes for the wrong reasons. Eli Whitney is best known for his invention of the cotton gin and for introducing the practice of precision-made interchangeable parts that could be assembled by semiskilled workers in large quantity. However, few people know that in 1818 he created another major device, the milling machine, which could cut and shape metal parts with far greater precision and speed than could be done by hand. The miller soon became a staple of any shop that needed intricate and precise metal parts.

Despite their contributions, the majority of inventors toiled in obscurity. The most impressive and versatile of their number in the early nineteenth century, Oliver Evans, never reaped the fame or fortune that his genius deserved. During the 1780s Evans invented several improvements in milling (embodied in United States Patent #3) culminating in his automatic flour mill, which was widely copied and improved over the years. Having shown how one of the young nation's core businesses, flour milling, could be mechanized, Evans turned to designing a steam engine, which he patented in 1804. He installed the engine in two mills and set up a machine shop to produce engines for a variety of uses. At his death in 1819 he left behind two sophisticated machine shops along with a corps of skilled machinists.

By the century's end, although exploits of individual genius still drew headlines, invention and innovation had become largely the business of research laboratories sponsored by corporations or other agencies. Edison, who amassed more patents than any other American (1,093), led the way with his research facilities first at Menlo Park and then at West Orange, New Jersey, where the work force reached 3,600. In 1911 he swept together no fewer than thirty of his enterprises into Thomas A. Edison, Inc. George Westinghouse took out 361 patents in areas ranging from the air brake for railroad cars to the friction draft gear to a host of electrical devices. Although renowned as an inventor, Westinghouse oversaw a complex research operation that stressed teamwork and strong project management. Shrewd industrialists soon realized the value of inventors, researchers, and engineers to their enterprises. When John D. Rockefeller needed someone who could solve the problem of removing sulfur from the oil in the huge Lima fields, he hired Herman Frasch, a noted chemist. Frasch's work in the laboratory enabled Rockefeller to exploit this enormous source of oil.

Invention, like so many other areas of American life, was fast becoming institutionalized. Much of it took place in the laboratories and other facilities of giant corporations, which created research and development departments for that purpose. "Modern science-based industry," noted historian David Noble, " . . . was the product of significant advances in chemistry and physics and also of the growing willingness of the capitalist to embark upon the costly, time-consuming, and uncertain path of research and development." Companies could give inventors what they most needed: funds, facilities, staff, and a fast track to market if their devices proved useful. The more complex industry became, the more it required people who understood the principles of science and mathematics. Gradually the tinkerers evolved into professionally trained scientists and engineers who became a staple of the corporate as well as academic worlds.

Well before 1900 technology established itself at the center of American life. For some people it became a defining characteristic of Americans, who seemed infatuated if not obsessed with the power and promise of new machines. It lay at the heart of American optimism with its belief that tomorrow would always bring more and better things, and with them a better life. "America is a land of wonders," marveled Tocqueville, "in which everything is in constant motion and every change seems an improvement. . . . [T]hey all consider . . . humanity as a changing scene, in which nothing is, or ought to be, permanent; and they admit that what appears to them today to be good, may be superseded by something better tomorrow."

2

The Lure of Lovely and Lucrative Land

It was all prices to them: they never looked at it: why should they look at the
land? they were Empire Builders: it was all in the bid and the asked and the
ink on their books.

                        – Archibald MacLeish

THE AMERICAN ECONOMIC HOTHOUSE BEGAN LIFE WITH
more soil than anyone had ever imagined. Since ancient times land
has served as the major source of wealth and productivity. Not by accident
did ruling classes everywhere consist of those who owned or controlled the
land. From the very beginning the promise of American life, the appeal
it held out to newcomers, revolved around land – boundless acres of a
commodity so unavailable in their native countries. The lure of land for
settlers involved not only sustenance but independence, the prospect of
enhanced dignity and self-worth, and the hope of passing a material legacy
onto one's children. For the vast majority of Americans in the preindustrial
era, farming was both their livelihood and their way of life, whether on a
small New England plot wrested from the rocky soil, a sprawling southern
plantation, or a prairie spread where the sky seemed never to end.

    Land helped shape the American character in many ways. It encouraged
attitudes of independence, self-reliance, and individualism that many
observers found typical of Americans. It promoted an almost mystical
faith in the promise of the future as well as a realm in which a person
could escape from his past. The American Dream itself was a product of
the possibilities land offered to settlers. At the same time it fostered an
attitude of waste and almost wanton carelessness toward resources that
seemed so boundless. Why take care of the land when one could simply

work it to exhaustion and then move on to fresh fields? Much of the southeastern seaboard did in fact get farmed nearly to death long before the Civil War. And the land had to be tamed. Contrary to myth, it did not bring farmers into a harmonious relationship with nature so much as one in which nature remained an unrelenting adversary to be subdued.

Apart from all its other roles in American life, land became the foundation for many of the nation's fortunes. Since the first settlers stepped ashore at Plymouth and Jamestown, Americans have grown rich – and sometimes poor – by dealing in land. For many families the surest road to financial security lay in buying land and holding it through generations for its rise in value. John Jacob Astor started work in the fur trade and funneled his profits into Manhattan real estate. Eventually he sold the fur business to concentrate on his real estate holdings. Over time the Astors became the largest landholders and landlords in Manhattan, and the family fortune soared.

In 1892 the New York *Tribune* compiled a list of all the millionaires in the United States by state and city. It found a total of 4,047 members of this exclusive club. Only 2 percent of them traced their fortunes to agricultural enterprises, but land and real estate figured in 36 percent of all the fortunes. The real figure is doubtless higher, since in many other cases the source of the fortune is simply listed as "investments." For California and Texas, the only western states with a sizable number of millionaires in 1892, a whopping 55 percent of the fortunes were rooted in land or real estate. For all the wonders produced by industrialization, land in its diverse forms and functions has remained the primary source of fortunes.

Land as a Business

The lure of land enchanted nearly everyone. As the primary form of wealth in preindustrial America, land became the favorite vehicle for speculation long before the stock market came into existence. Settlers in both Massachusetts and Virginia brought to the new continent the concept of land as private property. Building on this foundation, the American Revolution swept away all ancient obstacles and established the fee-simple form of ownership that persists to this day. Under this approach, as historian Sam Bass Warner observed, "land could be leased, bought, sold, and bequeathed with great simplicity." This system encouraged rapid settlement on farms small and large, but it also enabled speculators to acquire enormous tracts cheaply and hold them for resale at higher prices. Anyone who had the capital, or could borrow it, could invest in land. The Founding Fathers, most notably George Washington and Thomas Jefferson, were no more immune to the lure than ordinary citizens.

Speculation in land assumed many forms. At first it involved the boundless tracts of the wild frontier, to which settlers might not find their way for years. Some investors looked for key locations that might serve as town or village sites. When the mania for land moved to towns or cities, it became real estate – a commodity that embraced much smaller pieces of land but even more volatile movements in price. Although people of every class indulged in land speculation, it tended after the Civil War to concentrate in the hands of large corporations, including railroads, and wealthy individuals. As economist Willard W. Cochrane noted, "the land speculator, whether absentee or resident, squatter or banker, local politician or eastern senator, was present on every frontier. He affected every phase of agricultural development on the western frontier."

Historian Paul W. Gates has charted the course of speculation in public lands and identified three peak periods prior to the Civil War: 1818–19, 1836, and 1855–6. In each case the frenzy was fueled by "the favorable balance of trade from the sale of . . . American food and fiber abroad; loose experiments in state banking which produced huge increases in the circulating medium and bank credit; a swelling tide of immigration and of westward migration, and, for the second and third peaks, extraordinary expenditures of public and private funds on internal improvements." All three peaks collapsed into a financial depression or recession in which land prices fell almost as quickly as the demand for it. Overextended speculators, saddled with interest and tax bills they could no longer meet, surrendered their holdings to larger investors or settlers.

During the land manias a new business appeared in the form of agencies designed to handle transactions for eastern investors who rarely saw the land they bought. For a commission the agent entered the claim, secured the patent, paid all taxes, collected any rents due, and sold the parcel when instructed to do so. Speculation during the 1850s grew especially frantic because of the mania for building railroads. The news or even rumor of forthcoming rails sent every alert speculator scrambling for land at points where towns or other facilities might arise on the route. No class of individuals was immune to the disease. Even squatters lacking both capital and credit sometimes improved their quarter claim in order to sell it when demand rose, then moved on to repeat the process. Men of small means risked a few hundred dollars scraped together, while eastern capitalists plunked down thousands for land they had no intention of settling, using, or even seeing.

Not surprisingly, companies were formed to systematize the process. A group of New York and Boston men organized the American Land Company in 1835 with a capital of $1 million. The company bought $400,000 worth of cotton lands in Mississippi and $250,000 in Arkansas land, and spent the rest on city lots and rural tracts in six different western and southern states. Numerous other companies acquired several million acres of land altogether; one of them alone claimed to own 900,000 acres. Erastus Corning, an immensely successful Albany, New York, businessman, owned shares in four major land investment companies, including American, and thousands of acres outright in Indiana and Michigan. Other wealthy individuals maintained portfolios of land investments much as a later generation would hold in stocks.

"Speculation in real estate has for many years been the ruling occupation of the Western mind," wrote D. W. Mitchell, an Englishman who spent a decade in the United States. "Clerks, labourers, farmers, storekeepers, merely followed their callings for a living, while they were speculating for their fortunes. . . . The people of the West became dealers in land, rather than its cultivators. . . . Millions of acres were bought and sold without buyer or seller knowing where they were, or whether they were anywhere." However, most of the capital came from the East. Some investors advanced schemes to operate large-scale model enterprises using tenant farmers. Henry L. Ellsworth of Connecticut, best known for his role as commissioner of patents, bought 18,000 acres of prairie land in Indiana as lead investor for a group with such a plan. In all, Ellsworth funneled nearly $200,000 of eastern capital into the Wabash Valley, where several enormous (20,000–40,000 acres) tenant farms eventually operated.

This system meant that huge portions of the West belonged to absentee owners, who might pay taxes to local communities but otherwise made no contribution to their growth or betterment. After the Civil War speculators and large holders continued to dominate land ownership despite hopes that the Homestead Act and its interminable amendments might democratize the process. As new towns appeared, many of them along railroad lines, and as villages grew into towns and towns into cities, the land mania grew more intensive. Industrialization and urbanization worked strange wonders on past land practices. Land in the city turned out to be quite a different matter from that in the country, as a later chapter will show.

Land has both a social and an economic function, as does whatever is put on it. Using a parcel for one purpose usually precludes using it for another. To exploit a tract for economic gain means it cannot serve a social function such as a park or forest or just plain scenery. Choices must be made as to its use, and from those decisions flow a pattern of both land use and social values. The question is whether land is to be regarded in narrow terms as simply property or in broader terms as a social resource. The former conceives of land in economic terms, the latter in social terms. With few exceptions, the American response has always followed the first approach. The continent was settled on the basis of private individual ownership. Every early attempt to organize settlements along other lines, mostly feudal in origin, failed miserably. The right of private property became no less revered than that of freedom of speech, worship, or assembly.

After the Revolution, the Constitution and the Northwest Ordnance adopted the fee-simple principle as the basis for disposing of lands west of the Allegheny Mountains. To function effectively, it had to limit the extent to which public agencies could step between a man and his property. For most of the nineteenth century, government land policy focused chiefly on finding the most equitable ways of releasing land into the hands of private citizens. Once having let the land go, government hesitated to interfere with it again except under unusual circumstances. This approach guaranteed that Americans would enjoy the freest land system anywhere in the world. By allowing people to decide the use to which the land would be put, it defined property as private. The contrary notion of land as a social resource shriveled away. So long as land remained plentiful, the socially harmful effects of individual usage tended to be ignored. When public and private interests clashed, the law usually defended private property rights above all other considerations.

In short, land was released to the free play of the market. To get it, one needed only money or credit, which meant that those with the most capital got most of the land and the best of it. Rural and urban America alike suffered unfortunate and often unexpected consequences from this approach to land. Homesteaders and farmers struggled to wrest good land from the clutches of speculators and large holders. City residents watched helplessly as the choicest parcels went not to parks or schools or public space but to factories, warehouses, railroad facilities, and offices. The riverfront of nearly every city featured not open space but wharves, refineries, warehouses, railroad tracks, and other facilities requiring access to water travel. Later, when land became more scarce, Americans would launch movements to reclaim or protect key parcels of it from the private interests eager to exploit them.

The Business of Farming

The sheer abundance of land overwhelmed the imagination. By 1862, having already sold off an immense amount of land, the federal government still possessed about a billion acres of public domain, two-thirds of which was not considered arable. That year Congress passed the landmark Homestead Act after four decades of agitation. It allowed any citizen to claim 160 acres of the public domain for a $10 fee. Final title would be granted after continuous residence and improvement of the land for five years and payment of a fee ranging from $26 in most states to $34 on the Pacific coast. When the Civil War ended, thousands of settlers, many of them former soldiers, heeded the advice of Horace Greeley to "Go West, young man, and grow up with the country."

Go west they did. The emphasis on two great population shifts – the arrival of millions of immigrants and the incursion of rural people into towns and cities – sometimes obscures a third profound population migration: the westward movement. While the urban population tripled between 1870 and 1900, the farm population did not decrease but actually doubled. So did the number of farms, which rose from 2.6 million to 5.7 million during those same years, and farm acreage, which jumped from nearly 408 million to 841 million. The total value of farm property more than doubled from $9.4 billion to $20.4 billion. Most of this expansion took place on the Great Plains, once labeled the Great American Desert. In Kansas, Nebraska, and the Dakotas alone, according to historian David B. Danbom, the 50,000 farms existing in 1870 mushroomed to nearly 400,000 by the century's end.

During the 1870s American farmers put into cultivation an area equal to that of France. Over the next two decades they planted acreage matching the combined size of France, Germany, England, and Wales. Between 1867 and 1900 they opened more new land to cultivation than in the country's entire history since 1607. The invading army of settlers included not only farmers but miners, cowmen, sheepmen, express company operatives, railroaders, telegraphers, businessmen of all kinds hoping to profit from the new towns springing up everywhere, and adventurers seeking a new life in untamed territory. The myth invoked by the westward movement had this army of settlers spreading across the region on lands claimed under the Homestead Act, thereby creating the moving frontier that historian Frederick Jackson Turner hailed as the fount of American democracy. While the myth contains a kernel of truth, it ignores the role played by corporations and speculators in settling the West.

Proponents of the Homestead Act praised it as the cornerstone of democracy by offering the little man a chance to acquire his own farm and live independently. But as historian Ray Allen Billington pointed out, "the farmer benefited only slightly from the Homestead Act, and the laborer not at all. The latter, whose annual wages seldom exceeded $250, had neither the entry fees to file a claim, the considerable sum necessary to move his family to the frontier, nor the money to buy expensive tools and farm equipment." Historian Fred A. Shannon was even more emphatic: "An astonishing number of homesteaders were merely the pawns of land monopolists who took over the land as soon as the final patents [titles] were received. . . . [T]he bona fide homesteader usually got only the least desirable tracts, on poorer lands, far from transportation and society, while the ubiquitous monopolist and speculator held the better tracts for resale at a price too high for the class of persons the Homestead Act had presumably been intended to benefit."

Speculators and other large interests had not only the funds to acquire land but also the ingenuity for finding ways to circumvent the law. Some even built tiny houses twelve by fourteen inches so they could swear to meeting the requirement of a "twelve by fourteen dwelling." And the law itself contained major flaws. Billington explained one of them:

> In the Mississippi Valley a unit of 160 acres was generous; few frontiers-men bought more than eighty acres. . . . A farmer on the Great Plains needed far more or much less – 2,000 to 5,000 acres if he was a rancher, 360 to 640 acres if he practiced extensive agriculture, 40 to 60 acres if he used irrigation. Nowhere west of the 98th meridian was 160 acres a workable agricultural unit.

By one estimate it cost about $1,500 to put a 160-acre farm into production. Few laborers or immigrants could accumulate that sum on a daily wage of $1.50.

Later efforts to improve the act, and they were numerous, usually had the opposite result. The Timber Culture Act (1873) did promote some forestation and enabled homesteaders to expand their holdings into a workable farm. However, the Desert Land Act (1877) benefited the cattlemen who had lobbied hard for it; Billington labeled it "an open invitation to fraud." Of the 9.1 million acres claimed under the act, only 2.6 million received final patents. The lumber interests got their due in the Timber and Stone Act (1878), which timber companies exploited by rounding up gangs of dummy claimants to file for sections of forest land and then turn them over to the corporation for a fee. By 1900 nearly 3.6 million acres of prime forest land had been claimed under this measure. Some mineral and lumber interests simply ignored the law and induced compliant land office clerks to sell them large parcels.

An enormous amount of land went not to settlers but to states and railroads. The Morrill Act (1862) granted every state 30,000 acres of western land for each of its senators and representatives to fund the creation of agricultural colleges. The total acreage allotted came to 140 million. Land grants to railroads between 1850 and 1871 consumed another 181 million acres, more than 131 million of which went to transcontinental railroads alone. Another 49 million acres were donated through the states, while local governments, towns, and individuals contributed another 840,000 acres. Altogether these grants made railroads the largest landowners in the nation. Billington estimated that the amount of land "given or sold to speculators and corporations" totaled 521 million acres while only 600,000 homestead patents were issued for 80 million acres – many of them to "dummy entrymen, cattlemen, and representatives of mining or lumbering companies."

Yet the story has another wrinkle that defies myth. For decades historians have portrayed the railroads as greedy gobblers of land and resources. In selling their land at inflated prices or clinging to it in hopes of rising values, they slowed or actively resisted settlement of the West. Much of the condemnation was heaped on the transcontinental roads as recipients of most of the land grants. The emblem of this interpretation became the Southern Pacific Railroad (SP), immortalized as the "Octopus" in Frank Norris's 1901 novel of the same name. As the largest transportation system in the world, the SP cast a giant shadow across western development, which Norris and others depicted as entirely negative.

However, as historian Richard Orsi has shown in *Sunset Limited* (2005), the SP played a very different role. Far from retarding the settlement and economic development of the West, the SP vigorously pursued the dispersal of its land grant, especially to small farmers despite obstacles that would have dissuaded less determined companies. In the water-starved desert territories as well as less parched regions, the company took the lead in developing water supplies and irrigation systems. It promoted scientific farming techniques, encouraged newcomers to grow crops suited to their location, and sponsored popular farm demonstration trains to bring information to farmers across its territory. It devised new marketing and shipping techniques, such as the fruit trains that brought western produce to distant markets. Much of the initiative and work for these efforts came from middle managers, especially the men who served as land agents for the company.

Critics have long viewed the railroad as a machine that laid waste the natural environment of the West. Orsi concedes the negative impacts but shows how the SP also spearheaded major programs of environmental conservation and reform. Especially was it instrumental in the struggle to create national parks at Yosemite, Sequoia, and Lake Tahoe, all of which were threatened by developmental destruction. In a variety of areas it preached and practiced policies of resource conservation designed to put its "properties on the most conservative and scientific basis." The company pursued these policies not as a form of charity but rather as a blend of self-interest and close identification with the communities and regions it served. Research in the papers of the Union Pacific Railroad confirms similar if not as far-reaching activities on the part of that company as well. Other transcontinental roads, most notably the Great Northern, did important work in promoting rather than retarding the development of the West simply because such policies served their corporate interests. The railroads, after all, needed as many paying customers as possible.

Nevertheless, a huge portion of the nation's land fell into the hands not of individual farmers but of corporations and speculators who sold their holdings at the highest possible price. Farming had always been the nation's biggest business, but after the Civil War it became increasingly a big business for the same reasons that transformed other enterprises. At first glance it might seem that the reach of industrialization and the organizational revolution did not extend beyond the confines of urban America, but these forces influenced rural America and farming as well. The threat posed to the small businessmen by giant corporations in other industries had its counterpart in agriculture, where large firms arose in virtually every sector.

Farming has always been a hard business beset with difficulties beyond the farmer's control. He never knew how much of what he planted would come to harvest because his crops were subject to the whims of nature. Drought, frost, flooding, storms, or insect plagues could devastate him without warning. Nor could he influence the price he got for his crop or what he paid for machinery, transportation, tools, storage, or supplies. He toiled long hours for uncertain pay under harsh circumstances in living conditions that were often crude and always isolated from other people. While myth portrayed the farmer as self-reliant, he had long before the Civil War entered the market economy in which he depended on selling his crops to obtain the cash needed for buying what he required. Like every other sector of that economy, his situation changed radically under the impact of industrialization and the advent of new technologies.

During the 1850s the railroad and the telegraph transformed the marketing and financing of cotton and wheat, the nation's two most important export crops. Other commodities felt this same influence after the Civil War as the rail and wire networks spread rapidly. Their presence moved crops to market faster and made possible the rise of such enterprises as grain elevators, warehouses, cotton presses, and commodity exchanges. For example, Illinois doubled in population during the decade. Its output of wheat soared from 9.4 million bushels in 1849 to 23.8 million bushels in

1859, and its corn crop from 57.6 million to 115 million bushels. Much of this harvest flowed into Chicago, which soon emerged as the leading grain terminal in the nation as well as the hub of a growing railroad network running in every direction from the city.

By 1860 a significant new transportation and distribution system had arisen in the Old Northwest. A steadily expanding rail network fed shipments of grain, livestock, and other products into Chicago, where they were processed and/or shipped eastward on barges over the Great Lakes. Beginning in 1848, huge storage elevators were erected to handle the mountain of grain. Buffalo lined the shore of Lake Erie with elevators to receive grain in enormous quantities. An earlier generation had moved grain by loading it into sacks and stacking them in barges, trains, and wagons. The new system freed farmers from their dependence on local millers and merchants. Distant growers, who paid the largest portion of their costs for transportation and storage, especially benefited from the new arrangement.

As the rail system reached deeper into the West, the center of wheat and corn production moved steadily westward with it. The opening of vast stretches of prairie to cultivation so increased output of the major staple crops that smaller producers in more urbanized regions were obliged to switch to other crops. Technology also helped farmers to increase output. Cyrus McCormick's first reaper, produced in 1831, could clear ten acres a day with the help of eight men and a horse or two at a cost of about a dollar an acre. By hand it took five men with scythes and ten helpers to harvest the same ten acres, their labor costs running two to three dollars per acre. It did not take farmers long to grasp the savings offered by reapers. Other versions soon appeared, most notably the machines of Obed Hussey and John H. Manny, and spirited competitions were staged among rival versions. However, McCormick's reaper alone incorporated what came to be regarded as the seven essential parts of the modern reaper.

The Civil War accelerated the farmer's dependence on machinery. Early versions of harrows, planters, mowers, reapers, threshers, and new types of plows had already appeared by 1860 but, like the newfangled mower, were not yet in widespread use. However, as thousands of farm boys and men left to join the army, women, children, and older men had to shoulder the heavy field work. Eager manufacturers like McCormick sniffed a bonanza market. In 1864 his factory alone turned out 6,000 reapers, while overall output of mowers reached 70,000 that year or twice that of 1862. Other machines such as the horse-rake, cultivators, corn planters, new harrows, steam threshers, and grain drills also came onto the market. Mechanization helped northern farmers produce enough wheat, corn, and other crops to fill domestic needs and still sell surpluses to England for badly needed funds. The number of hogs and cattle rose sharply, and the sheep population doubled, swelling wool production from 60 million pounds in 1860 to 140 million pounds in 1865.

After the war, the parade of technological innovations continued at an even faster pace. In 1871 alone, 160 patents were issued for reapers, 72 for threshers and separators, 13 for cornhuskers, and 160 for plows and their attachments. Stronger plows made of cast iron and steel expedited that tedious work. In 1837 John Deere introduced his self-polishing steel plow, which transformed an implement that dated back to biblical times. By 1852 his company was producing 10,000 plows a year. During the 1870s the sulky plow made its appearance and spread rapidly. By enabling the farmer to ride rather than walk behind his team, it doubled the amount of ground he could cover.

Seed sowers put down seed efficiently and economically while disk harrows broke up heavy soils and turned under stubble. Those who grew corn welcomed the help of checkrow planters, cultivators, huskers, and binders. Improved mowers, rakers, and balers expedited the gathering of hay. Dairy farmers saw their routines eased by the invention of the centrifugal cream separator and the centrifugal cream tester, which, according to Shannon, "did more than all others in revolutionizing the dairy industry in the later decades of the century." The new devices captured virtually all the cream and produced it at any thickness desired while saving a considerable amount of labor in the process. More than 40,000 of the separators were in use by 1900. Even the lowly churn received close attention from inventors, who took out more than 2,700 patents for various improvements on it.

In farming, too, the steam engine worked its wonders. Jerome I. Case, who opened his business in Racine, Wisconsin, was less an inventor than a brilliant mechanic. He designed and built a succession of threshing machines during the 1840s, then turned his attention to adapting a steam engine to farm machinery. In 1860 he introduced an eight-horsepower portable engine drawn by horses. His fame grew when his engines won several gold medals at the Paris Exposition in 1878. Case and his firm took the lead in manufacturing engines for steam-powered farm machinery. Altogether his company turned out 35,737 engines before it stopped making them in 1926.

Gradually farmers felt the now familiar pattern of technological innovations that came ever faster. They embraced harvesters rapidly until more than 100,000 of them had been sold by 1879. Four years earlier, John Appleby invented the first effective binder. Using twine instead of wire, it featured a tying principle that reapers employed for another half century. During the 1880s the self-binding harvester drove its predecessor machines from the market. By one estimate the binder saved the equivalent of two men's labor over the harvester and that of five men over the reaper. Lumbering threshers, driven by steam engines, saved the labor of two men by knocking grain free of the straw, carrying it away, and dumping it into a stack. Over the years the capacity of threshers doubled and their functions increased thanks to the invention of numerous attachments. Later, too, the cumbersome steam engine gave way to more powerful and efficient internal combustion engines powered by gasoline.

Cyrus McCormick probably did more than any other man to revolutionize the way farmers worked. Unlike his rivals, McCormick envisioned a huge market if he could produce in quantity, maintain strict quality control, and forge a network of agents to sell machines and provide service for them afterward. To realize this vision, he left his native Virginia in 1848 and moved to Chicago, where he built a factory. Prior to 1848 he had sold a total of 1,278 reapers. Between 1848 and 1850 he sold about 4,000 machines, and by 1856 his factory was turning out forty a day. Once established in Chicago, he forged not only an efficient production system but also an innovative marketing and distribution system as well.

Since he sold a seasonal product, McCormick took care to improve every year's model. He added a mowing attachment in the 1850s and introduced the self-rake reaper in 1862, although by then he had long since left invention to the skilled mechanics and engineers he hired. McCormick devoted himself to upgrading the manufacturing process and to devising a marketing organization suitable for his unique product and clientele. He pioneered in constant and lavish advertising but backed his claims with a fixed price, a written guarantee, and a solid service organization. "He recruited an able agent corps," wrote historian Robert Sobel, "provided them with literature, brought them to the factory to see how the machines were produced, and even instituted an *ad hoc* training program."

Farmers seldom had the cash to buy outright and rarely the mechanical skill to deal with newfangled machines. McCormick kept his own credit solid and cheerfully sold on the installment plan with only a slight charge for the convenience. His agents showed customers how to operate and care for their machines, left them product literature, and were quick to send help when a machine malfunctioned. No one had tried to market so complex a machine to so broad a market before, yet McCormick succeeded brilliantly. During the depression years 1872–5 his company doubled its sales even as many of his competitors sank into bankruptcy. In 1878 McCormick sold more than 18,000 machines and earned a net profit exceeding $600,000. The next year he incorporated as the McCormick Harvesting Machinery Company.

When the disastrous Chicago fire of 1871 wiped out his factory, all his stores, and most of his residences, McCormick swallowed his $600,000 net loss and rebuilt on a larger scale. His new fireproofed factory, heated by steam and lit by gas, could turn out nearly 15,000 implements a season. Through the years McCormick waged an interminable number of patent fights with rival firms. Although expensive and time-consuming, the endless suits did not prevent him from buying important patents or increasing his sales. In 1883, the year before his death, McCormick sold about 48,000 machines. His son, Cyrus McCormick, Jr., continued the business until 1902, when J. P. Morgan partner George W. Perkins merged the company with the Deering Harvester Company and three smaller firms. The new International Harvester Company controlled about 85 percent of the harvester and reaper market.

Thus did McCormick follow a familiar trajectory of partnership and family firm to giant corporation. By 1906 the company had centralized its administration and begun to produce other types of agricultural implements such as plows, harrows, seeders, and spreaders. It also began to expand its overseas operations. In response, rival firms such as John Deere and Moline Plow moved into the harvester and reaper field and strengthened their overseas operations. The agricultural machinery business became one more group of corporate giants on the economic landscape. In the process they transformed the business of farming. A growing variety of useful machines greatly increased output but also raised the stakes in terms of the capital required to farm. This in turn encouraged the growth of large agricultural organizations designed to produce on a large scale.

In one area at least, the corporation came early to agriculture. The Great Plains region west of the 98th meridian received much less rainfall than the area east of it. Cattle raisers became the first industry to utilize the region, thanks in large part to the government's allowing herds to graze freely on public land. The cattle trade on the High Plains began as early as the 1840s in response to the needs of settlers heading west over the Oregon Trail. The building of the Kansas Pacific Railroad opened a market for Texas longhorn cattle, which were driven north to railheads such as Abilene and Dodge City that soon became legendary cow towns. During the years 1878–85 the cattle kingdom in both the northern and southern plains underwent rapid expansion as rail lines proliferated, the growth of urban markets increased demand, and a full-blown meat-processing industry emerged. Cattle moved via rail directly from the range to Omaha, Kansas City, or St. Louis, and often from there to Chicago.

The soaring demand for meat also created a reverse traffic flowing westward to stock the range with young cattle. Historian Ernest Staples Osgood has calculated that between 1882 and 1884 as many cattle were shipped west as east. Stories about the fabulous profits to be had in the business attracted a rush of eastern and foreign (mostly British) capital. As Osgood observed, "It was all so simple. The United States furnished the grass; the East, the capital; and the western stockman, the experience." Cattle corporations organized with unseemly haste; in 1883 twenty companies with a total capitalization of more than $12 million incorporated in Wyoming territory alone. Cheap American beef started moving overseas as early as 1868, first as live cattle and then as dressed meat when refrigeration methods developed.

Predictably, this orgy of investment soon led to a market glut. The open range filled up with more cattle than even its vast expanses could sustain. As the situation grew more volatile, cattlemen formed their own organizations to impose some sense of order on the growing chaos. The Laramie County Stock Growers' Association began life in November 1873, changed its name to the Wyoming Stock Growers' Association six years later, and by 1885 had 363 members who together owned two million head of cattle.

Montana followed suit, but these organizations faced a growing list of issues besides overcrowding on the range. Rustling remained a problem, farmers kept moving westward onto public lands cattlemen considered their own, and sheepmen also wanted part of the range. Another major problem, the threat of disease, finally nudged the federal government into action. In 1884 Congress passed a bill creating the Bureau of Animal Industry, which was to make rules and regulations for curbing cattle diseases such as pleuro-pneumonia and Texas fever.

Disaster soon befell the cattle kingdom. The boom had occurred during years of relatively heavy rainfall and mild winters on the Great Plains, both of which encouraged overstocking of the range. In 1885 the weather cycle turned sharply against the cattlemen. Two devastating winters between 1885 and 1887 destroyed herds from Canada down through Texas. The ghastly sight of countless dead cattle stacked up amid weak, emaciated survivors moved even hardened cattlemen. "A business that had been fascinating to me before, suddenly became distasteful," wrote one of them years later. "I never wanted to own again an animal that I could not feed and shelter." The day of the open range came to an end along with many of the corporations that had rushed to profit from it. Those that survived, and some new firms, turned to ranching – owning the land their cattle grazed, fencing it, and growing hay to feed the herds in winter.

The farmers who settled west of the 98th meridian endured tough times until they adapted to the unique demands of the Plains. One solution lay in a technique known as dry farming, which created large farms but let half the land lay fallow each year to accumulate moisture. The use of crop rotation and fertilizers helped improve the soil while silos, which first appeared in 1873, enabled farmers to store grass and other plant stalks and thereby convert them into nourishing feed for animals through biochemical reaction. The steady advance of railroads and the telegraph gave western farmers access to distant markets and sped the flow of information. Increasingly the movement of crops became tied to the new commodity exchanges that systematized marketing, improved methods of financing, and lowered the cost of moving crops by allowing them to be bought and sold before they were shipped or even harvested.

The new system came first to the grain trade. As historian John G. Clark explained, the telegraph brought western markets news of price changes in eastern markets, and the railroad enabled grain to move eastward quickly enough to exploit any favorable change in price. This led to larger purchases of grain in major markets like Chicago and Buffalo. The telegraph also allowed a dealer in New York to buy directly at the place of production. This system reduced both risk and the time needed for grain to reach its destination, which in turn cut the time that the purchaser had to pay interest on the funds he had borrowed to make the transaction.

These new storage and shipment methods needed weighing and inspecting facilities as well as some standardized method of grading wheat. The Chicago Board of Trade, which opened in 1848, assumed these tasks during the 1850s, as did similar organizations in other cities. Their efforts soon created a body of national standards for these functions. A new type of contract, the futures agreement, encouraged new practices that helped stabilize prices, lower credit costs, and transfer much of the risk in shipments to speculators on the grain exchanges. The merchants who had once dominated the grain trade gave way to commodity dealers, not only in wheat but in the marketing of cotton, corn, rye, oats, and barley as well. In this manner organization came to agricultural marketing as it had to other sectors of the economy.

Farmers could never approach the degree of consolidation achieved by manufacturing and industrial firms, but attempts were made during the late 1870s and early 1880s to produce crops on a mass scale. Known as "bonanza farms," these bold ventures tried to leverage the advantages of cheap land and rapidly improving machinery. At first the plentiful rainfall of those years favored their efforts. One such farm on the Red River contained an estimated 61,500 acres, an area five times the size of Manhattan Island. Another farm in the same area boasted a single field embracing 13,000 acres.

Michael L. Sullivant started his expansive career with a 5,000-acre farm near Columbus, Ohio. In 1852 he began acquiring land in eastern Illinois until he had amassed 80,000 acres in the state. Using a corps of 100 hired hands, most of them immigrants, 125 yoke of oxen, and 50 horses, he planted 3,000 acres in corn and a lesser amount in wheat while erecting miles of hedge fencing to keep cattle out of his fields. Sullivant sold 23,000 acres of his land to John T. Alexander. Before the purchase, Alexander already owned 80,000 acres on which he planted 16,000 acres of corn and raised 32,000 head of cattle and 15,000 hogs. Later he added another 26,500 acres for another stock farm. After selling the tract to Alexander,

Sullivant went on to develop another 40,000 acres that included 18,000 acres planted in corn and 5,000 in other crops. Within five years he attained a yield of 450,000 bushels of corn.

The work force on most bonanza farms resembled the organization found in factories in that superintendents managed gangs of migrant workers. The sight of these crews at work across a sea of wheat or corn inspired military metaphors among observers. "We encounter a squadron of war chariots . . . doing the work of human hands," noted a writer for *Harper's New Monthly Magazine* after visiting a bonanza farm in North Dakota. "There are twenty-five of them in this one brigade of the grand army of 115, under the marshalship of this Dakota farmer." Oliver Dalrymple, who developed and managed a bonanza farm west of Fargo, North Dakota, raised 75,000 bushels of wheat in 1877, his second year. He divided the fields into subdivisions ranging from 1,280 to 5,000 acres and built houses on each one for the local foreman and the laborers he hired. His equipment included sixty-six plows of various types, twenty-one seeders, sixty harrows, thirty self-binding harvesters, and five steam-powered threshers along with eighty horses and thirty wagons.

Predictably, the early success of the bonanza farms triggered a land and wheat boom in the Red River Valley. As the area became more widely publicized, large amounts of eastern capital flowed into it. A booklet issued by the St. Paul, Minneapolis & Manitoba Railroad in 1883 rhapsodized that "Any land will pay for itself at present prices in one or two crops" in what the writer called "the farmer's Elysium – a realm of peace, plenty and prosperity." Homesteaders too rushed into the valley seeking government or railroad land for wheat farms. Between 1879 and 1889 wheat acreage in six Minnesota and nine North Dakota counties mushroomed from 130,877 to nearly 2.5 million.

The bonanza farms enjoyed a few years of success until the slackened rainfall of the late 1880s reduced yields, soaring national production reduced prices, and taxes on land continued to rise. Smaller farms, like other small businesses, either perished in the face of large competitors or adapted to a changed environment by shifting to different or more diversified crops. The bonanza farms could not easily make such adjustments. Nor could they escape the ancient strictures on farming at any scale. No agricultural entrepreneur, however ingenious, could create new systems or organizations to exploit economies of scale in the manner of his industrial counterpart. The farmer on any scale could control neither his production, his costs, the market for his goods, nor the climatic factors that influenced and often determined his output.

Despite their demise, the bonanza farms pointed the way to the future in some respects. A congressional committee learned in 1886 that some twenty-nine companies, all controlled by foreigners, owned a total of 20.7 million acres of farmland in the United States. One English company alone held 3 million acres in Texas, while the Holland Company owned 4.5 million acres in New Mexico. Critics denounced these holdings as monopolies in much the same rhetoric as they directed at corporations. In fact, agriculture did eventually turn into a big business, but not in the manner feared by nineteenth-century critics. New techniques and advances increased the speed of production but rarely created new ways to integrate and coordinate the process.

Not until the twentieth century did technology and other factors begin to transform farming into an "agri-business" dominated by large companies. In 1920 American farms still consumed 24 billion man-hours of labor; by 1970 that figure had shrunk to 6.5 billion man-hours. Yet total farm output increased by more than 30 percent in that same period. The man-hours required for an acre of wheat dropped from 35 in 1840 to 20 in 1880 to 2.9 in 1970, that of corn from 69 to 46 to 5.2, and of cotton from 135 to 119 to 24 for the same years. Put another way, the man-hours needed to produce a hundred bushels of wheat fell from 233 in 1840 to 152 in 1880 to 9 in 1970. Corn went from 276 in 1840 to 180 in 1880 to 7 in 1970. The man-hours required to produce a single bale of cotton declined from 438 in 1840 to 303 in 1880 to 26 in 1970.

Despite hard times and other difficulties, the number of farms continued to increase, going from about 4 million in 1880 to 6.5 million in 1920. During that same period the number of small farms (ten acres or less) grew only from 139,000 to 162,000 while the number of farms with a thousand or more acres jumped from 29,000 to 151,000. Farms planted with between 500 and 999 acres soared from 76,000 to 216,000. The amount of cropland actually harvested grew steadily from 166 million acres in 1880 to 283 million in 1900 and 348 million in 1920. Although the rural population declined as a percentage of the total population, it continued to grow in raw numbers from nearly 22 million in 1880 to nearly 30 million in 1900 and nearly 32 million in 1920. Where the farm population accounted for almost 44 percent of the nation's people in 1880, it dropped to 30 percent by 1920.

The difference between industrial and agricultural production revealed itself clearly in the new process flour mills that appeared during the 1870s. Two of these mills alone could grind in a single day all the wheat grown on 225,000 acres of land. The new transportation and marketing system described earlier arose precisely to feed these giant mills, which swallowed eight to ten carloads of grain every day to keep operating. The number of mills could be multiplied at will if investors so chose and a market existed for the flour. However, no amount of technology, technique, or expanded acreage could enable wheat growers to match this quantum leap in processing, let alone guarantee its regularity of output.

The family farmer was a small businessman, and like other small businessmen often lacked the ability to survive in what was a very hard business. In good times, when prices were high and rainfall plentiful, he borrowed money to buy more land and equipment to increase output. But his very success worked against him. The more corn or wheat or any commodity that was produced, the lower the price tended to fall. Farmers could not compensate by planting fewer acres, for who knew how much of what they planted would actually come to harvest? Moreover, the farmer happened to be a debtor in an era that proved to be the longest unbroken period of *deflation* in American history. Many failed to survive and either quit the land or worked as tenants on the land they once owned. By 1880 tenants already worked 26 percent of American farms; twenty years later that figure had increased to 35 percent.[*]

Caught in this whirlpool of difficulties, farmers blamed banks, railroads, grain elevators, country stores, machinery manufacturers and salesmen, Wall Street, the new currency exchanges, and the monetary system for their ills. Sometimes their suspicions were well founded; more often their diagnosis and proposed solutions never got beyond the simplistic and

---

[*] Deflation always benefits creditors and works against debtors because it increases the purchasing power of each dollar. For example, if the farmer had borrowed $5,000 to buy land and equipment and paid 10 percent interest, he owed $500 in interest every year. If wheat sold at $2 a bushel when he took out the loan, he needed to sell 250 bushels of wheat just to pay his interest. If the price of wheat fell (deflated) to $1 a bushel, he had to sell 500 bushels of wheat to pay the same amount of interest. The creditor also can buy wheat for half the price it cost him earlier.

the conspiratorial. In the eyes of rural America, the same forces that oppressed the farmer seemed also to be corrupting the very foundation of American values. Gradually their discontent swelled into the urge to join forces against these evils. Organization did not come easily to people so independent of spirit and living so far apart from one another, yet between 1870 and 1900 farmers created an impressive network of organizations to improve their lot.

Like other movements, theirs began with local societies that expanded into state and then national associations. The first of these larger efforts, the Granger movement, lasted from 1867 to the late 1870s and counted more than 858,000 members at its peak. What began as an effort to educate farmers and bring them together socially escalated into attempts at economic reform and then political action at every level. The movement faltered and died because its makeshift character and loose organization proved no match in a contest against business enterprises that were closely integrated, more efficient, better financed, and more adept at the political process.

During the 1880s local and state farm groups gave rise to the northern and southern alliances as well as a separate one formed by black farmers in the South that enlisted more than 1.2 million members. Like the Granges, the alliances developed programs of social, economic, and educational betterment for farmers. Some even created cooperative ventures to buy goods, market crops, and even manufacture farm machinery. Like the Granges, too, the alliances achieved some success but eventually failed for the same two reasons: They could not maintain their internal cohesion, and they tried to seek remedies by going into politics. Where the Grangers sought relief from the short-lived Greenback party (1874), many alliance members abandoned the traditional parties and turned to the Populist party, which formed in 1890. Despite some early success at the state and local levels, the Populist party foundered in the national arena and wilted away during the late 1890s.

These early efforts failed because farmers failed to create cohesive, effective organizations. "Some of the farmers," complained one sympathizer, "cannot or will not pull together." Race, region, and type of crops continued to divide them, as did the lack of experience at organizing that urbanites learned so readily in so many ways. Technological advances did ease their burden, especially the gasoline-powered tractor, which could be adapted not only to field work but also to other chores such as pumping water and running other machines. When the tractor replaced the horse and mule, it opened land once used for pasture or hay to be sown with crops. Cheap, versatile, and easy to maintain, the tractor did more to help the farmer than any other invention.

Organization, too, came gradually to the farmer's aid, but not in the form he expected. Increasingly after 1900 the family farm gave way to large-scale agricultural enterprises that usually incorporated even when still family owned. These entities joined forces to create not broad-based reform organizations or parties but smaller, more tightly focused advocacy groups such as the American Farm Bureau Federation and the National Farmers Union. Like labor, farmers learned that greater gains could be obtained through such pressure groups than through diffuse parties or organizations. The larger agricultural enterprises mastered this approach first and discovered as well how to exploit government at every level to their advantage. Rural America came late to the organizational revolution, but once it arrived, the business of farming became a more successful business than it had ever been, at least for some.

3

The Defeat of Distance and Desolation

Between 1850 and 1880 rates were reduced on the average to about one half
their former figures.... We no longer produce for the home market, but for
the world's market. It is by the world's supply and demand that prices are
made. The development of transportation has been the main instrument of
this change.

– Professor Arthur T. Hadley, 1885

THE GREATEST ASSET OWNED BY THE AMERICAN PEOPLE
proved also to be their greatest obstacle. Before them lay a vast
continent, most of it still unexplored as the nineteenth century opened. In
an age when land was the principal source of wealth, there seemed no end
to the promise offered by this enormous expanse of territory. But how to get
at it? The celebrated expedition of Meriwether Lewis and William Clark
(1804–6) gave Americans their first important clue as to just how vast and
varied the western landscape was. For more than a century, however, they
could reach land even close to them only by foot or horse, and sometimes
by water. But if they traveled by river, they could not return the same
way because boats could move only downstream. Going by horse or wagon
required roads, which scarcely existed westward and became impassable
in winter or wet weather.

Transportation and communication held the key to settling and exploiting the American continent. New technologies in both areas enabled
settlers and businessmen alike to conquer time and space in unique
ways, and in the process turn wilderness into civilization. It enabled
them to develop distant resources and move them to distant markets.
Not surprisingly, transportation and communication became important

57

businesses in themselves. Railroads became the nation's first big business and its dominant industry for more than half a century. The telegraph also became a major industry as well as an indispensable partner to the railroad.

Moving Goods and People

In 1800 the business of America was commerce. It resided in the nation's few cities, all of which were ports, and it looked to the sea or river because these were the only practical ways to move goods and people. The country had only six cities with 10,000 or more people and only twenty-seven others with 2,500 or more residents. Twenty years later it counted a mere thirteen cities with more than 8,500 people. Only two of them, New Orleans and Cincinnati, lay west of the Allegheny Mountains. Eleven of the thirteen were ports; only Albany and Cincinnati sat alongside rivers. Four cities had much larger populations than the others: New York with nearly 124,000, Philadelphia with 113,000, Baltimore with nearly 63,000, and Boston with more than 43,000. By 1815 New York conducted twice as much foreign trade as its nearest rivals, Philadelphia and Boston.

The future of both settlement and business lay in the back country, where large numbers of people were migrating in a steady stream. Although the nation had an excellent river system, it could take travelers only so far into the interior. Roads were needed, and by the early nineteenth century the young nation had an impressive road system in number if not quality. Most of them were little more than broad paths hewed through the forest on which stumps and stones were sometimes removed and sometimes not. Some swampy areas had "corduroy roads," featuring logs laid across the muddy path. Crude wooden bridges crossed some rivers and streams, but most relied on fords or ferries. The roads followed basic needs, connecting farms to the nearest village, store, mill, or cotton gin. A few "turnpikes" ran between the larger towns or crossed the mountains at low points.

To grow and prosper, the young nation desperately needed improved transportation to the interior. Attempts to get the federal government to underwrite a system of what became known as internal improvements bogged down in local jealousies, financial intrigues, and clashes over constitutional issues. The construction of a federally funded National Road aroused fierce controversy and moved westward at a glacial pace;

by midcentury it finally reached Vandalia, Illinois, where the project was abandoned. States did somewhat better in building roads, and some private toll roads were built by early corporations that usually failed to reap the expected profits from them. The short-lived craze for turnpikes soon gave way to one for canals, thanks to the astounding success of one of the first and most ambitious projects.

Funded by the state of New York and promoted by the determination of Governor De Witt Clinton, the Erie Canal began work in July 1817 and took eight years to complete. At its opening in October 1825 the 364-mile canal connected the city of Buffalo on Lake Erie to Albany on the Hudson River, giving the upper West a direct link to the Atlantic seaboard. At the time no canal longer than twenty-eight miles had been built, and much of the Erie ran through remote wilderness. Nay-sayers predicted financial ruin and embarrassment for the state if "Clinton's Big Ditch" went forward. Instead it poured into New York City what historian John Lauritz Larson called "a 'river of gold' far exceeding that which its early friends had predicted." Settlers hurried west to take up lands in upstate New York while lumber, grain, flour, and other goods flowed down to New York City and into markets on both sides of the Atlantic from the growing population of the upper Midwest. Only ten years after its completion New York state felt obliged to enlarge the canal. Tonnage carried on the Erie Canal did not even reach its peak until 1880.

The spectacular success of the Erie Canal triggered a frenzy of canal projects. Many of them never reached completion and none even approached the record of the Erie. Some, like those built in Ohio, did good business; others, including most of those constructed in Pennsylvania and Indiana, proved to be financial disasters that undermined the credit of the states funding them. By 1840 the American people had built 3,326 miles of canals at a cost of about $125 million. Three states struggled to avoid bankruptcy from overspending on canals. After 1840 the canal mania subsided and those that could not pay their way were abandoned. An economic downturn beginning in 1837 and lasting until 1844 helped deflate hopes, as did the lack of suitable routes for new canals once so many had been built. More important, a new form of transportation vied for investor funds after 1830 and became an even greater craze: railroads.

Even before the railroad entered the scene the steam engine transformed traffic on the nation's rivers. Prior to the steamboat, goods moved downriver on crude rafts and barges. At journey's end in New Orleans they were broken up for scrap and the crew trekked home. A few keelboats and barges tried to return against the current, sailing when the river was wide and poling, rowing, or hauling by cordelle (a heavy rope) when it was not. The trip downriver from Pittsburgh to New Orleans took a month to six weeks; struggling upriver consumed four months or more, a thankless task at best. In 1807 Robert Fulton demonstrated the feasibility of applying steam power to a riverboat on the Hudson River. Two years later John Stevens did likewise on the Delaware River. A new era in river transportation was born.

By 1830 the rivers were crowded with steamboats, which came to dominate river traffic. The Mississippi Valley especially came to depend on the steamboat for its economic development. But the price came high on hazardous western rivers. At least 30 percent of all western steamboats built before 1849 were lost in accidents while in service. Gradually steam technology spread to the Great Lakes, where sailing vessels still offered stiff competition, and to the Atlantic Ocean, where in the 1850s monster steamships like the Great Eastern plied the route to Great Britain. Important as steamboats became to the movement of goods and people, they still had serious limitations. The most obvious one was that they could go only where the river went, and then only part of the year. Ice shut down northern lakes and rivers for two to five months in the winter, while low water often closed western rivers for long periods during the summer. Something more versatile and reliable was needed.

That something proved to be the railroad, which in one generation changed the world of transportation more decisively than any technology since the invention of the wheel. The locomotive was one more marvelous application of steam power. It was in essence a boiler laid on its side with a complex apparatus that enabled the steam to drive flanged wheels along rails with as little friction as possible while hauling a string of cars filled with goods or people. The world's first railroad was built in England in 1825, the same year the Erie Canal opened for business. In the United States three cities lacking good inland waterway connections began ambitious rail projects to reach interior markets. The Baltimore & Ohio, chartered in 1828, constructed thirteen miles of line within two years. Charleston, South Carolina, built a 136-mile line to Hamburg on the Savannah River. Once completed in 1833, it became the longest railroad in the world under single management. By 1835 three Boston companies had opened roads running north to Lowell, west to Worcester, and south to Providence, Rhode Island.

Nearly all of these and other rail projects relied on private rather than public funding and used the corporation as their organizational vehicle. The canal and turnpike manias had soured people in most states on the use of public funds for internal improvements. The result was a fateful shift to private capital to construct transportation facilities providing a public service. This in itself was not new; toll roads, ferries, and the new steamboats did the same, but the railroad dwarfed all of them in scale and complexity of operation. The Boston & Worcester turned out to be a major pioneer in this respect. As Larson explained, "Freer than other public works to embrace innovation and solve novel technical or business problems, the directors of the Boston & Worcester set precedents for governing a railroad in behalf of private interest narrowly conceived that would not likely have evolved under public control. The result was extraordinarily rapid development of railroad business and operating principles – and the roots of a conflict of interest that for two later generations would be known to Americans as the 'railroad question.'"

Some public funds did go into railroad investment, especially after the economic depression lifted in 1844. Southern states in particular put money into what they deemed key rail lines. Georgia completed the Western & Atlantic Railroad from Atlanta to Chattanooga in 1851. Four other states built some track but eventually turned the projects over to private companies. States aided railroads chiefly by providing new companies with liberal charters to expedite their work. In Georgia the state granted two key roads, the Central Railroad of Georgia and the Georgia Railroad, the privilege of operating a bank as well as a railroad. Other charters granted monopoly privileges on traffic, gave railroads generous provisions for issuing securities, or provided tax exemptions. Local aid also boosted railroad construction greatly as communities scrambled eagerly to be located on the line of any proposed road. Historian George Rogers Taylor calculated that prior to 1860 southern state and local authorities contributed more than 55 percent of railroad capital in that region.

During the 1850s the federal government ventured into the subsidy business. Earlier it had helped railroads by allowing its engineers to survey some lines at government expense, and by lowering the tariff on iron used for railroad construction. In 1850 Congress went further by approving a land grant to help build what became the Illinois Central Railroad from Illinois to Alabama – a rare north-south line in a country where most roads ran east-west. A feeding frenzy promptly broke out as promoters sought federal grants for other projects, especially for a transcontinental line from the Missouri River to California. Rival groups promoting different routes fought to obtain this subsidy, which was not granted until the Republicans came to power and southern representatives had left Congress. Nevertheless, the financing of American railroads shifted increasingly to private investors, thanks in part to the deep public disillusionment with government handling of internal improvements. This change was to have profound significance for the future of American business as well as transportation.

The railroad mania raged throughout the rest of the nineteenth century. By 1860 the nation already boasted 30,626 miles of track compared to 3,698 miles of canals at their peak in 1850. One immediate result was a sharp decline in the cost of land transport, a fall significant enough to underwrite what Taylor called "a major revolution in domestic commerce." Most of these prewar roads were local enterprises built to serve local interests competing for trade with rival cities and towns. They did not constitute a rail system in any way, having been built with a variety of gauges and uneven quality of construction. Once the Civil War ended, however, the economic hothouse spurred a frenzy of construction and consolidation that by 1900 created an integrated network totaling 193,246 miles, more than the rest of the world combined. In less than a single lifetime the rail system became the lifeline of industrial America as well as the largest industry in the nation.

The career of one man, Cornelius "Commodore" Vanderbilt, illustrates not only the revolution in transportation but also the American Dream itself. Born on Staten Island in 1794, Vanderbilt revealed early a robust constitution, a fierce appetite for hard work, and a driving ambition to succeed in life. Starting with one small boat he worked to buy at age sixteen, he built lucrative ferrying and shipping businesses first on the Raritan and then on the Hudson rivers. When steamboats showed their superiority and cut into his business, Vanderbilt sold his sailing fleet and switched to the new technology. He mastered steam power well enough to design his own ships. On both river routes he proved so formidable a competitor that rival lines bought him out. Vanderbilt turned his attention to Long Island Sound and then to the coastal Atlantic route to Central America.

In business as in life the Commodore competed ruthlessly and gave no quarter. Once, upon learning that two associates had betrayed him, he wrote them in his barely literate scrawl, "Gentlemen: You have undertaken to cheat me. I won't sue you, for the law is too slow. I'll ruin you." And he did.

At fifty Vanderbilt already embodied the American rags-to-riches story. He prospered at business and possessed a fortune exceeding $1 million, but he had no intention of slowing down. He continued to expand his shipping enterprises for another twenty years before retiring from them in 1864, when at the age of seventy he launched yet another new career. Having dabbled in railroads for some years, he entered the field in earnest by gaining control of the New York & Harlem and Hudson River railroads. These two roads provided access to New York City for the New York Central Railroad, itself a patchwork of lines between Albany and Buffalo. Using his usual strong-arm tactics, Vanderbilt in 1867 forced the stockholders of the Central to admit him to their board. He promptly took command of the road and merged it with his Hudson River line, giving the combined line an astounding capitalization of $90 million. Critics denounced the watered stock and predicted doom for the new company, but Vanderbilt's tough, efficient management turned the road into a first-class line and squeezed the water out of the stock as he said he would do. "If you have been running a road and you spend nine or ten millions to run it," he declared, "if I cannot do it for eight, and do it as well, I am ready to go from the road. . . . [T]hat has been my principle with steamships."

Once in command of the Central, the Commodore's restless eye looked past Buffalo to the three railroads connecting that city to distant Chicago. Vanderbilt acquired all three roads and merged them into the Lake Shore & Michigan Southern Railroad, giving him a through line from New York to Chicago. He also built the first Grand Central Station as a monument to himself and his company. During the depression of the 1870s, Vanderbilt not only expanded westward but also doubled the capacity of the New York Central from two to four tracks, modernized equipment, and made other improvements, including a new administrative structure. However, he left no legacy in the area of management. The New York Central remained a rare case of a road being run by three generations of the same family. At his death in 1877 Vanderbilt bequeathed his family $100 million, the largest American fortune at that time, along with one of the finest rail systems in the land. In one lifetime he spanned two transportation revolutions and introduced the process of consolidation that would characterize the development of the American rail system in future decades.

Railroads transformed American life in a variety of ways. They opened new markets and developed old ones by connecting them to new outlets. By lowering the cost of shipping, they rendered distant markets not only accessible but economically feasible as well. They hastened the settlement of whole regions, especially those west of the Mississippi River. Unlike boats, railroads could go almost anywhere in a straighter line at faster speeds through nearly any kind of weather. They could run on regular schedules and devise equipment to fit their customers' needs. They created towns and cities where none existed, and turned sleepy villages into booming economic centers. As historian Albro Martin wrote, "The railroads made small-town America." In the process they eliminated much of the isolation that was so large a part of life on a vast continent by bringing the outside world to towns in the form of goods, salesmen, settlers, touring performers, and visitors.

But railroads did much more. Their construction and operation made them a prime market for other key industries, especially iron and steel, coal, lumber, and heavy machinery. The iron and steel industry in particular owed its rapid development after 1865 to the lucrative market for its products offered by railroads. Locomotive works, foundries, car builders, bridge companies, and many other suppliers and manufacturers of equipment counted railroads as their chief and sometimes only customer. As the first industry to handle large and varied labor forces scattered across a wide region, railroads created a template for relations between a large, far-flung firm and its workers. As private corporations providing a public service, they were also the first industry to confront the complexities of competition and to undergo regulation by state and federal governments. In these and other areas the railroads set precedents that were later followed by giant industrial corporations.

As the nation's first big business, railroads provided a model for large corporations seeking to do business across an entire region. They pioneered in methods of finance, accounting, and organization, and in raising large sums of money in public markets. As business historian Alfred D.

Chandler, Jr., wrote, "The railroads were the first private business enterprises in the United States to acquire large amounts of capital from outside
their own regions.... Those seeking funds for the new roads in the late
1840s came increasingly to New York City." Wall Street sprang to life
once a flood of railroad securities began to dominate its activities. European funds also began to flow into American railroad construction, and
new firms opened on Wall Street to specialize in the handling of such
investments.

These activities helped make New York the nation's financial center and
capital market. They also ushered in a host of modern financial practices.
"As soon as the American capital market became centralized and institutionalized in New York City," declared Chandler, "all the present-day
instruments of finance were perfected; so too were nearly all the techniques of modern securities marketing and speculation." In these ways
the railroads transformed Wall Street, bringing to the New York Stock
Exchange the modern form of buying and selling securities utilizing such
techniques as buying on margin, call loans, and the use of puts and calls.
It also attracted a new breed of professional speculator who learned to
operate on an unprecedented scale with no other goal than to make transactional profits in an increasingly busy and complex market. For the next
half century railroad securities dominated the New York Stock Exchange
in company with such related industries as the telegraph and express
companies.

The railroads also revamped the construction industry by offering contractors far larger projects than ever before, and plenty of them. Early
turnpikes, canals, and railroads had been built largely by local, part-time
contractors who undertook to complete one portion of the project. Some-
time around 1850 there emerged professional contractors who formed
companies of their own to build an entire road. They supplied all the
equipment, recruited the work force, and found subcontractors to handle
parts of the task. In return they received a flat fee either per mile of construction or based on the total cost, and they usually took part of their
payment in securities of the new road. This arrangement got them deeply
involved in railroad finance. It also positioned them to obtain contracts
from the host of growing cities that needed everything from sidewalks and
paved streets to municipal buildings, schools, water and sewage systems,
and transit facilities.

The management of railroads produced striking innovations that forged a pattern for future large companies. The scale and scope of railroad operation required a new form of administration for which the only precedent even remotely relevant was that of the military. Army officers understood the role of such things as an administrative structure, hierarchical command, bureaucratic procedures, internal communication, and staff operations. Moreover, many rail executives had been trained as engineers, giving them direct experience in railroad or bridge construction. As railroads grew larger through construction and consolidation, the demand for new organizational techniques grew more pressing. The Civil War accelerated this relationship by creating a small army not only of entrepreneurs but also of retired military officers familiar with the hierarchal structure that characterized railroad management. After the war, as railroads multiplied in number and size, former officers came increasingly to dominate their management.

Most American businesses were still run by their owners. Since railroads required vastly more capital than any mill or plantation or shipping fleet, few men or families could afford to own one outright. Ownership quickly became separated from management, and the men who managed them made careers of that work. The many and varied needs of a railroad required a variety of specialized skills and training as well as an administrative hierarchy broken down into specialized departments and functions. The men who performed these specialized tasks – and they were all men – became professionals in their own newly emerging fields. Full-time salaried employees took charge of managing operations, maintenance, equipment, scheduling, accounting, billing, traffic, and repairs. Often they had to create a system where none existed in whatever function they came to perform.

The number and diversity of these functions dwarfed any business that had preceded the railroad, as did its scale of operations. A railroad company had to orchestrate the flow of goods and people on a preset schedule. Most roads ran trains in opposite directions on a single track, which required careful planning and execution. Companies had to keep track of trains, crews, workers, shipments, and cars coming and going from its line. Inspections and maintenance had to be performed, often daily, on everything from rolling stock to track and bridges. Large sums of money gathered in many places by many hands had to be accounted for, and payments made to an army of vendors for a wide variety of expenses. Systems had to be devised for keeping track of a flood of paperwork, for determining whether the road was making or losing money, and how much to charge for a given service. Reports of all kinds had to be generated, read, and synthesized for important data on every aspect of the road's operation. Facilities ranging from shops to offices to roundhouses to fuel and water stops had to be kept in order. The company even needed a "foreign policy" to handle relations with connecting and competing roads.

The need to perform all these tasks led railroads to innovate in many areas of organization. Most railroads came to adopt either the divisional or departmental form of organization. The divisional approach separated the functions of the railroad, appointed superintendents to take charge of each one, and evolved a staff-and-line structure through which responsibility flowed upward from the superintendents to their superior officers. The different functions came to include operations, transportation, motive power, traffic (subdivided into freight and passenger), maintenance, accounting, legal, purchasing, and telegraph. Within each of these realms the superintendent or chief officer reported to a general superintendent or other divisional head, who in turn reported to the top officers of the railroad: the vice president(s), chief legal counsel, secretary, and treasurer. These officials reported to the president of the road, who was responsible to the board of directors.

In effect the divisional structure created largely autonomous realms overseen by general superintendents. By contrast the departmental structure maintained centralized control over the entire road. The president, general superintendent, and other top officers did not surrender autonomy to division officers. Instead the officers at the functional levels reported directly upward to superiors in their department. For example, every superintendent or officer in the transportation department of every geographical division reported not to the general superintendent of that division but to his superior officer in the road's central offices. This tighter centralized control tended to grow more cumbersome and inefficient as the railroad grew in size, prompting many roads eventually to move from the departmental to the divisional structure with its clear delegation of authority from the central office to divisional officers.

Accounting posed a special problem for railroads because they needed so much data, much of it on a daily basis, and no precedents existed for what they needed. Their officers had to invent statistical systems to measure and record the road's activities. Thus did the railroads literally create the profession of accounting, which made startling advances on the ancient world of bookkeeping. As Chandler explained, the new practices involved three categories: financial, capital, and cost accounting. At the most basic level financial accounting involved "the recording, compiling, collating, and auditing of the hundreds of financial transactions carried out daily on the large roads. It also required the synthesizing of these data to provide the information needed for compiling the road's performance." As early as 1857 the Pennsylvania Railroad already had 144 basic sets of accounting records.

But the innovations went much farther. This mass of data enabled railroads not only to strike meaningful balance sheets but also to utilize the "operating ratio" as the standard tool for measuring financial performance. The operating ratio, a statistic still used by railroads, reflected the percentage of gross revenue needed to meet operating costs. Capital accounting aimed at solving several thorny problems. The sums spent on building a railroad went into the construction or capital account, which became an asset on the balance sheet once the road was completed. But what to do with depreciation once the road started operating? Gradually it was determined that defining renewal and repair charges as operating costs kept the capital account honest. To make funds available for this work, most roads set up a reserve or surplus fund into which all earnings went after paying expenses, taxes, interest, and dividends if any. This amounted to a bookkeeping device that worked reasonably well but posed a number of problems over time.

The most devilish accounting problem during the early years was the basic question of how to determine actual costs. The pioneer in this regard was Albert Fink, a civil engineer, who became a top officer on the Louisville & Nashville Railroad. Fink developed complex formulas of measurement out of a simple basis, the ton mile, which showed the cost of moving one ton of freight one mile. "In order to make use of this formula," Fink said of his final computation, "it is necessary to know . . . fifty-eight items of expense, all of which vary on different roads, and enter into different combinations with each other." It took a steady stream of information to compile the ton-mile calculation, but so useful was it that railroad managers soon made it the primary criterion for evaluating the performance of the road and the subordinates who ran it.

The railroads pioneered in modern business accounting out of necessity. Their efforts created methods adopted later by industrial corporations and other enterprises. They remained the standard accounting techniques for American business well into the twentieth century. These organizational innovations, along with new technologies, did much to improve railroad efficiency between 1850 and 1890. During these same years the industry moved steadily away from its early pattern of isolated local roads toward an integrated rail network. A host of issues confronted the foreign policy of every road: differences of gauge, equipment, and techniques, agreements for the exchange of cars between lines, through bills of lading, rate and traffic agreements, and even the matter of schedules through different time zones. All these questions arose as small roads built and merged themselves into larger ones and connected with neighboring lines.

As the national economy grew and cities developed, through traffic – that is, traffic that did not both originate and terminate on one line – became more important. Unlike local traffic, through shipments required arrangements with connecting lines. Through traffic imposed new demands on rail lines. Connections between them had to be seamless, rolling stock compatible, schedules coordinated, and billing methods prearranged. From these needs arose a number of major changes that helped integrate the rail network. The patchwork of different gauges (the distance between the two tracks) led many roads to adopt what became the standard gauge of four feet eight-and-a-half inches. In one remarkable day during the spring of 1886 the last remaining holdouts, all southern roads, moved their tracks to the standard measure.

The crazy-quilt pattern of local times that plagued scheduling disappeared in 1883 when the railroads agreed to adopt the standard time system, which divided the nation into four time zones. Some Americans grumbled that they would rather operate on "God's time – not Vanderbilt's," but the new system became popular enough that Congress made it official in 1918. Professional associations did much to advance standardization. The American Railway Master Mechanics Association, founded in 1868, worked to standardize motive power. Rail officials meeting in conventions also agreed to standardize much of their rolling stock, making interchanges between lines more efficient. So did technical innovations such as automatic couplers, air brakes, and block signal systems. The through bill of lading, which first appeared in the 1850s, enabled goods to move smoothly across several roads. Another innovation, the car accountant office, tracked the location and mileage of the company's cars over other lines and those of other lines over the company's track.

The same forces that brought many of these improvements also confronted railroads with a major dilemma in the form of competition. Small local roads did not vie for traffic with other local roads, but as these lines expanded they reached markets already served by other roads. This sort of competition was something entirely new in the American experience. For the first time large enterprises with high fixed costs competed for the same business, and none could afford to lose. The key characteristic of rail service was that the cost of running a train – which had to follow its schedule – varied little whether the cars being hauled were full or empty. To remain solvent, let alone profitable, a company had to be assured of its share of traffic.

The process of growth evolved through two basic stages: the territorial era during the 1850s and 1860s and the interterritorial era of the 1870s and 1880s. Early American railroads tended to be built by local interests who conceived them as weapons in the growing commercial rivalry between their city and other cities or interior points. Three goals dominated their thinking: (1) funnel traffic to the principal terminus, (2) develop the economic resources of the region tributary to the road as sources of traffic, and (3) earn long-term investment profits. The territorial approach assumed that the road existed to serve its key terminus, and therefore a territory should have only one primary railroad. City, territory, and company alike had to recognize their mutual interdependency. Historian Julius Grodinsky described the concept this way:

> An exclusively controlled local territory . . . was perhaps the most important strategic advantage of a railroad, provided, of course, the monopolized area either originated valuable traffic or served as a market for goods produced in other areas. Territory thus controlled was looked upon as "natural" territory. It belonged to the road that first reached the area. The construction of a line by a competitor was an "invasion."

But defending a road's territory proved far more difficult than anyone imagined. In the postwar environment changing conditions conspired to render the territorial strategy obsolete. The emergence of New York as the nation's leading capital market in the 1850s made investment funds more readily available. Ambitious entrepreneurs organized a flood of new railroad projects. Often these men were neither local nor represented local interests, and they were more interested in short-term profits from the sale of securities and construction of the road than from long-term investment returns. The most ambitious and talented of them looked beyond the territory to an enlarged strategic chessboard that embraced whole regions. Inevitably some of the new mileage competed with existing routes directly or by connecting with other lines.

Defenders of the territorial strategy met this challenge by expanding their road either through construction of new lines or buying connecting lines. Both approaches proved expensive and ineffective. The economic depression of 1873–9 aggravated the situation by throwing a large number of roads into receivership, making them ripe for acquisition by rival companies. Moreover, a road in receivership, freed of its obligations to pay interest on its debt, could slash rates. Gradually it became clear that the territorial strategy was fast becoming obsolete. The alternative was for every major road to extend its reach beyond the territory so as to compete for traffic in as many key points as possible. Thus arose the interterritorial strategy, and with it the specter of competition on a much greater scale than ever before.

In their relations with other lines rail managers utilized three tactics: cooperation, construction, and consolidation. On the simplest level cooperation consisted of agreements among connecting lines to promote through traffic at common rates. As early as the 1850s fast freight lines arose to expedite the shipment of goods over long distances; by the 1870s they had multiplied to the point of hauling most of the nation's through freight. Sometimes roads formed an alliance to create a competitive through line or to extend into hitherto untapped territory. Or they might unite against invading lines or competing routes. The most ambitious forms of cooperation took the form of pools or associations to maintain rates and/or share revenues on traffic to competitive points. Since rate wars meant loss of income for every road involved, most railroad managers genuinely desired cooperative policies and organized the most elaborate and sophisticated associations to maintain stability of rates.

However, all these arrangements lacked any standing in law. They were gentlemen's agreements among executives who seldom behaved like gentlemen. The temptation to ignore agreements and grab short-term advantages by lowering rates proved irresistible, especially to roads hungry for income. The opening of some new invading line might alter the competitive situation dramatically and cause a shuffling of alliances. Any alliance or agreement once made could be unmade, leading to renewed warfare or tedious negotiations to restore harmony. The years between 1870 and 1893 witnessed an endless parade of bitter rate wars, all of which had the effect of driving the cost of transportation lower. These wars, and the inability of the pools and associations to curb them, led rail managers in every section of the country to conclude that cooperation could not produce stability within the industry. Increasingly the more aggressive rail leaders turned instead to construction and consolidation to achieve their goals.

The basic premise seemed clear: If a territory could not be protected from invaders, then the best hope lay in expanding the field of battle and thereby diversifying the outlets for both through and local traffic. This desire to penetrate new territory provided the main impetus for the orgy of construction and consolidation among American railroads after 1880. The completion of a road of any length not only opened new territory for local traffic but might also serve as a link in a new through route, multiplying the number of competitors for traffic at distant points. Major roads enlarged their domains by building new mileage but more often by acquiring existing roads. This approach naturally bred friction, resentment, and suspicion as one company's lines invaded the territory of rival lines. It prompted the latter to respond with expansion moves of their own, ratcheting up the arms race. "The basic motive of system-building" declared Chandler, "was . . . defensive: to assure a continuing flow of freight and passengers across the roads' facilities by fully controlling connections with major sources of traffic."

Whatever the motive, the interterritorial strategy transformed the railroad map of the United States. It produced large, sprawling rail systems that competed with one another on a greatly enlarged landscape. The strategy also contained serious flaws. It assumed that enlarged systems would generate expanding business, which indeed happened. However, steadily declining rates kept earnings from increasing in like proportion. Both construction and consolidation swelled the funded debt of the parent company, and the new mileage often did not pay its way. Nor did the tactic of absorbing rival roads entirely reduce competition. The emerging giant systems had to battle not only each other but also a host of smaller local lines built during the flush of prosperity in the 1880s. They also had to contend with blackmail projects – roads put under construction for the sole purpose of being bought out by an existing line with which they would compete. The face of competition changed considerably, but its presence lingered in rivals large and small.

Perhaps most important, the interterritorial strategy resulted in a great excess of mileage. Many regions found themselves with more railroad lines than even a growing amount of traffic could support. As a result many roads struggled to maintain solvency amid fierce competition that drove rates – and therefore income – steadily downward. Unable to support their bloated capital structures, these roads drifted into receivership. The onset of depression accelerated this process; between 1893 and 1897 nearly a fourth of the nation's railroad mileage sank into bankruptcy, including such major systems as the Union Pacific, Northern Pacific, Atchison, Topeka & Santa Fe, Erie, Richmond Terminal (a holding company of southern railroads), and Philadelphia & Reading. The depression exposed the broader weaknesses of the rail industry with cruel clarity: bloated capital structures lacking sufficient income to service their debt, too many roads chasing too little business in hard times, physical plants that were outmoded on older roads and flimsily built on newer lines, managements that were hidebound in their ways, and organizations lacking the efficiency and flexibility to adjust to changing conditions.

As these roads struggled out of receivership, they faced a new era in which the bankers who had funded much of their expansion, underwritten their consolidations, and orchestrated their reorganization played an enlarged role in their management. One banker in particular emerged from relative obscurity to galvanize the industry with bold new ideas and methods. E. H. Harriman took charge of the reorganized Union Pacific Railroad, modernized it, pieced together a slimmed-down system from the remnants of the old one, gave strong, able officers the leeway to carry out his plans, reorganized the management in a manner considered heretical by most traditional railroad men, and ushered in a new era of railroad organization and management. In 1900 he proceeded to acquire the Southern Pacific, then the largest transportation system in the world, and made his influence felt across the industry with other acquisitions actual or threatened.

With prosperity returning in 1898, Harriman understood as most of his peers did not that the future belonged to those railroads capable of hauling greater loads longer distances at lower rates as cheaply as possible. He spent lavishly to improve the efficiency of his roads and turned most of them into cash cows. As his influence in the industry grew, he promoted what came to be known as a "community of interest" in which a handful of rail leaders would impose order on the rail industry with help from the bankers, who always craved stability. Although this effort failed, Harriman succeeded in imposing on the industry his credo that spending huge sums on modernization reaped dividends in the end. By 1900 a rejuvenated railroad industry resumed its pattern of growth. Total railroad mileage in the United States did not reach its peak of 259,705 until 1916.

Moving Information

The transportation revolution could not have advanced so rapidly without a parallel breakthrough in communications. As the nation expanded, businesses grew ever more dependent on the flow of information. Here, too, the railroads played a pivotal role by making the delivery of mail faster, cheaper, and more efficient. In 1847 railroads carried less than 11 percent of the country's mail, most of which went by horseback or stagecoach. A decade later nearly a third went by rail, and by 1870 the reorganized American postal service had become the largest in the world with its heavy reliance on movement by rail. A new system of distribution utilized special mail cars on which letters could be sorted en route to their destination. A national rail network made possible the efficient operation of a national postal system.

Postal service also benefited from a decrease in the cost of sending a single letter in 1883, the same year that the Post Office added special delivery service. Four years later the free delivery of mail, formerly confined to larger cities, was extended to all towns with 10,000 or more people. An even greater innovation came in 1896 when rural free delivery was introduced. This new service helped transform the buying habits of rural America by fostering the growth of the great mail-order houses, notably Sears, Roebuck and Montgomery Ward. Despite the leaps in technology described below, the Post Office remained the backbone of communication. The number of post offices jumped from 18,417 in 1850 to 76,688 in 1900, when these offices handled more than seven billion items of mail, a volume nearly twice that of only fourteen years earlier.

The most startling advance in communication involved a new technology that was truly a revolutionary innovation. The telegraph enabled messages for the first time to travel faster than man or beast could carry them. It was also the first industry to rely on what was still a mysterious force of nature: electricity. Yet it was a simple instrument that even amateurs could grasp without having to understand the principles of electricity or other scientific concepts. For that reason it was the first industry to utilize electricity as a power source.

The telegraph developed a symbiotic relationship with the railroads, which relied on the "lightning wire" to move trains safely. Dispatching by telegraph enabled trains to travel in one day a distance that earlier might have taken four days. Once the railroads realized the advantages offered by the new technology, telegraph wires were strung alongside railroad tracks and moved west with or sometimes ahead of the lines under construction. Thanks to a federal subsidy, the first telegraph line to California was completed in October 1861, nearly eight years before the first transcontinental railroad linked that state to the rest of the nation. Mutually beneficial contracts gave the railroad a telegraph line along its tracks while assuring the telegraph company of a protected route and an office inside small-town train depots across America.

Railroads ultimately relied on the telegraph to move trains; other businesses used it to move information. Transactions that once took weeks or even months by letter could be completed in days or even hours by parties located in distant cities. This ability to move information quickly changed the way bankers, brokers, merchants, and speculators did business. In the process it also fostered the rise of New York as the nation's commercial hub and of Wall Street as the center of financial markets. Later it enabled growing companies to centralize their operations in one city while maintaining close touch with plants or stores or other facilities across the nation. In this way the telegraph helped create the rise of regional and national markets.

The telegraph also launched the age of media when newspapers seized on it as a competitive edge. The Mexican War in 1846 became the first American conflict to receive extensive newspaper coverage using telegraph dispatches. The reporters who flocked to the scene could not satisfy an excited populace with letters that took seven days to reach the East. At that time only patches of line existed between New York and New Orleans, but rapid work completed the connection late in 1847. So popular did telegraph dispatches become that newspapers clamored for access to the limited capacity of available wires. In 1848 six major New York papers joined together to form what became the Associated Press to share telegraphic news. For more than a decade it dominated the news-gathering scene.

Within two decades the telegraph, like the railroad, became an indispensable part of American life. In 1852 the Superintendent of the Census devoted no fewer than twelve pages of his report to the new industry. By then the United States had 23,283 miles of wire in operation and another 10,000 miles under construction. The telegraph office became, among other things, a training school for many bright young men who later became famous businessmen, including Thomas A. Edison and Andrew Carnegie. It also became a magnet for inventors who devised one improvement or innovation after another for the new technology. In this work no one exceeded Edison, who counted the duplex and quadruplex among his many brainstorms. The duplex enabled an operator to send two messages across a wire at the same time; the quadruplex doubled this output to four, two in each direction.

Although the work of many inventors in several nations, the telegraph reached fruition in the hands of Samuel F. B. Morse, who gave Americans its first public demonstration in 1844. The results astonished an unsuspecting public. "What has become of space?" exclaimed the New York *Herald* shortly afterward. "The magnetic telegraph at Washington has totally annihilated what there was left of it by steam locomotives and steam-ships." Two years later the *Herald* could boast of a rapidly improving telegraphic news service:

> We now publish regularly, in our morning edition, the Southern news received in Washington up to six o'clock the previous evening, together with the Congressional news of that day. Our dispatches are sent from Washington to Baltimore by telegraph, and thence to Wilmington by special steam and horse express, from which point they are telegraphed to Jersey City. In a few days we shall have an uninterrupted communication by telegraph from Washington to New York, and then we shall be able to give the Southern news in full, together with a more particular report of the Congressional proceedings, simultaneously with the Washington papers.

Known better as a painter at the time, Morse became fascinated with the telegraph and devised the celebrated code that became a staple for telegraphic dispatches. Like Whitney with his cotton gin, Morse spent much of his remaining life fending off others who claimed to have invented the code. In effect Morse provided a language for rapid communication and in the process triggered changes in the use of language itself. The leisurely, flowery flow of Victorian prose found itself challenged by the terse, snappy vignettes of the telegram, where more words meant higher costs. In broader terms, the telegraph became one more instrument speeding up the pace of American life, which in turn pressured language to become more succinct as well.

Like the railroad, the telegraph began as a motley assortment of local lines that made little sense without connection to wires reaching more distant points. The trend toward consolidation began early in the telegraph industry and led to the so-called "Six Nations' Alliance" of 1857 in which six leading companies agreed to cooperate with each other and divide territory. However, fabulous profits during the Civil War so strengthened one of these companies, Western Union, that in 1866 it absorbed its rivals into a powerful new corporation capitalized at $40 million. The new Western Union held a virtual monopoly on the nation's telegraph business and became one of America's largest and most powerful firms. In 1866, too, another communication milestone was reached when the first cable linking the United States with Europe opened for business.

By 1870 Western Union operated 3,972 offices linked by 112,000 miles of wire that produced $6.7 million in revenues. Impressive as these figures are, later growth soon dwarfed them. In 1915 Western Union could boast more than 25,142 offices, nearly 1.6 million miles of wire, and $51 million in revenues. Despite the advent of the telephone, radio, and other new technologies, the telegram sent in Morse code remained a staple of American life through World War II. Western Union did not send its last Morse telegram until 1960, 116 years after Samuel Morse first stunned the nation with his memorable first message: "What hath God wrought!"

But the telegraph had some major limitations. The Morse code required an operator to translate every message. Learning the code amounted to mastering a new albeit simple language. Moreover, the telegraph was strictly a station-to-station medium. Every telegraph line was a private connection between two parties. If a firm wished to send messages to five different people or places, each of those recipients needed a separate wire connecting them to the sender. As a result the streets of large cities soon took on thick clusters of overhead wires that were vulnerable to storms and other damage.

Another new technology, the telephone, astonished people even more than the telegraph. The latter sent messages over wires through the mysterious "ether," while the former transmitted actual voices speaking in real time from distant places. Hearing a disembodied voice confronted people with a radically different experience than reading a telegram. Early in the telephone's history a writer in *Scientific American* predicted confidently that the device would never catch on with people. After all, he observed sagely, "The dignity of talking consists of having a listener, and it seems absurd to be addressing a piece of iron." Nor was it a pleasant experience at first. "To use it a person, after briskly turning a crank, screamed into a crude mouthpiece," recounted historian Arthur M. Schlesinger, "and then, if the satanic screechings and groanings of static permitted, faintly heard the return message." Nevertheless, progress on improving its performance went steadily forward.

Although credit for invention of the telephone has always belonged to Alexander Graham Bell, who patented it in 1876, Thomas Edison had as much to do with its development as Bell. He designed a competing instrument for Western Union, but the latter company sold the rights to the Bell Company in 1879 to avoid protracted litigation. It was a transaction that Western Union would come to regret. Like many new technologies, the telephone posed the question of what use to make of it. Some regarded it as a mere entertainment novelty; others saw in it an enormous business market if certain technical improvements could be made. Apart from upgrading the instrument itself, the most significant new piece of equipment was the switchboard, which first appeared in 1878. A year later L. B. Firman devised the multiple switchboard, which enabled the telephone to do what the telegraph could not: connect a host of different users to each other through a central station.

Still, enormous problems remained. The instrument itself had to be improved, as did the technology for transmitting its signal over distance. No infrastructure existed to support a telephone system; it would have to be built from scratch at great cost. Any such large investment involved great risk, especially since the Bell patents would expire in 1893 and no one knew what would happen then. Businessmen had to be convinced that the instrument would be useful to them. At first, hardly anyone conceived of the telephone as a social instrument or thought in terms of a mass market among ordinary people. As with the telegraph, the focus was almost entirely on business usage.

The entrepreneur who did more than anyone else to move the telephone from a curiosity to a staple of everyday life was Theodore N. Vail. Under his leadership the Bell Company solved every one of these problems. Although he had no background in science or engineering, Vail transformed the Bell system into the very model of a modern corporation grounded in technological innovation. While others puzzled over what to do with the new contraption, Vail developed a vision of a national communications network providing integrated service within a framework that amounted to a monopoly. In 1908 he embodied this vision in a compelling slogan: "One policy, one system, universal service."

During the early 1880s Vail helped build the original Bell system; in 1885 he became president of a new subsidiary, American Telephone & Telegraph Company, which was created to develop long distance service. He hoped to forge a national telephone system but could not obtain the capital needed from the owners. In 1887 he left the company to pursue other interests and did not return until twenty years later. By that time the industry had undergone profound changes. The original Bell patents had expired, opening the door for independent companies to jump into the business. By 1902 some 295 independent telephone companies competed with Bell subsidiaries across the nation. Most of them had inferior equipment and little capital, but, like the railroads, they might become a formidable competitor if some aggressive investor scooped them up, combined them, and upgraded their service.

The Bell system met this competition by expanding but failed either to stifle its rivals or to maintain a superior quality of service. It had, however, overextended itself financially and tarnished its public image in an era growing darkly suspicious of giant firms seeking to hold monopoly power. During Vail's absence, too, AT&T had become the parent holding company of the system, presiding over a group of local companies that possessed considerable autonomy in their operations. Summoned back to the presidency of AT&T in 1907, Vail gave the company vigorous, hands-on leadership and a bold new direction. He met the threat of the independent companies with a policy of friendly mergers, absorbing rivals on generous terms and upgrading their service. He reorganized Western Electric, a subsidiary company he had created in 1881, into the nation's dominant manufacturer of telephone equipment and a first-rate research facility.

To strengthen AT&T's position in both the local and long-distance markets, Vail pushed a policy of rigorous standardization and innovation. Service could be efficient only if the entire system had equipment that enabled it to operate seamlessly. That equipment should also be state of the art. As historian Louis Galambos observed, Vail imposed upon the Bell system the tenet that "there would never be a time when technical innovation would no longer be needed or even when it would pay diminishing returns." To that end research facilities played a critical role. For years the major responsibility for research and development fell under the aegis of Western Electric. In 1924, five years after Vail stepped down as president, a separate entity, the Bell Telephone Laboratories, was created to house research and development work. It became the most famous research laboratory in the nation.

In 1915 one of the company's innovations, the electronic repeater, enabled Vail to establish transcontinental long-distance service for the first time. By then AT&T, thanks to Vail's reorganization efforts, presided over an efficient, centralized system that exercised strong control over its operating companies. By then, too, he had also blunted the public outcry against a telephone monopoly. Vail managed this feat by proposing an extraordinary policy that most top leaders shunned. Instead of fighting public regulation he welcomed it as the logical course for a public service that, he insisted, must be a monopoly to operate efficiently. In 1909 Vail actually bought Western Union but cheerfully surrendered control of it as part of an agreement to avoid an antitrust suit. By improving service, keeping rates low, favoring public service commissions, and showing the public the benefits of a unified telephone system, Vail realized his vision of "One policy, one system, universal service."

The monopoly was hardly complete. Some small companies remained, mostly in lightly populated rural areas. Vail sold them equipment and encouraged their connection to the Bell system. By endorsing the concept of state regulation, he blunted the threat of municipal systems in an era that saw rising enthusiasm for cities to own utilities. As historian Robert Sobel concluded, "He formulated a theory of utility monopoly under private control . . . and convinced political leaders of its soundness." Vail also identified and trained a cadre of superior managers to carry on his policies after his retirement. When Vail left the presidency in 1919, AT&T boasted assets of $1.5 billion, second only to United States Steel and twice those of Standard Oil. By then the nation had nearly 12.7 million telephones. The Bell system included more than 7.7 million of these phones and employed nearly 210,000 people.

4

The Potential of Plentiful Power

With the advent of the dynamo electricity has taken a new and very much larger place in the commercial activities of the world. It runs and warms our cars, it furnishes our light, it plates our metals, it runs our elevators, it electrocutes our criminals; and a thousand other things it performs for us with secrecy and dispatch in its silent and forceful way.

– Edward W. Byrn, 1900

BEHIND THE ADVANCES DISCUSSED EARLIER LAY THE MOST fundamental revolution of all: the creation and spread of new sources of power. The power revolution laid the foundation for the new technologies that transformed transportation, communication, and production. It hastened the settling of the continent, multiplied the productivity of a people short on labor, and became the indispensable engine driving material progress. Between 1870 and 1920 American consumption of energy increased about 440 percent, and its sources changed dramatically. In 1870 wood accounted for about 73 percent of all energy used, with coal supplying nearly all the remainder. By 1920 wood provided less than 8 percent of energy used, coal soared to 73 percent, oil contributed 12 percent, and natural gas chipped in 4 percent. By the 1880s a growing proportion of energy went into producing a new source of power that became the most vital technology of the twentieth century: electricity.

Without new sources of power, the industrial revolution would never have occurred. Without plentiful new sources of fuel, the power revolution would have stalled out. Once the steam engine entered the world, wood became its primary fuel. However, even in the New World the seemingly endless supply of wood was finite. The early settlers of America carved giant gashes into the forests, but they were hardly the first to do so. By the time of their arrival native American tribes had already cleared large swatches of forest for their own use. As the white population increased and penetrated deeper into the continent, the forests receded steadily. Coal was available but the Northeast had to import it from either Virginia or England.

Industrialization required two key ingredients for its development: fuel and iron in large quantities at reasonable prices. Prior to 1830 most American machines tended to be small, flimsy, and made of wood. Most of them, especially in the manufacture of textiles, relied on water power because other forms of energy were too scarce or expensive. Coal was mined only at a few locations along the James River in Virginia. Iron was either imported or produced on plantations utilizing charcoal for fuel. A tectonic shift on the industrial landscape began with the opening of the vast Pennsylvania anthracite coal fields in the 1830s. In 1825 these fields produced less than 389,000 tons of coal; by 1849 they yielded more than 3.8 million tons. Clean-burning anthracite provided cheap fuel for the Northeast, which had long depended on water or expensive imported coal for fuel. In broader terms it expedited the spread and diversification of steam power, which in turn enabled more industries to utilize the factory system of production.

No industry underwent a more profound change than the production of iron once anthracite replaced charcoal as the major fuel. A ton of anthracite did the equivalent work of 200 bushels of charcoal, cost less, burned cleaner, and required less attention. Anthracite, with its lower cost, higher heat, and fewer impurities, encouraged the introduction of such new techniques as the hot blast furnace (1840) and the Bessemer process for converting pig iron into steel (1850s). American iron makers borrowed two innovations from the British: the rolling mill (a machine that reduced the labor needed to refine and shape iron into bars) and the puddling process, which enabled iron manufacturers to use coal for fuel and produce on a grander scale. The scattered plantations gave way to much larger iron works that separated production from mining.

As iron makers switched to anthracite, they triggered a major shift in how and where iron was made. Many works located in eastern Pennsylvania to be near their source of fuel. The ability to increase production led owners to move their works from the countryside into cites and towns, and to hire more workers. The first furnace utilizing the hot-blast technique began operation in 1840 in Pennsylvania. By 1849 eastern Pennsylvania alone boasted more than sixty anthracite furnaces with an average work force of eighty persons. American-made iron not only improved in quality but became cheaper and more plentiful. It also ensured the Northeast's domination of manufacturing in many sectors.

The soaring increase in production of American iron made possible by cheap anthracite fuel created a ripple effect throughout the American economy. It made possible the rise of the machine-tool industry, which became a critical component in industrialization. It also enabled other fuel-intensive industries that relied on heat in the production process to adopt the factory system and thereby increase their output. These included glass, paper, and the makers of a wide variety of finished metal products – everything from tools to farm implements to stoves to railroad equipment – as well as the textile industry, which began substituting steam for water power. Most important, coal became a staple fuel for the most crucial machine of the industrial age, the steam engine in all its varied uses from pumping to running machinery, locomotives, and steamboats.

The Steam Revolution

The power revolution began with the steam engine, which by the mid-nineteenth century had generated startling new technologies for such diverse fields as transportation, manufacturing, mining, smelting, agriculture, and construction. Heralded as a miracle of invention, the steam engine in all its forms set in motion the forces that transformed the United States from a rural, agricultural society to an urban, industrial one. Prior to its coming, the only available sources of power remained the ancient ones of wind, wood, water, and muscle, human and animal. Nothing could be moved, lifted, hauled, or produced that required more power than these sources could provide. Small wonder that one writer hailed the coming of the steam engine as "a grand triumph over the material which nature has placed at our disposal. There is no limit as to the sphere of its usefulness."

Although people had dabbled with the concept and application of steam since ancient times, real progress did not occur until the Englishman Thomas Newcomen built the first successful working engine in 1712. No one improved on Newcomen's engine for sixty years. Then, in a series of patents, James Watt and his partner Matthew Boulton added features that created the prototype of the modern steam engine. The Watt engine, like Newcomen's, was first applied to pumping water out of mines or lifting water to higher elevations. Other possible applications required a rotative rather than a simple reciprocating motion. Aware that other inventors were trying to develop a rotative engine, Boulton prodded Watt to devise one. Watt obliged with a rotative version, the final step of which he called "one of the most ingenious, simple pieces of mechanism I have contrived."

The new engine was a major breakthrough because it promised a variety of applications. In particular it could drive the machinery used in textile mills, which had become a staple of the British economy. By 1800 Boulton & Watt had built 496 engines, of which 38 percent were used for pumping and the rest went mostly to the textile industry. Great Britain held the undisputed lead in steam technology, but inventors there and elsewhere were hard at work designing improvements, enhancements, and alternatives to Watt's basic engine. Watt had set in motion the basic pattern of technological progress in which a machine, once brought into existence, became the launching pad for newer, bigger, and better versions of itself. In the United States the leading figure in steam-engine development became that multitalented genius, Oliver Evans.

American inventors came slowly to the steam engine. British historian H. W. Dickinson counted only six engines in the United States in 1803, noting that "mechanical construction and skill were at least fifty years behind those of England." Oliver Evans closed that gap brilliantly. He saw very early the need for smaller, lighter, more powerful engines that could be moved by the power they generated. As early as 1786 he began conceiving engines for both mills and a land carriage. In 1801 he built a small stationary engine to power a grinding mill and patented it three years later. This first high-pressure engine differed from Watt's bigger, heavier models in two key respects: It lacked a condenser and placed the cylinder and crankshaft at the same end of the beam.

In 1805 Evans unveiled his boldest creation to date: the giant "Oruktor Amphibolis" or "Amphibious Digger." Weighing 40,000 pounds and thirty feet long, it was in essence a flat-bottomed scow on wheels with a steam engine mounted inside it. The machine lumbered awkwardly under its own power from Evans's workshop to the Schuylkill River, where the engine was switched to power a paddlewheel in the rear. The engine also powered a shovel, and for some months the monster saw service as a dredging machine. A year later Evans built the first of two high-pressure engines that were perhaps the first to power gristmills entirely by steam. He began constructing steam engines in his Philadelphia workshop and later opened another workshop in Pittsburgh, where his men constructed their first engine for a steamboat.

Evans never received the encouragement, fame, or fortune that was heaped on Watt, but his vision and his legacy endured. "I have no doubt that my engines will propel boats against the current of the Mississippi and wagons on turnpike roads with great profit," he declared. "The time will come when people will travel in stages moved by steam-engines from one city to another, almost as fast as birds can fly, 15 or 20 miles an hour." He realized only part of that ambition before his death in 1819, but other inventors took up the challenge. Robert Fulton put his steamboat on the Hudson River in 1807 and John Stevens his version on the Delaware River two years later. By 1820 steamboats could be found on all the major rivers of the East Coast and in Chesapeake Bay. Five years earlier, the first steamboat had made its way up the Mississippi River from New Orleans. In 1817 only seventeen steamboats operated on western rivers; by 1855 that number had mushroomed to 727.

Among other accomplishments, Evans and those who followed him succeeded in making the steam engine an important business in itself. Robert Fulton brought the engine for his first steamboat from England along with a mechanic to tend it. So too with locomotives. Richard Trevithick and George Stephenson of England built the first steam locomotives, and the first versions to appear in the United States came from England. But American mechanics mastered these prototypes and quickly came up with locomotives of their own. The first locomotive to haul cars in regular train service appeared in 1831 on the Charleston & Hamburg Railroad; it was built in New York City. Several other American-made locomotives went into operation that same year, including a small engine built by Matthias Baldwin of Elizabethtown, New Jersey. A year later Baldwin introduced his *Old Ironsides*, a new engine that became an immediate success and launched its designer onto a career as the country's premier engine manufacturer. By 1839 the Baldwin Locomotive Works had turned out 136 steam locomotives. The company's output increased steadily until by 1864 it was producing 130 locomotives every year. Within a decade of its first appearance, the locomotive became a significant American business.

Steam engines provided power for ships, trains, mills, mines, and other general uses. Like the locomotive, they grew in size, power, and utility through a constant stream of innovations. No American pioneered more innovations or achieved more fame as an engine builder than George H. Corliss, a Rhode Islander with no background in engineering. At twenty-seven Corliss went to work for an engine builder in Providence. In three years he became head of the firm and launched a series of inventions that established his reputation. The first of these in 1848, the "automatic drop-cutoff," controlled the amount of steam entering the cylinder and resulted in an impressive increase in efficiency. A year later he introduced cylindrical rocking valves and followed with a series of patented innovations aimed at reducing fuel consumption and improving efficiency.

By the Civil War Corliss had become the best-known engine builder in the nation. He not only manufactured engines and boilers but also licensed them to other builders. To emphasize the superiority of his engines he worked out a bold sales ploy similar to one used by Watt: Customers could pay a fixed price or base their payment on how much their fuel bill had been reduced after a year's service. The Corliss valves became as popular abroad as at home, especially in engines that drove the textile mills in Lancashire, England. When the basic Corliss patents expired in 1870 other builders rushed to turn out their own versions of the Corliss engine. In this way the Corliss steam engine remained dominant for most of the nineteenth century. As late as 1925 the Allis-Chalmers company still had heavy-duty Corliss engines in its catalog.

The peak of Corliss's fame, and that of the steam engine, came with the giant twin engines he constructed for the great Philadelphia Centennial Exhibition of 1876. Housed within the giant expanse of Machinery Hall with its fourteen acres of exhibits, these monster engines loomed forty feet high, weighed 700 tons, and churned out 2,500 horsepower, enough to power every working machine in the building. Spectators flocked eagerly to see them and went away shaking their heads in disbelief at the spectacle of so much power flowing out with only a single attendant to provide a sip of oil every so often. Seventeen years later Chicago would host another world's fair intended to show off the marvelous advances Americans had made in technology. By then the steam engine had taken a back seat to a newer, even more amazing, and infinitely more versatile form of power: electricity.

The Electric Revolution

For all its wondrous accomplishments, the steam engine even in its more refined forms embodied serious shortcomings. A complex machine with its furnace, boiler, pumps, valves, coal bunkers, ash pans, and other parts that required an engineer to tend, it transferred power awkwardly and could not transmit over distance. It was neither portable nor flexible in its use. Factories requiring steam power, for example, could not organize their machines in the most efficient manner for production; rather the machines requiring the most power had to be placed closest to the source of power. Factory interiors became a jungle of belts and pulleys, creating a cramped, noisy, dirty, and dangerous workplace. There could be no truly efficient assembly-line method of production with machinery driven by steam power. Nor could steam provide direct power for communication or illumination devices as it had for transportation in the form of the locomotive and steamboat. And always there hovered the fear of a boiler explosion, the cause of many ghastly accidents, especially on steamboats.

For these and other reasons, ambitious inventors sought alternative sources of power. The most promising line of development lay in experiments with one of the most elusive forces known to man. Electricity was known to the ancients in the form of lightning and magnetism in the lodestone, but neither force was understood or used in any way except for the compass. In 1801 Alessandro Volta devised the first battery that enabled the flow of electric current, but its nature remained a mystery eagerly explored by a host of inventors and scientists. By the century's end, electricity advanced from a mere curiosity to the most vital source of energy in industrial society. In the process it also spawned several of the largest businesses in the United States.

Electricity can be utilized in three forms: heat, light, and mechanical energy. Two key discoveries paved the way for its practical use. In 1820 Hans Christian Oersted discovered that an electric current flowing from a battery produced a magnetic effect. Eleven years later Michael Faraday found that he could produce an electric current by a mechanical action such as moving a conductor through a field. From these two discoveries emerged two crucial elements in understanding electricity. Oersted had shown that an electric current would produce a magnetic field and with it a force – that electrical energy could be converted into mechanical energy. Faraday demonstrated the reverse: that mechanical energy could be converted into electrical energy.

Two major problems dogged efforts to find practical applications: how to produce power in quantities comparable to the steam engine or even the horse, and how to transmit that power from its source to the user. Although progress had been made in the development of batteries, they remained too feeble to power any substantial machinery. Electricity found its first practical use in communication largely because the telegraph required only modest amounts of power. However, the telegraph taught people little if anything about the nature and potential of electricity. It was a simple instrument that required no theoretical understanding, and that understanding was slow to develop. The telephone, too, required only a small amount of electric power. By the 1870s, however, inventors and entrepreneurs were struggling to realize far more ambitious applications in the fields of illumination and transportation.

By mid-century gas lighting had come to dominate American cities. In 1850 the nation had thirty gas companies; twenty years later it had 390. Kerosene lamps also came into widespread use after the discovery of oil in Pennsylvania in 1859. But gas lighting had some major drawbacks. It was dim, flickered, left a residue on the fixture and walls, consumed oxygen, and posed the threat of fire. In summer it made rooms even hotter, and wall fixtures could not be moved. A potentially vast market awaited anyone who could devise a better system of lighting. One new industry got its start in 1878 when Cleveland inventor Charles F. Brush introduced his arc-light system consisting of simple arc lamps and an improved direct current generator to run them. The arc lamp provided a bright, glaring, unvarying light that was suitable for city streets and commercial use such as department-store windows, but it would not do for indoor use.

The pivotal breakthrough in electric lighting came in 1879 when Thomas Edison displayed the first incandescent light bulb. Edison came late to the race among inventors to devise a workable electric alternative to gas lighting. No one had succeeded in creating a bulb that could provide suitable light at a price and durability that would rival gas. Edison not only came up with a workable bulb but also took the next giant step by creating an entire system to install and power it. In effect he put together the first electric power system. His famous Pearl Street Station in New York City began operating in 1882 and within two years provided power for 500 homes in the surrounding neighborhood. "The Pearl Street Station was the biggest and most responsible thing I had ever undertaken," Edison recalled. "It was a gigantic problem.... All our apparatus, devices, and parts were home-devised and home-made. Our men were completely new and without central station experience."

Edison formed several companies, one of which built and operated power stations while others manufactured the needed lamps, generators, and other equipment. Although business was brisk, especially among hotels, companies, and public buildings that acquired individual power stations to furnish them with lighting, Edison's system had one serious flaw that stunted its growth. It operated on direct current (dc), which had major limitations. Direct current flows in one direction and has to be transmitted at low voltage because it must be used at low voltages and cannot easily be reduced from a high transmission voltage to a lower one. Nor does it lend itself readily to production by a generator of large capacity. Since some current is always lost in transmission, any effort to send direct current over long distance required a large investment in expensive copper wiring. This factor made the cost of transmitting direct current prohibitive for any distance beyond a mile.

However, dc was not the only option. Alternating current (ac) does not flow only in one direction but reverses itself periodically. (The term "frequency" refers to the number of times per second alternating current reverses itself.) This quality made ac relatively easy to transmit over long distances at high voltages with little loss. The problem lay in how to step this flow down to lower voltages for practical use at the destination. Moreover, wires carrying ac current, unlike those handling dc, posed significant dangers because of their high voltage. By 1885 several inventors had helped devise the transformer, which could raise the voltage of generated power at the point of origin and reduce it again at the destination. This crucial appliance made possible the efficient transmission of power over long distances.

Given his pioneering role as an entrepreneur in electricity, Edison might have been expected to dominate important new innovations in the field. But his attention turned to several other inventions, and he never resumed the focus on things electrical that had led to his earlier triumphs. As a result, other inventors overtook him in devising improvements and developing new inventions. Even worse, Edison's early success with his dc-based system led him to ignore the obvious advantages offered by ac current. Not only did he cling doggedly to the dc system, he fought every innovation geared to the creation of a rival ac system with a viciousness that stained his reputation. Here, as elsewhere, Edison showed his uncanny ability to be spectacularly right in some areas of invention and spectacularly wrong in others.

For a time Edison's dc system did well. By 1885 his company had installed 494 isolated power stations for lighting everything from oil refineries to banks to hospitals. Between 1884 and 1888 the firm also licensed 515 central stations for cities and towns, all of which bought their lamps from Edison. During these same years an important new industry sprang into existence that became by far the largest user of electric power. After several promising but flawed early projects, the electric trolley became a reality in 1888 when Frank J. Sprague built an entire system in Richmond, Virginia, that applied electric power to a twelve-mile rail network with thirty cars in service. Sprague was a former employee of Edison, who had himself worked on railway motors early in the decade but abandoned his efforts in 1883.

Sprague brought to his venture only a motor he had designed. Everything else had to be improvised on the job without benefit of previous experience or testing, and he had rashly agreed to a contract requiring him to complete the entire system in ninety days. No existing system had utilized more than twelve cars at a time. Even worse, Sprague had never even seen Richmond, the hills of which would give his system fits. Yet he succeeded, and the success of his bold venture sparked the rise of what became the giant electrical streetcar or traction industry. Urban transportation, strained by steadily rising populations, had long relied on streetcars hauled by horses, each of which ate its original cost in feed every year and lasted only about four years in harness. By 1882 investors had poured more than $150 million into horsecars. When the century closed, 99 percent of these lines had been converted to electric trolleys totaling 22,576 miles of track with an investment of $2 billion.

The rapid growth of demand for electric lighting and trolleys spurred another round of technical innovations. Apart from improvements in the lights themselves, better and more powerful generators were needed to run them. Transmission systems capable of delivering large amounts of power had to be developed. Trolleys lacked efficient motors and control systems. Better motors were needed to drive machinery in plants. New uses for electricity loomed on the horizon if these and other problems could be solved. During the mid-1880s two men, an entrepreneur and an inventor, did much to launch what proved to be a new era in the use of electricity. George Westinghouse pioneered in the creation of power systems utilizing alternating current. Nikola Tesla contributed the induction motor, which could be adapted to run almost any type of machine.

Westinghouse made his early reputation as an inventor in the railroad industry, most notably with the air brake he patented in 1869. Between 1880 and 1890 he poured out a stream of new inventions and innovations, averaging more than a patent a month. Along with contributions to railroad brakes, the little known but extremely important friction draft gear, switches, and signaling, he devised a delivery system for natural gas and became deeply interested in electric power. Especially did he immerse himself in the possibilities of utilizing alternating current. Apart from being a gifted inventor in his own right, Westinghouse also possessed a rare ability to organize and direct research teams of talented scientists and engineers within the numerous companies he founded. His talent for inspiration matched that of invention. Although not formally trained, his mind was open and hungry for new information. Along with his own inventions, Westinghouse kept a close watch for new developments and was quick to acquire patent rights from other inventors.

Once his interest in electricity was aroused, Westinghouse founded a separate company in 1886 to develop products for both dc and ac systems, but his attention turned early to the possibilities of ac. He and his top engineers perfected a more efficient transformer that became the heart of an ac system, and in November 1886 Westinghouse installed the nation's first commercial ac power plant in Buffalo, New York. In four years the company built 300 central power stations, all using alternating current, and positioned itself as the chief rival to the Edison company with its dc systems. During the late 1880s Edison waged a bitter war against the spread of ac current, insisting that it was far too dangerous. Known popularly as "the War of the Currents," the fight, in the words of historian Jill Jonnes, led Edison into an unsavory role as the "self-appointed crusader against the 'damnable current,' a man whose stated goal was the legislative end of . . . the AC companies."

Westinghouse met this challenge with typical fortitude. In the end not even Edison's influence could overcome the obvious superiority of ac systems. The third major electric company, Thomson-Houston, stayed clear of the fight but had early switched from selling dc systems to marketing ac ones. In 1889 Edison encouraged financier Henry Villard to merge his lighting and manufacturing companies into one big firm, Edison General Electric. Villard also acquired Sprague's traction company. As the current war heated up, Villard tried to lure the managers of Thomson-Houston into a merger despite Edison's objections. At the same time he tried to woo Westinghouse into merging with Edison General Electric even as Charles Coffin, the head of Thomson-Houston, approached Westinghouse with the idea of combining their firms. None of these efforts went anywhere even though Westinghouse desperately needed cash for his capital-starved companies.

Where Villard failed, J. P. Morgan succeeded. In 1892 he orchestrated a merger between Edison General Electric and Thomson-Houston. Capitalized at $50 million, the new General Electric company unceremoniously dumped the names of all its founding fathers from the title. Thomson-Houston's managers took charge of the new company, and a disillusioned Edison left the field of electricity never to return. Westinghouse survived his own financial crisis thanks to a reorganization in 1891 that left his company stronger than ever. Nevertheless, many observers predicted that General Electric would soon swallow its only remaining rival. They reckoned without the ingenuity and stubbornness of George Westinghouse, whose major flaw had always been trying to do too many things at one time with limited resources.

Despite the enervating war of the currents, Westinghouse made important strides during those years. In 1888 he learned of some patents taken out by Nikola Tesla on an ac induction motor. The brilliant but eccentric Tesla's creation promised huge advantages over conventional dc motors if it could be adapted to an ac power system. Westinghouse immediately grasped the importance of Tesla's motor. He secured the rights to it and brought Tesla to Pittsburgh to oversee development. Earlier Tesla had worked briefly for Edison but did not get along with him. Westinghouse he found to be an entirely different kind of person. "He is one of the few men," said Tesla, "who conscientiously respect intellectual property, and who acquire their right to use inventions by fair and equitable means."

Work on the Tesla motor dragged on for seven discouraging years. Technical problems dogged the engineers, and early efforts to adapt the Tesla motor to traction work flopped. In 1890 the financial crunch forced

Westinghouse to suspend work on the motor for nearly two years until the reorganization put his company back on solid footing. By 1893 Westinghouse had progressed enough to offer ac power equipment to commercial customers on a regular basis. An unexpected opportunity gave him a stage on which to showcase his system in grand style. The World's Columbian Exposition opened in Chicago that year. In the competitive bidding to light the fairgrounds, Westinghouse outfoxed General Electric and won the contract. He responded with the most dazzling display of electric power and light ever seen.

When the fair opened on May 1, 1893, Westinghouse had in place twelve giant dynamos weighing 75 tons each, utilizing a multiphase system devised by Tesla and powered by a 2,000-horsepower steam engine. A marble switchboard 1,000 square feet in size controlled more than 200,000 incandescent lamps, only 180,000 of which operated at any one time. One of the fair's most popular attractions, the giant 250-foot-high wheel of George Washington Ferris, alone contained 3,000 lights. In daylight the fabulous White City enchanted visitors; at night it became a wonderland of lights in many colors. Electricity ran everything – not only the elevated railway that circled the grounds but even the battery-powered gondolas in the canals. No overhead wires threatened visitors; they were all tucked underground in corridors tall enough for a man to stand. Electrical exhibits, especially the electric kitchen, attracted large crowds, although the most revolutionary of them, the complete ac system assembled by Tesla, impressed only those knowledgeable about electricity.

Thwarted in its effort to light the fair, General Electric made its presence known in the huge Electricity Building, gorgeously lit and featuring an enormous eight-foot-tall Edison incandescent bulb with dancing multicolored lights created by five thousand prisms inside it. Westinghouse countered with the whirling Egg of Columbus, a large copper egg demonstrating the rotating fields of polyphase currents. Other exhibits designed by Tesla dazzled onlookers with the mysteries of electricity. The fair succeeded in providing Westinghouse with a compelling advertisement for ac power, and the company even turned a modest profit on the contract. Two other inventions helped ensure the superiority of the ac system. In 1892 Westinghouse had devised the first rotary converter, which converted ac power to dc, and one of his engineers came up with a meter suitable for alternating current.

The ac system displayed by Westinghouse at the World's Fair included a complete polyphase ac system: an ac generator, transformers for raising and lowering the voltage for transmission, induction motors, and a rotary converter, which supplied dc for a railway motor. The implications for future use of electricity went far beyond lighting to supplying power for everything from trolleys to industrial plants. For this to happen on a large scale, generators powerful enough to provide hitherto unprecedented amounts of power had to be created. Bigger generators in turn required more powerful steam engines to drive them. The problem was how to develop more power from a steam engine without making it too large and heavy for practical use. The answer lay in the development of the steam turbine, and here, too, Westinghouse played a vital role.

The first patent secured by George Westinghouse in 1865 had been for a crude rotary steam engine. His interest in the rotary engine remained strong even while he busied himself with a host of other activities. He followed the work of English inventor Charles A. Parsons, who built the first steam turbo-generator in 1884 and devised his first turbo-alternator or ac generator four years later. Knowing observers dubbed the steam turbine the greatest advance in primary power since Watt's steam engine. It enabled the use of steam at high pressure and temperature in a relatively small body compared to standard steam engines. By increasing the potential speeds of generators, it ushered in a new era of power generation. In 1895 Westinghouse licensed the Parson's patent and proceeded to manufacture turbines that incorporated his own improvements as well. By 1902 he was building turbo-generators with a capacity of 6,000 kilowatts. At the time of the founder's death in 1914, Westinghouse Electric had increased the output to 30,000 kilowatts. Later models would dwarf these units.

The war of the currents culminated in a project that unexpectedly ushered in a new era of power usage. Since the mid-nineteenth century attempts had been made to harness the power of Niagara Falls for commercial purposes. Apart from their scenic majesty, the falls offered ideal conditions for power generation. The flow of the Niagara River was heavy and constant, thanks to the four Great Lakes that served it as reservoirs. The first successful effort in 1875 produced only about 7,000 horsepower by 1882. One problem concerned the sheer potential output of the falls and what might be done with large amounts of power if it could be generated. The village of Niagara Falls had only about 10,000 people and little industry. The city of Buffalo consumed some 50,000 horsepower of energy a day but lay twenty miles from the falls. It would require a transmission system capable of sending large quantities of electricity over that distance. To complicate matters, New York state in 1885 acquired land on both sides of the falls to preserve its scenic beauty for tourists. No power facilities or industrial development could occur within this area.

In 1886 Thomas Evershed, a civil engineer, devised a plan for developing power at the falls outside the reserved land. Three years later a group of investment bankers formed the Cataract Construction Company to carry out some plan of development. Edward Dean Adams, the president of the new company, researched the matter thoroughly in both Europe and the United States. In 1890 he created an international commission of prominent experts and held a contest for the best proposals from domestic and foreign firms. Westinghouse declined to enter, saying the prize was not worth the value of the advice sought. "When the Niagara people are ready to do business," he said, "we shall make them a proposal." Already some businessmen in Buffalo in 1887 had offered a prize of $100,000 to any inventor(s) for a design that could successfully transmit power from the falls to the vicinity of Buffalo. No one had yet claimed it.

The technical obstacles were formidable. No one had ever transmitted so much power that far. Electricity was not the only way to transmit power; wire, manila rope, water pressure, and even compressed air (which Westinghouse suggested in 1889) had also been used. Four of the awards given by the commission in 1891 were for compressed air systems, though none were ever implemented. If electricity was chosen, should the system be ac or dc? The largest existing alternator produced only 1,000 horsepower, much less than the Niagara project would need. But breakthroughs in electric technology came steadily during the early 1890s, including the induction motor and the rotary converter. Moreover, Westinghouse had in 1891 successfully transmitted ac current four miles from a dynamo to a working motor at a mine in Telluride, Colorado. This modest project became the first ac power transmission system in the nation. Then came the triumphant display of ac power at the Chicago fair.

In May 1892 Westinghouse finally told Cataract that he was willing to submit plans for generators to power the Niagara project. Many experts, including the distinguished Lord Kelvin, urged Adams and his committee to employ a dc system. However, early in 1893 Westinghouse completed a thirty-five-mile hydroelectric ac transmission system in Pomona, California. That May the committee chose to go with ac power. This decision was as bold as it was historic in its results. Both Westinghouse and General Electric had submitted plans for complete ac systems, but Adams and his committee rejected both and asked one of their technical experts, British engineer George Forbes, to design the generators and other apparatus. When Forbes had finished, the committee asked Westinghouse to build the generators. The Westinghouse engineers saw several technical problems with the design, however, and refused to do the work until the committee allowed them to make modifications.

Despite the formidable technical obstacles in constructing 5,000-horsepower generators as well as the switchboard and auxiliary equipment, Westinghouse installed the system successfully in 1895. The village of Niagara Falls received power that summer, and in November 1896 the first electricity flowed from the falls to Buffalo. For the first time large amounts of power were produced and transmitted to a distant locale. Growth came quickly to the Niagara facility; by 1905 the original three generators had grown to twenty-one located in two powerhouses. The spectacular success of the Niagara project settled the war of the currents once and for all. It blazed the trail for the creation of large centralized electric power plants, and its pioneering role did not stop there. To the surprise of even knowledgeable observers, it also spurred the stunning rise of a formidable electrochemical industry close to the falls.

For years the output of several industries had remained modest because their production required exceptionally high heat. The most conspicuous of these were aluminum and abrasive products. Electricity provided not only a high but a pure temperature because it did not contaminate the application receiving it. The process for manufacturing aluminum had been discovered in 1886, but production barely reached three tons a year until the Aluminum Company of America (Alcoa) built a plant at Niagara and launched what proved to be a major new industry. Giant electric furnaces also turned out large quantities of artificial graphite, carborundum, alundum, ferrosilicon, ferrochromium, vanadium, molybdenum, nitric acid, and other electrochemical products. Electric power also began moving steadily into the factory to power not only lighting but also motors for machinery that triggered a revolution in the internal organization and efficiency of production. From the advent of electric motors would flow, among other innovations, the assembly line pioneered by Henry Ford.

Electricity had moved from lighting to traction to industry, but it had not yet become widespread in American life. At the century's end it remained a luxury of the rich. Ordinary people could not afford electric lights, let alone the cost of retro-wiring their homes for its use. It took the pioneering efforts of a man not nearly as well known as Edison or Westinghouse to move electricity from the wholesale to the retail era. Samuel Insull devised a system for distributing and selling electric power that transformed it from an exotic technology into the key component of American daily life and work. He brought to the American home not only cheap, efficient lighting but a power source capable of operating a host of appliances that could never have come into existence without the availability of electricity. In that sense he created an entire industrial sector.

An Englishman by birth, Insull came to the United States in 1881 at the age of twenty-two to serve as private secretary to Thomas Edison. The timing of his arrival proved crucial to Insull's future. He became Edison's indispensable man just as the inventor was preparing the Pearl Street Station and ushering in the new electrical industry. In 1883 Edison created his construction department and told Insull to go sell and build central power stations. Insull showed an immediate talent for both promotion and salesmanship. Three years later the Edison electrical business had grown so extensive that the inventor needed enlarged facilities to manufacture his component products. He acquired a defunct locomotive factory in Schenectady and put Insull in charge of it. "Do it big, Sammy," he said. "Make it either a big success or a big failure."

Insull made it a huge success, quadrupling sales and generating a profit of 30 percent in two years. The plant mushroomed from its original 200 workers to 6,000 men in six years. In managing the operation Insull mastered the intricacies not only of manufacturing but of finance as well. The experience gave him a lifelong loathing for Wall Street bankers. When J. P. Morgan created the new General Electric in 1892, Insull was the only Edison executive offered a high position in the company. He accepted but left a short time later to become president of the Chicago Edison Company. In that post he would in little over a decade revolutionize the electric industry and turn Chicago into the heart and showcase of electric power in the United States if not the world.

Put simply, what Insull did was solve the tangle of problems involved in how to cost, price, distribute, and generate electric power on a scale grand enough to make it a staple retail product. As Insull himself later admitted, "no one in the central station business at the time really understood its fundamental economics." He managed this transformation by standing the industry's conventional wisdom on its head, and by displaying a political acumen rare in businessmen. Cruising the shark-infested waters of Chicago politics, Insull spent six years acquiring a virtual monopoly of power stations within the Loop before turning his attention to the broader problems of how best to run them. Edison and later industry leaders had used the gas industry as their model for operations and rates, but this model had a fatal flaw. Gas could be stored and its delivery load evened by using reserves to handle peak demands. Electricity could not be stored, which meant that production had to remain at whatever level peak demand required to avoid blackouts or damage to equipment.

Insull recognized early that solving the load factor was a critical element in creating a new model for electricity. Traction consumed by far the largest amount of power, and its usage peaked during the morning and late afternoon rush hours. To spread their use into Sundays, many streetcar companies had developed amusement parks near the end of their lines as a draw. Little usage took place at night. Insull saw that broadening the base of consumer use would do much to balance loads, since most home use occurred in the evening. However, Chicago Edison and the other Loop companies he acquired were dc-current systems, which limited their ability to distribute power efficiently beyond the downtown district. To realize his ambition, Insull needed both a better distribution system and the means to increase electricity consumption dramatically. The obvious solution to a better distribution system was ac current. Insull confined Chicago Edison's delivery area to barely a mile beyond the Loop and used another company, Commonwealth Electric, to create an ac company capable of furnishing power to the rest of the city.

The problem of increasing the consumption of electricity had long baffled the industry. Insull stumbled onto the answer during a trip back to his native England in 1894, when he learned about a new device called a demand meter. Invented by Arthur Wright, the meter recorded not only how much electricity a customer used but also when it was used and the maximum level of demand. After installing the new meters in Chicago,

Insull worked out an entirely new method of calculating the relationship between costs and pricing. In 1897 he stunned the electric utility industry by unveiling his new two-tier pricing system, which featured a fixed cost for a customer's minimum usage and a second sliding-scale charge for all usage beyond the minimum. This ingenious new system resulted in lower charges for both heavy and light users of electricity, and encouraged every type of consumer to use more power.

From that moment Insull launched a crusade to transform the way electric utilities did business. The emphasis moved from increasing production to a gospel of mass consumption that promised not only to increase demand but also to spread the usage load over twenty-four hours. Besides increasing both the number of customers and the amount of electricity they consumed, the new approach offered the important political benefit of driving electric rates steadily downward. Average rates dropped nearly a third at once and kept going down. A master promoter, Insull enticed new customers with an offer to install six lighting outlets in their homes free of charge. So successful was he in this work that his rate-making pattern became the standard throughout the world. As his biographer Forrest McDonald wrote, "He knew that the electric man's promised land lay in the almost unimaginably vast potential market in industrial power and commercial and residential lighting. . . . To win customers, Insull sold electricity at rates so low they appalled other central station men."

Selling power on a grand scale meant that Insull had to produce and distribute it in mass quantities. Here, too, he transformed the industry by introducing a system that his publicists called "mass production" well before Henry Ford exemplified that technique. Rapid improvements in the technology of electrical equipment enabled him to create a network of central power stations that distributed ac current at high voltage via underground wires to substations, where rotary converters changed the current to dc for distribution to customers. This enabled Insull to supply all of Chicago with power from one central location, the Fisk Street Station. To spread the load, Insull used his political as well as sales acumen to secure the business of Chicago's traction companies, which by 1909 consumed nearly twice as much power as all other customers.

To meet the soaring demand created by Insull's policies, his companies had to generate more power than had ever been possible in the past. Insull pushed General Electric to develop the revolutionary turbo-generator beyond the limits of existing technology. The turbo-generator had one outstanding characteristic: The larger it was, the more cost effective it became. Insull wanted 5,000-kilowatt units; both General Electric and his own engineers said it couldn't be done. Insull persisted until in 1903 GE managed to construct the world's first 5,000-kilowatt steam-electric turbine. Then he promptly raised the stakes. Eighteen months later GE engineers came up with units twice that size. Within a decade Insull demanded and got generators as large as 35,000 kilowatts. By the 1920s he was installing units five times that size.

The steady escalation of power output coupled with an efficient distribution system enabled Insull to pursue his gospel of consumption vigorously. To pay for his rapidly expanding system, Insull proved no less original. He pioneered the open-end mortgage and other financial innovations. His dislike of the New York bankers led him to dismiss them as part of a breed who, he snorted, "will lend you umbrellas only when it doesn't look like rain." Instead he allied with Chicago bankers, especially H. L. Stuart, who made an art of retailing bonds to small customers. During the 1920s Stuart became Insull's financial right arm, selling $200 million worth of bonds in one year. Insull preached tirelessly the gospel of customer ownership and established departments in each of his companies to sell securities to the public. These methods enabled him to finance rapid growth independent of New York; it also earned him the enmity of Wall Street.

In politics, too, Insull proved to be an innovator. Like Theodore Vail with the telephone, he argued that electric utility service worked best as a monopoly subject to government regulation. Where other utility executives cringed at the prospect of public regulation, Insull championed it. His policy, after all, was to run lean companies, provide the best possible service, and push electric rates ever lower. Once he had mastered Chicago, Insull expanded his empire to the suburbs and beyond. He even worked out a formula for extending electric power to rural areas profitably. Insull's approach proved so sound that he advanced rural and small-town electrification by almost a generation. In all his companies he introduced a program of welfare capitalism that included a forty-hour work week, medical benefits, a retirement plan, profit-sharing, company-sponsored night schools, and numerous other benefits.

During the 1920s Insull's empire expanded steadily. He controlled not only five major utility companies but also the Chicago elevated railway and three interurban rail systems. The largest utility operator outside of New York, he created an impossibly complex web of holding companies to protect his empire from New York raiders. Altogether his properties exceeded $3 billion in value, served more than 4 million customers, and produced nearly 13 percent of the electricity and gas consumed in the nation. The stock-market craze of the 1920s sent the prices of stocks in his companies soaring. During the frantic summer of 1929 their combined worth increased at the rate of $7,000 a minute around the clock.

When the market crashed, Insull made several tough decisions to defend his empire from possible takeover. They proved to be miscalculations. The steady decline of the economy enabled the New York bankers he so despised to gain control of his companies in December 1931. Within several months they ousted Insull and cast him in the role of a scoundrel bent on ruining his stockholders. Both the federal government and the state of Illinois brought charges against Insull for mail fraud and embezzlement. The prosecutors tried to make Insull a symbol and scapegoat for the disgraced business and financial communities. They succeeded in humiliating Insull personally, but he won acquittal on all charges. In fact, his supposedly looted companies weathered the depression better than most companies. Not one of them went into bankruptcy, and owners of their securities lost less than 1 percent of their investment.

Despite the scandal that unjustly tarnished his later life, Insull remains one of the most important entrepreneurs in American history. His innovations democratized electricity, spreading it into broad new areas of American life until it became as much a staple as the automobile. Once electricity began reaching the homes of average Americans, it changed their lives forever. It made possible the astonishing rise of the huge appliance industry. Insull himself foresaw this symbiotic relationship between electricity and a host of household machines. His own stores promoted and sold appliances vigorously; by 1925, according to historian Harold L. Platt, the average Chicago resident owned three appliances, and between 92 and 95 percent of the city's families received electricity from central stations. For most of urban America, at least, the future had arrived and it was brightly lit.

5

The Fabrication of Familiar Forms

Take from me all the ore mines, railroads, manufacturing plants and leave me my organization, and in a few years I promise to duplicate the Carnegie Company.

— Andrew Carnegie

FOR THE VAST MAJORITY OF AMERICAN BUSINESSES, ORGAnization posed no problem at all. Small businesses have always been the staple of the American economy. Like the skyline of a great city, they are overshadowed by the towering skyscrapers of big firms, but they more than make up in number what they lack in size. The vast majority of American businesses have always been small operations run by one or two individuals or a family. These individuals became the folk heroes of American economic life, the seekers after that most cherished goal of being one's own boss. In preindustrial America they dominated virtually every sector of economic activity, whether they be farmer, merchant, fisherman, innkeeper, or artisan. Predictably, many small enterprises had short life spans, perishing from poor management, bad luck, hard times, or the mortality of owners. A select few firms survived through more than one generation or succeeded so well that they became large companies.

The coming of industrialization drastically revamped the role of small business in American life. It enabled companies to produce a greater volume of goods at a lower cost per unit. As large firms applied these economies of scale, they pushed smaller competitors out of the industry and made it all but impossible for smaller rivals to enter. The rise of big business forced smaller firms to find niches in the more specialized areas of economic activity left untouched by large companies. Increasingly they moved into the retail, service, and construction sectors, where they have remained vibrant despite the growth of formidable large competitors in these areas. In this way the growth of large corporations did much to shape the nature and direction of small business as well. Hardly anyone in America escaped the influence of the organizational revolution that proceeded through two distinct phases: the corporate economy and its offspring, the corporate society.

No one planned the organizational revolution. The product of drift rather than design, it occurred not in the form of sudden, sweeping changes but rather as a process of accretion – the unexpected result of countless decisions and actions made by people who gave little thought to the broader or cumulative consequences of their actions. It came into being when ambitious entrepreneurs succeeded so well at their work that they were forced to devise new means of organizing and administering their creations. In solving these immediate problems they also restructured both the business and social landscape of the nation. Although a gradual process, these changes shocked most Americans because no one saw it coming.

Traditional family firms increasingly gave way to large enterprises managed by hierarchies of professional managers. As these giant organizations came to dominate both the production and distribution of goods, they began to preside over activities once left to the free play of the market. As Albert D. Chandler, Jr., put it, "In many sectors of the economy the visible hand of management replaced what Adam Smith referred to as the invisible hand of market forces. . . . As modern business enterprise acquired functions hitherto carried out by the market, it became the most powerful institution in the American economy and its managers the most influential group of economic decision makers."

The corporation became the instrument through which this transformation took place. As late as the Civil War no one could have foreseen that the corporation would become the chief institutional model for American civilization. Early American businesses utilized three forms of organization. The *proprietorship* featured one person who owned and operated the business. A *partnership* involved two or more people as owners and managers. The *unincorporated shareholder company* had several shareholders bound by a written agreement, any one of whom could leave the business by selling his shares. Such an arrangement was private and had no standing in law beyond the written pact that created it. These arrangements were simple, direct, and personal. They suited an economy of small firms serving local markets. They might even serve growing firms for a time, but they posed serious problems for larger enterprises.

Neither the partnership nor the shareholder company made any legal distinction between the business and its owners. All three forms of organization had unlimited liability, meaning that the owner or partners remained personally responsible for all debts incurred by their business. This fact alone led men to hesitate before undertaking large or risky ventures. Moreover, the death of a partner dissolved the firm and required new arrangements, as did a falling out among them. Since the shareholder company relied on a private agreement, ample room remained for disagreement among the stockholders. Nor could any of these arrangements raise large amounts of capital.

The corporate form met all of these objections. Chartered by the state, it had a clear legal status and a separate identity from its stockholders. Ownership could easily be transferred through a sale of shares without disturbing operations. As a legal entity it outlived its creators and was unaffected by their demise or departure. Large amounts of capital could be raised by selling stock or issuing bonds, which gave it mechanisms for perpetual growth under favorable conditions. And it offered shareholders limited liability. The corporation alone was responsible for its debts; the stockholder could lose no more than his investment if the company went under. The charter gave the corporation clear privileges that might later be expanded. Taken together, these advantages made the corporate form a superb instrument for planned, rational business enterprise on a large scale.

The corporation was no stranger to American life, but neither was it an overly familiar form. It originated in England as a device for furthering public policy by granting special privileges in unusual circumstances. In the United States it remained an instrument of public policy even after the Revolution. Between 1775 and 1801, states granted 326 corporate charters, mostly for public undertakings such as wharves, turnpikes, and water works. Some thirty-four went to banks, thirty-three to insurance companies, and only eight to manufacturing enterprises. After 1800, however, the number of charters increased sharply as the public attitude toward the purpose and function of corporations underwent a dramatic shift. By the 1830s the granting of corporate charters had become engulfed in fierce political controversy.

Entrepreneurs, seeking ways to raise capital for large projects such as railroads, agitated to have corporate charters broadened from a limited privilege to a universal right. Instead of requiring a special act of the legislature, they wanted the right of incorporation made available to anyone who paid a reasonable fee and met some minimal requirements. Those who opposed this change argued that corporations were a tool of moneyed interests and a threat to democracy. "The very object . . . of the act of incorporation is to produce inequality, either in rights or in the division of property," declared lawyer Daniel Raymond as early as 1820. "They are always created for the benefit of the rich, and never for the poor." Others worried about the ethical implications of the corporation. "As directors of a company," wrote William M. Gouge in 1833, "men will sanction actions of which they would scorn to be guilty in their private capacity. A crime which would press heavily on the conscience of one man, becomes quite endurable when divided among many." Wealthy Bostonian Peter C. Brooks was even more blunt. "Corporations," he declared, "will do what individuals would not dare do."

To modern readers these warnings sound ominously prophetic, but at the time they were ignored. As the movement to broaden the law gained momentum, not only the wealthy but those on the make threw their support behind it. Some even portrayed the corporation as a democratizing force that would enhance competition. Connecticut responded first by passing a general incorporation law in 1837; by 1850 most other states had followed suit. Gradually the corporation evolved from a guarded instrument of public policy into a general vehicle for private enterprises of many types. By the eve of the Civil War the corporation had set down strong roots as a preferred form of business organization, although most firms continued to be incorporated by special legislative acts rather than the general statutes because they could gain more liberal charters and often special privileges that way.

As the corporation mutated from a specially granted instrument of public policy into a general vehicle for private enterprise, irony abounded in the transformation. As historian Arthur M. Schlesinger, Jr., observed wryly, "The general laws sprinkled holy water on corporations, cleansing them of the legal status of monopoly and sending them forth as benevolent agencies of free competition." One striking result was a clear shift in the decision-making power within the American economy from the public to the private sector. During the next half century the corporation became the structural norm for large enterprise. In conquering the problems of size and longevity, it simply transcended human limitations. This was the heart of corporate innovation and of the organizational revolution itself. Conceived as an instrument to organize business enterprises on a large scale, it became in the hands of talented entrepreneurs a leviathan that dwarfed its creators and assumed a life, a character, and an identity of its own. Intended as a servant of its founders, its spectacular growth compelled them to serve its needs and redefine their own visions along lines dictated by the necessities of corporate development.

For several decades nearly all of the major large corporations were railroads, which pioneered in corporate development as in so many other areas of American business life. Most early lines were financed and built by local interests to serve their own communities. As these roads folded into systems through absorption by larger companies, control passed into the hands of managements that had little interest or involvement in local communities other than as markets. Among other things this separation brought a growing hostility toward railroads by local shippers who accused them of charging exorbitant rates. After 1880 industrial and manufacturing firms began to follow this same pattern, creating the modern multiunit business enterprise with its hierarchy of managers dedicated to increasing productivity, cutting costs, and boosting profits. Here, as with railroads, competition acted as a catalyst propelling firms down the path of growth and consolidation.

In manufacturing and industry, producers can determine their output and to some extent their costs, prices, markets, and other factors. Given enough capital, machines, raw materials, labor, good transportation, and an efficient organization, they can expand production tremendously. The problem then becomes one of finding markets in which to sell this outpouring of goods. As firms became capable of reaching regional and national markets, they competed with other companies on an enlarged scale. In the intense clashes that followed, some firms emerged powerful enough to dominate their industry and shut rivals out of markets. They might also acquire or merge with their competitors and seek to control an entire market. Ambition on this scale required an organizational form like the corporation capable of commanding resources and conducting operations on a scale unprecedented in human history.

As long as a market kept growing, it could absorb and even welcome new competitors. Eventually, however, production capacity outstripped the market's capacity to absorb goods, at which point competition grew more savage. John D. Rockefeller was one of the first to understand and master this new business environment. He entered the oil-refining business in 1863 because it offered a promising future for a relatively small investment. But others saw the same advantages. "Naturally all sorts of the people went into it," he recalled; "the butcher, the baker, the candlestick maker began to refine oil, and it was only a matter of time before more of the finished product was put on the market than could possibly be consumed." Andrew Carnegie found the same pattern unfolding in the iron and steel industry and, like Rockefeller, determined to outperform all his competitors in every aspect of the business.

Born in 1835, Carnegie was the quintessential poor boy made good. The son of a Scottish weaver who lost his job to mechanization, he came to America with his family at the age of thirteen. Impoverished and brokenhearted over the loss of his craft, his father, Will Carnegie, never found a place in the new world and died seven years later in 1855. By contrast young Andrew took hold with a vengeance. Bolstered by his iron-willed mother, he climbed the ladder of success in the telegraph and railroad industries with a zeal and intelligence that impressed everyone who employed him. On a loan of $817 he erected an early fortune of $400,000 that earned him more than $56,000 a year by the age of thirty-three. Having demonstrated his brilliance at both work and investing, Carnegie shed his other interests and in 1872 formed a company to manufacture steel.

Convinced that iron and steel lay at the heart of industrialization, Carnegie concluded that they could be produced in huge quantities by maximizing efficiency of operation. With fanatical zeal he lowered costs and sought new technologies that promised superior performance. If a better method or technology appeared, he did not hesitate to scuttle even a new facility to install it. To his shops he brought strict costing and careful accounting. He invested in the Siemens gas furnace because his calculations told him it would raise profits by cutting unit costs, a basic principle that did not dawn on many of his competitors for years. When times were hard, Carnegie kept his furnaces operating and even expanded because costs were low. As economist Jonathan Hughes observed, "He bought in depressions, rebuilt in depressions, restaffed in depressions, then undercut his competitors when business was good." This ruthless policy of efficiency made Carnegie wealthy beyond his wildest dreams. It also drove the price of iron and steel goods steadily downward. Steel rails, for example, dropped from $160 a ton in 1875 to $17 a ton in 1898.

Rockefeller pursued a similar course of reducing costs relentlessly. Like Carnegie, he believed that the way to eliminate rivals was to *eliminate* them – either by forcing them to the wall or absorbing them. The latter policy both expanded his Standard Oil empire and brought him many talented executives who had once been competitors. By 1877 he had rationalized the oil-refining business and controlled 90 percent of the oil refined in the United States. He then expanded rapidly into transportation and production until he dominated 25 percent of all American crude oil production and bullied the railroads into giving him rebates on the shipment of his own oil *and* that of rival companies as well. Still not content, he proceeded to built a pipeline network to lessen his dependence on railroads.

Both Carnegie and Rockefeller relied heavily on superior organization to forge their empires. However, Carnegie never incorporated his company, preferring to maintain a somewhat cumbersome partnership arrangement. By contrast, Rockefeller pioneered in new forms of corporate organization, first with the trust in 1882 and then the holding company in 1889. The latter enabled Standard Oil to perfect its trail-blazing style of organization based on the committee system governed by a corps of executives among whom Rockefeller served not as dictator but as first among equals. From their efforts emerged a colossus that shipped oil from 20,000 wells via 5,000 tank cars and 4,000 miles of pipelines to giant refineries in key locations. The company employed 100,000 workers and exported 50,000 barrels of oil daily to Europe. "That he created one of the first multinational corporations," concluded biographer Ron Chernow, "selling kerosene around the world and setting a business pattern for the next century was arguably his greatest feat."

What Carnegie and Rockefeller did in their fields, Henry O. Havemeyer did in sugar, Charles A. Pillsbury in flour milling, Gustavus Swift and Philip D. Armour in meat, James "Buck" Duke in cigarettes, and George Eastman in cameras and film, to mention but a few of the great entrepreneurs who created organizations that long outlived them. Carnegie sold his company to J. P. Morgan, who combined it with some rival firms in

1901 to form United States Steel, the nation's first billion-dollar corporation. Rockefeller quietly retired from active management in Standard Oil during the mid-1890s and, like Carnegie, devoted much of his remaining life to philanthropy. In their place came what Chandler called "a new subspecies of economic man," the salaried professional manager. Some did well at the work, others not so well. Great entrepreneurs spawned great corporations, but great corporations did not always produce or recruit great managers.

Methods of distribution and retailing also underwent a metamorphosis of organization. During the first half of the nineteenth century agricultural products dominated the national economy. Goods, whether domestic or imported, traveled chiefly by water. Since all trade routes led to the seaboard, eastern coastal cities emerged as centers of distribution. At the wholesale level a complex and unwieldy system included importers, shipping merchants, commission merchants, jobbers, brokers, and auctioneers. The functions of these operatives often overlapped. Importers usually conducted both wholesale and retail operations. They received goods from abroad and sold them to retail merchants from the interior who made one or two buying trips a year to the seaboard. Although most importers handled a general business, many began after 1830 to specialize in particular lines of goods such as groceries, hardware, dry goods, or house wares.

Shipping merchants usually confined their business to wholesaling and often owned all or part of the ships carrying the goods they handled. They, too, began to specialize in certain trades, which meant that interior merchants had to make the rounds of numerous importers or shipping merchants to get everything they wanted. This growing inconvenience led to the emergence of the jobber, who acted as a middleman between the wholesalers and the retail merchants. Jobbers stocked goods from the specialized wholesalers and resold them to retailers in smaller or "broken-lot" quantities – a godsend for country merchants who could not afford to buy in large quantities from wholesalers.

Commission merchants comprised the largest and most important group of wholesalers. They acted as agents both for Americans buying or selling goods abroad and for foreign firms selling products in the United States. In these roles they performed an impressive variety of functions. For foreign companies they handled, sold, and distributed goods, took care of all the financial transactions involved, and even offered advice on market conditions. American planters relied on them to sell cotton, sugar, tobacco, and other crops abroad, purchase supplies of all kinds, and handle all financial arrangements. They performed similar services for textile companies and other manufacturers as well. In the financial realm they made advances, collected due payments and other debts, and handled bills of exchange. Commission merchants also took care of transportation – buying, selling, or chartering ships, outfitting vessels, gathering cargos, and arranging for insurance. It was a busy and dangerous profession, full of opportunities and subtle pitfalls. Not surprisingly, a large number of prominent American business figures got their start acting as commission merchants.

Brokers were the most literal of middlemen, bringing together buyers and sellers for a fee. Since most brokers concentrated on one commodity, their presence signaled a growing specialization wrought by the advance of industrialization. By the 1850s they had already begun to cluster in those cities that had established formal commodity exchanges. Auctioneers were the bearers of a hoary American tradition undergoing significant change. Where auctions once served primarily to dispose of goods acquired secondhand through court orders or bankruptcies, they became after 1800 a vehicle for the quick sale of imported goods in large lots. Auctions remained popular because they were convenient, required no permanent establishment, kept overhead costs to a minimum, and could handle a wide variety of goods.

Unlike this maze of wholesalers, retailing remained simple. Well into the nineteenth century it still relied on the public market, fairs, peddlers, and drovers, all of which traced back to medieval if not ancient times. In rural areas, which is to say most of the nation, the ubiquitous general store carried an impressive array of hard and soft goods acquired by the proprietor on his buying trips to the seaboard. In the hinterland the general store held a retailing monopoly. Since cash was scarce among farmers, the store offered liberal credit at high rates. Proprietor and customer still haggled over prices, and the owner's reputation was the buyer's only guarantee. Urban retail stores began to specialize in particular lines of goods as towns grew and the volume of trade increased. By the eve of the Civil War cities and large towns had shops selling books, cutlery, boots and shoes, china and glassware, clothing, millinery, and numerous other items.

This cumbersome preindustrial distribution web could hardly be called a system, but it suited an environment characterized by local or at best regional markets, modest domestic industrial output, and water transportation. The coming of industrialization doomed it to extinction. The rising productivity of American factories reduced dependence on foreign goods and spurred a rapid growth in the volume of domestic goods. In 1860 factories employed about 1.3 million workers to produce nearly $2 billion in products; by 1914 these figures mushroomed to 7 million workers and $24 billion worth of goods. The railroad and the telegraph enabled mass producers of goods to reach distant markets. Chicago and St. Louis emerged as rail centers, triggering a shift in the distribution of consumer goods from the East Coast to the Midwest and forcing eastern wholesalers to flood the West with salesmen and catalogs in their effort to hold the trade.

As the volume of domestic trade expanded, it drove merchants steadily down the road to specialization. The wholesaler became an endangered species as producing firms expanded into distribution and marketing while retailers took steps to gain greater control over their supply of goods than could be obtained through the old clumsy labyrinth of middlemen. Gradually retailers squeezed out many of the wholesalers by forging direct links with their suppliers. Manufacturers, too, required a more sophisticated system of distribution to ensure themselves of markets as well as reduced costs. Some large firms undertook vertical integration by establishing their own branch plants, warehouses, wholesale supply systems, and retail outlets. A larger number resorted to horizontal integration by uniting several large companies to expedite marketing. Standard Oil, United States Rubber, Singer Sewing Machine, National Biscuit Company, International Paper, and American Tobacco Company all pursued these strategies.

The entry of these corporate giants into marketing doomed the independent wholesaler in their domains. A new breed of jobbers struggled to maintain their existence by forging large buying networks to obtain goods directly from manufacturers and marketing organizations and selling them to general stores and urban specialty shops. They relied heavily on a corps of salesmen or "drummers" who roamed the countryside to peddle goods and gather vital marketing information. Jobbers also put together efficient purchasing organizations, using scattered buying offices and buyers operating out of the home office. From this refurbished system of distribution arose the great mercantile firms such as Marshall Field in Chicago and

A. T. Stewart in New York. As early as 1870 Stewart did $50 million in sales, only $8 million of which was retail business. Marshall Field grew from $9.1 million ($1.5 million retail) in 1865 to $36.4 million ($12.5 million retail) in 1900.

As similar companies sprang up across the country, they destroyed the traditional eastern domination of distribution. Like other growing enterprises, they soon developed departments for such specialized functions as shipping, accounting, and credit. At the same time, they had to compete on one side with the relentless vertical expansion of giant retailers, who began buying directly from manufacturers and selling directly to consumers, and on the other with manufacturers who began creating their own wholesale distribution and marketing networks and purchasing agencies. This higher level of competition generated yet another major change in the distribution and marketing of consumer goods.

Mass retailers began to replace wholesalers once they could exploit a market as large as that covered by the wholesalers. Giant retailers could generate an enormous sales volume by establishing their own purchasing organizations to buy directly from manufacturers. They already had the advantage of dealing directly with their customers. Three new types of retailer came to dominate the market: the department store, the mail-order house, and the chain store. Each one utilized the same principles in different ways: high volume of sales, low margins, economies of scale, rapid turnover of stock, and an efficient organization. Thus did the organizational revolution work its magic in the store no less than in the factory.

The department store emerged during the 1860s and became the first institution to employ the techniques of mass selling. This approach required a large customer base, which confined it to larger cities. In its diversity of stock the department store resembled the old general store writ large, but it was organized far more efficiently and operated on very different principles. Within the confines of one huge building it offered a broad array of goods organized around departments, thereby sparing customers the need to wander from one store to another to get what they needed. The guiding principle was often to have every department outsell the city's leading specialty shop in that line of goods. Like other businesses, department stores started modestly and grew rapidly. Where stores might have only ten or fifteen departments in the 1880s, they often had more than a hundred by 1910.

Some of the department-store pioneers, most notably Stewart and Field, moved to retailing from wholesaling, while others such as Rowland Macy and John Wanamaker began in retail clothing or dry goods and expanded into new lines of goods. Between 1870 and 1930 the leading department stores perfected the techniques of centralization and diversification. So phenomenal was their success that most managed to finance expansion entirely from accumulated earnings and maintain ownership within the founding family. As with manufacturers, sales volume and cost efficiency held the key to profits. Stewart pioneered the approach but never expanded his operation beyond dry goods. Nevertheless, his imaginative techniques and large sales volume made him a model for the men who forged the modern department store: Macy, Field, the Gimbel brothers, Ebenezer Jordan, and especially Wanamaker.

No one outdid Wanamaker in devising innovations in retailing. From Stewart he borrowed the one-price rule that eliminated the old practice of haggling over price. He also backed every purchase with a money-back guarantee, which ensured customer loyalty, and he ordered sales people to let customers roam freely unless they asked for assistance. To move goods during slow periods like January and August, Wanamaker introduced special sales such as the "White Sale." A devout believer in promotion, he advertised heavily and often wrote the copy himself. His fertile mind came up with original promotions as well as campaigns, all of which aimed to keep the stock moving out the door. "We must move the goods," he told his executives. "If one of your salesmen sees an article around, unsold, until he gets tired of looking at it, how can you expect to find – ever – a satisfied purchaser for it?"

The department store moguls like Wanamaker freely utilized promotional gimmicks beyond the budget of smaller shops. So too with costs: They kept prices low and wages even lower while buying goods in volume from a wide variety of sources, sometimes through special arrangements directly with manufacturers. As their stores grew, they turned them into giant temples of consumption with lavish interiors and imaginatively designed display windows illuminated with lights of many hues. Here too no one outdid Wanamaker, who opened a new store in Philadelphia in 1911 that occupied a full city block with twelve stories above ground and three below. The largest building in the world devoted to retail merchandising, it featured a striking array of display areas, courts, halls, and galleries around a center court topped by a dome 150 feet high with marble arches. One gallery housed the largest organ in the world; two others graced the Greek and Egyptian halls, prompting Wanamaker to quip, "Surely we are well organized." Shopping became not an ordeal but a pleasurable experience in emporiums filled with amenities to pamper the customer.

Where department stores took business away from urban specialty shops, the mail-order houses struck at the rural general store. Their rise owed much to the growing rail and telegraph network along with major improvements in the mail system, especially the creation of special rates for catalogs in 1873, the establishment of rural free delivery in the 1890s, and the addition of parcel post service in 1912. As early as 1872 Aaron Montgomery Ward formed a company in Chicago to sell a variety of goods described in a catalog distributed by mail. By the late 1880s Montgomery Ward boasted a 540-page catalog listing more than 24,000 items. Its catalog circulated nationally and targeted rural markets in particular. Within only a few years, however, Montgomery Ward took a back seat to an even more ambitious and successful mail-order company, Sears, Roebuck.

A native of Minnesota, Richard Sears embodied the classic American success story. A succession of jobs in his youth gave him a solid grounding in the habits, thinking, and tastes of farmers. During the late 1880s he sold watches by mail, then tried banking in Iowa before joining with two friends in 1893 to create Sears, Roebuck & Company in Chicago. The new firm offered watches, jewelry, and other goods mostly to the sprawling rural market. Sears understood that farmers were always short of cash and slow to part with it, and that they would distrust any scheme urging them to buy goods sight unseen from unknown merchants in distant cities. Yet he also knew that farmers had no love for their local general store with its high prices and even higher interest rates.

To win the trust of farmers, Sears transformed his catalog into a masterpiece of sales propaganda. Drawing on his sure grasp of the rural mind, Sears described his wares in cheerful, homespun prose. He invited folks to come see his Chicago plant and hammered home his policies of low prices, high quality, and guaranteed satisfaction or money refunded with no questions asked. To keep prices low, he sold on a cash-only basis. His approach sought not only to melt buyer resistance but also to make Sears a household name. He succeeded spectacularly in both tasks, and helped his cause by advertising the catalog extensively in farm magazines. The result was a prolific growth in sales, bitter hostility from rural storekeepers who saw their business drifting away, and a financial crisis caused by Sears's tendency to expand faster than his resources permitted.

Business boomed because Sears delivered on his promise of selling high-quality goods at the lowest prices. "Sears guaranteed his $11.96 cookstove to cook," wrote the company historians. "It cooked. And it cooked for years and years. Sears's plows would plow, and Sear's washing machines would wash. That was what farm families wanted; and that was what they got from Sears." Sears himself declared that "the strongest argument for the average customer was a sensationally low price." Time and again he provided it. His sewing machines, for example, sold for $15.55 to $17.55 in 1897 when national brands went for three to six times that amount. That fall he reduced the $16.55 model to $13.50 and was deluged with orders. Not content, he then bullied his supplier to lower his price by a dollar so that Sears could cut the price again. By 1900, despite rising prices, the same machine carried a price tag of $7.65.

In 1895, amid a national depression, Sears took the bold step of buying out his timid partner, Alvah C. Roebuck, for $25,000. Within a few years that share of the business would be worth millions. Sears formed a new partnership with Julius Rosenwald and Aaron Nusbaum, reorganized the company, and launched an ambitious expansion program. A clash of personalities led to Nusbaum's departure shortly after 1900. Sears himself retired in 1908, leaving the firm under the brilliant leadership of Rosenwald, who remained president until 1921. Where Sears had been the consummate salesman, Rosenwald proved a genius at management and administration. As the mammoth company steadily expanded its line of wares, it integrated backward to control the supply of key products. By 1918 Sears owned all or part of thirty factories. Sales volume, which had been a modest $745,000 in 1895, raced past that of Montgomery Ward in 1900 to reach a stunning $166 million in 1917, more than double that of its old rival.

Having conquered rural America, the mail-order houses set their sights on the fast-growing urban market. By the 1920s, Sears had perfected a centralized and departmentalized structure for its mail-order business, but times were changing. The population continued to shift from rural to urban places, the automobile had begun to change shopping habits, and the rise of chain stores posed a major threat. Confronted by these and other pressures, Sears moved directly into retailing by opening stores in cities across the country. Montgomery Ward followed suit, and by 1929 each house owned hundreds of retail outlets. By that time, too, a third form of store had established a pattern of retailing that prevails to this day: the chain store.

Although versions of the chain store appeared as early as the 1870s, they made little impact until the 1900s. They usually specialized in goods not yet dominated by existing retail giants, such as groceries, drugs, furniture, shoes, and cigars, or they offered a broad range of smaller items that made them in effect a variety store. Their approach utilized a different mix of the same policies used by other mass retailers. When possible, they bought in quantity directly from the manufacturers. Instead of a high markup on goods, they relied on a high volume of sales at low prices coupled with a fast turnover of merchandise. This strategy of high volume and slender profit margins required a large and expanding market, which led the chains to target urban buyers. Yet they pursued different paths to this goal. Some, like the Great Atlantic & Pacific Tea Company (A&P), Woolworth's, and the early drugstore chains, targeted large and medium-sized cities while others, notably J. C. Penney, concentrated on the small-town trade.

The retailing of food products had long belonged to small local shops that charged high prices to compensate for their low turnover. Then, in 1878, George Huntington Hartford took over the management of A&P, which had sold tea since 1862. Hartford first moved to increase tea sales by expanding the number of stores until by 1900 he approached 200. Then he began to expand the line of goods carried in each store, adding baking powder and extracts, and only gradually going into groceries of other types. John Hartford, who succeeded his father as head of the company, saw that profits could be increased by selling in volume at low prices. In 1913 he opened the first of a new kind of establishment called the "economy store." Unlike the regular stores, these made no deliveries, took no orders by phone, sold only for cash, gave no premiums or trading stamps, and even closed when the manager went to lunch. This policy enabled them to sell at much lower prices.

The Hartfords gave their stores the same appearance inside and out. Between 1914 and 1916 they opened no less than 7,500 stores only to close nearly half of them to eliminate the weakest. By 1920 A&P's remaining 4,600 stores earned a profit of $4.8 million on sales of $235.3 million.

Within another decade it became by far the largest retail chain organization in the world and the fifth largest industrial corporation in the nation with 15,700 stores that earned $35 million in profits on sales of nearly $1.1 billion. Others were quick to copy the model. As early as 1890 at least half a dozen grocery chains had sprung up in different parts of the country.

F. W. Woolworth followed a similar course in variety stores. Beginning with a small store in 1879, he reworked an existing concept of stores selling goods for no more than a nickel into one featuring merchandise for ten cents or less. Thus was born the five and dime store. Woolworth early revealed a genius for buying. A tough bargainer, he chose only goods that moved quickly. He also introduced the partnership principle whereby a partner provided half the startup costs and managed the store in return for half its profits. This approach enabled Woolworth to expand rapidly, which in turn gave him buying leverage. After bitter struggles he managed to bypass jobbers and deal directly with manufacturers, which cut costs even more. He crusaded relentlessly against waste, attacked costs like a miser, and paid miserable wages on the premise that "We must have cheap help or we cannot sell cheap goods." After building an empire of nearly 200 stores by 1909, he moved boldly overseas and opened his first store in England. Despite dire warnings of disaster by critics, he turned his British venture into a chain with profits that exceeded those of the American stores.

What Woolworth did for novelties, James Cash Penney achieved for soft goods. His inspiration came not from Woolworth but from two partners who gave Penney a chance to manage his first store in Kemmerer, Wyoming, in 1902. From that tiny store Penney fashioned a gigantic chain empire that by 1941 embraced 1,605 stores with sales exceeding $377 million. From his first employers he borrowed a different version of the partnership: Put a good man in charge of a new store, sell him a one-third interest in it, and let him repeat the process by opening other stores on the same basis. This arrangement left Penney as senior partner and major investor in all the stores supported by a group of manager-owners dedicated to their work.

Penney, too, excelled at keeping costs low and standards high. His exacting requirements drove employees hard, but he introduced the term of "associates" rather than clerks because he realized that some of them would one day become partner-owners. In 1913 he incorporated as the J. C. Penney Stores Company and a year later formalized his basic rules

into the six Penney Principles. Like Woolworth he raged against waste
and ran a central organization utterly devoid of frills or amenities. To
his managers he hammered home the basic principles of keeping prices
low and goods moving, maintaining a clean store, and putting customer
satisfaction above all else, including profits. Late in life he impressed one
earnest young employee with these lessons: Sam Walton put them to good
use in creating his Wal-Mart stores.

To a lesser extent a similar pattern occurred in the financial sector as
well. Every element of the financial system – banks, brokerages, stock and
commodity exchanges, the money market, finance companies – evolved
from small, independent, often casual operations into larger and more formal institutions. Many bankers, brokers, and other financial agents, who
once did a general business, began concentrating on some narrower function. A surprising number of investment bankers, for example, got their
start as commission merchants. In finance as in manufacturing and distribution, elaborate pecking orders emerged within and among organizations.

For banks, organization became the primary problem and, for some,
the most profitable line of business. In 1870 the United States had 1,937
banks with assets totaling about $1.8 billion. By 1900 the nation boasted
13,053 banks with nearly $11.4 billion in assets; twenty years later the
number of banks had soared to 30,909 and their combined assets to more
than $53 billion. Most of these banks, like most businesses, remained
small and local with assets ranging from $25,000 to $300,000. In smaller
towns the bank was often owned by the proprietor of the dominant local
industry and run as an adjunct to it. The world of small banks, like that
of small business, was a precarious one characterized by slender profits
and a high death rate. The major banks followed the lead of industrial and
manufacturing firms in consolidating and integrating their functions. New
York City emerged early as the nation's financial center and home of its
largest, most powerful banks. Wall Street became not only a place but also
a symbol for the financial heart of the nation.

Banks tended to specialize in one of two types of business, although they
could perform both until 1933, when the Glass-Steagall Act forced them to
specialize in one of the functions. Commercial banks performed the whole
range of banking services for the public. Investment banks specialized in
underwriting and marketing securities for corporations. They did not deal
with the general public and undertook other banking services only for

select clients. The nation's best-known banker, J. P. Morgan, epitomized the breed. Industrialization magnified the influence of investment bankers by making them midwives to the great wave of mergers between 1895 and 1904. Railroads, the nation's first big business, brought Morgan and his peers into new prominence and power. When railroads needed capital to expand or buy equipment, the bankers sold the stock and bonds they issued to the public. When railroads decided to merge or acquire smaller lines, the bankers stepped forward with a financial plan and supplied the capital needed. They usually gained an influential voice in management as well.

Near the century's end, industrial firms began to rival and even supplant railroads as the core business for investment bankers. Growing firms incorporated or merged with erstwhile rivals; they needed capital for expansion or for new machinery and began offering their securities to the public as well. Between 1885 and 1900 corporate bond issues alone exceeded $6.4 billion, providing investment bankers with handsome profits and increased influence in the business arena. The grinding depression of 1893–7 threw nearly a quarter of the nation's railroad mileage into bankruptcy. Investment bankers with Morgan at the forefront prepared and underwrote the financial plans to resuscitate these roads. In both the reorganizations and industrial mergers the bankers provided not only capital but leadership as well as they moved onto the boards of client firms to influence management policies.

By 1913 the executives of four leading investment banks – J. P. Morgan & Company, National City Bank, First National Bank, and Bankers' Guaranty Trust Company – occupied 118 seats on the boards of thirty-four banks and trust companies, thirty-five seats on the boards of insurance companies, and 193 seats on the boards of industrial, manufacturing, and other firms. These and other activities fetched enormous profits for the banks, which paid astronomical dividends to their small band of stockholders while understating their true assets and funneling large sums into hidden reserves. The powerful First National Bank, for example, listed its working capital at a meager $500,000 while accumulating a surplus exceeding $11.6 million. On one occasion James Stillman, the powerful head of National City Bank, listened to a younger banker marvel at the generous return a transaction had brought and replied quietly, "You don't understand what profits we are in the habit of making."

National City Bank, under the astute leadership of Stillman and his protégé Frank Vanderlip, expanded from commercial into investment banking. Other banks followed suit by diversifying and integrating their operations and consolidating their organizations. Although the major banks apparently competed for business, they operated under the Gentleman Bankers Code, which the Morgans had imported from London and adapted to Wall Street. By its rules they did not advertise, offer lower rates, or try to steal the clients of other banks. Alliances soon formed among the top bankers. Stillman grew close to Jacob H. Schiff, head of Kuhn, Loeb, an investment banking house second only to Morgan. They in turn associated with William Rockefeller, brother of John D., and with railroad titan E. H. Harriman. Many bankers also developed close ties to the heads of major insurance firms, which invested huge sums of money into railroad and other securities.

This rapid concentration of financial and industrial power alarmed a public already uneasy over the seemingly sudden rise of huge enterprises in so many fields of business. By 1910 alarmed critics warned that the "Money Trust" posed an even graver threat to the nation's future than Rockefeller's Standard Oil trust. In banking as in distribution, centralization also led to territorial expansion. Branch banking emerged as a device for penetrating suburban or hinterland markets. It aroused fierce opposition, especially among small bankers, and prompted several states to outlaw it. Some bankers turned instead to chain banking either by buying stock in several banks or by joining to form a holding company that acquired control of other banks. Like First National, some commercial banks diversified their activities by opening bond departments, getting into the call loan business, opening trust departments, and lending money to consumer-credit agencies. Even before World War I many large banks were moving toward what came to be called department-store banking in the 1920s.

As the age of bureaucracy in business spread, organization became even more pressing a problem. Giant multiunit enterprises might produce more goods with greater efficiency at lower cost, but they also faced new problems. The larger the firm grew, the more challenging it became to maintain adequate coordination and clear lines of communication. Efficient organization became an urgent need in these areas, as did a clear sense of direction. A large company, like a large ship, could not easily be turned from its course. Its very size and complexity became a liability in a changing economic environment where smaller, more nimble firms could adapt far more quickly to new conditions. As administrative hierarchies grew larger and more specialized, employees lost contact with both the top management and the larger goals of the company.

Large corporations also embodied a huge capital investment, much of it in fixed costs such as plants and equipment. Fixed costs, unlike variable costs such as labor, raw materials, and transportation, must be paid regardless of whether or not the company sells its goods. When business slowed, the company might cut back production and lay off workers, but it could not lay off rent, utilities, interest charges, or taxes. As the units of production grew larger, the proportion of fixed to variable costs rose steadily. A sudden contraction or recession often caused serious cash flow problems and posed the threat of management's losing control of the firm to creditors. Hard times abounded during the years between 1870 and 1920. Two major depressions (1873–9 and 1893–7) wracked the economy along with severe panics in 1884 and 1907, two recessions (1913–16 and 1920–1), and numerous lesser slumps.

Once fixed costs assumed so large a share of total costs, regularity of output became as important as efficiency of production. This necessity to produce generated in turn a necessity to sell whether or not enough buyers existed to absorb the entire output. If demand did not exist, it had to be created; if the market proved inadequate, it must be developed and expanded. This was a novel dilemma for American manufacturers, who in the early years of industrial growth struggled to meet a swelling demand for goods and services of all kinds. By 1880, however, productive capacity had begun to exceed demand in several key industries. This new condition led to the recurring bouts of recession and depression as well as a steady decline in the price of most goods. The years 1865–97 marked the longest period of unbroken *deflation* in American history. Many companies responded to the problem of saturated markets by slashing prices, believing that it was better to get some business than none at all.

As the fights for markets grew in both scale and bitterness, they soon revealed a new imperative. Large enterprises demanded not only innovation but also stability to preserve and protect the huge investment in the corporation. Competition demonstrated an urgent need for stability and control as it entered this new and more desperate phase. In the early industrial period, the struggle between small firms rarely affected many people beyond the participants. Clashes between large national corporations, however, spread the carnage far beyond the original battlefields. If the fight brought down a major company, thousands of people might be thrown out of work. Subsidiary enterprises, suppliers, jobbers, retailers, and transportation lines could also suffer lost business. Security prices might drop and the money market tighten, sending waves of contraction through banks and brokerages. One stunning collapse, like that of banker Jay Cooke's firm in 1873, might trigger a panic or nudge the economy into a numbing depression through this ripple effect.

The dangers posed by saturated markets gave rise to a clear axiom of the corporate economy: The larger the capital investment at stake, the more intolerable competition and its resulting instability became. The economic hothouse had come into full flower and threatened to choke on its own thick overgrowth. Some way had to be found to weed out the tangle of plants competing for sunlight and survival in this most fecund of soils. Several attempts at experimentation and application gradually produced the neatly ordered garden of the corporate economy. In this process the investment bankers, most notably J. P. Morgan, served as the master gardeners.

Two basic solutions to the problem of competition soon emerged: collusion and combination. Collusion took several forms, the most common of which was a secret agreement among two or more competitors. The best known of these arrangements was the industrial pool, which usually sought to maintain prices at profitable levels. However, some pools also tried to divide markets on a prorated basis, restrict output, manage patents, consolidate sales agencies, or combine services. Some went public and even established formal organizations; most remained private and informal. The railroads first introduced this mechanism and made the most extensive use of it, but such diverse industries as rope, wallpaper, and whiskey later employed it.

Although the pool served for a time as a sort of halfway house between individual competition and cooperation, it proved inadequate for several reasons. Pools lacked any standing in either common or statutory law and so could not readily be enforced. They were in effect gentlemen's agreements among men not known for being gentlemen. Pool members did not hesitate to violate its provisions when it suited their immediate needs, especially in tough times. "A starving man will usually get bread if it is to be had," observed railroad magnate James J. Hill, "and a starving railway will not maintain rates." Pools also ran afoul of laws governing restraint of trade, and their presence was difficult to defend to a public increasingly suspicious of collusion among corporations. In 1887 Congress explicitly outlawed pooling as part of the Interstate Commerce Act, the first attempt by the federal government to regulate business.

The prohibition of pooling had little effect because by that time most businessmen had already turned to combination as a surer and safer way to achieve stability. Combination could be employed in two different ways. In *horizontal* integration companies moved to absorb direct competitors. Rockefeller's first stage of expansion was to acquire all the other oil refineries in Cleveland, after which he began to buy refineries elsewhere until he dominated the refining process. Later he moved toward *vertical* integration by reaching backward to acquire suppliers of oil and forward to dominate finishing processes and distribution outlets. This strategy led Standard Oil to acquire oil fields, warehouses, pipelines, barrel manufacturers, transportation and docking facilities, retail outlets, and other businesses.

Horizontal integration allowed a company to dominate its sector of an industry. Vertical integration went much farther by enabling the company to stabilize its whole production and marketing process. It ensured a steady flow of raw materials at predictable prices, guaranteed regular transportation connections, and provided a reliable network for distributing and selling the finished product. By controlling every stage of the production process, the company could minimize the dangers of interruption or breakdown, generate real economies, produce better quality control, and formulate dependable production schedules. By contrast, horizontal integration eliminated competitors, thereby enabling the company to set prices and control markets. Some competition always remained; no company ever achieved or desired a complete monopoly. The presence of smaller firms helped preserve the illusion of real competition and helped ward off political attacks.

In its quest for stability and dominance, Standard Oil developed the two new forms of organization that came to be embraced by many other companies: the trust and the holding company. Both were legal innovations that revolutionized the structure of American business. They were conceived as devices to skirt the same obstacle: the common-law prohibition against one corporation owning stock in another without a specific sanction in law to do so. This obstacle prevented one firm from controlling another or even coordinating their functions and policies. The trust placed the stock of every subsidiary company in the hands of a group of trustees, who were usually executives in the parent company, in exchange for certificates of ownership. This arrangement gave the parent corporation de facto but not legal control over all its subsidiaries, which meant that actual control still had to be exerted under the table.

After Standard Oil pioneered this innovation in 1882, companies in other industries began to employ it. By 1890 alarmed critics were plastering the "trust" label on every giant enterprise and flinging it about as a loose synonym for monopoly and big business in general. Despite the widespread popularity of the term, however, Chandler found only eight trusts that had actually operated in the national arena. Two of them soon folded while the other six prospered in the petroleum, sugar, whiskey, lead processing, cottonseed oil, and linseed oil industries. The trust was too cumbersome an instrument to endure. Like the pool, it lacked clear legal standing, and it soon became the target of attacks in state and federal courts as well as state legislatures. The holding company offered a simpler and far more versatile solution to the problem.

A holding company differed from an operating company in that it produced no goods or services but merely held securities in other companies. It was in effect a parent company through which control could be exerted over any number of subsidiaries, the controlling interest of which was owned by the holding company. Under this arrangement an entire business empire could be controlled simply by owning enough stock in the holding company to dominate it. Although versions of holding companies in railroads can be found as early as 1870, they existed only through charters obtained by special acts of state legislatures. Not until 1889 did New Jersey ease the path toward holding companies by passing a landmark law permitting corporations in that state to own and manage companies in other states, to capitalize at any amount, and to own property and operate in other states. Although other states soon followed suit, New Jersey became the home base of many large corporations, most notably Standard Oil, eager to unify their far-flung interests into one cohesive organization.

New Jersey's law proved a milestone in the organizational revolution. Throughout the nineteenth century, the dominant trend in American law had been to broaden the range of individual freedom of action. In effect

New Jersey granted the same privilege to corporations, which had already been defined as individuals in the eyes of the law. As more companies rushed to reorganize under this and similar laws, the holding company entrenched itself as the vehicle of choice for large-scale enterprise in American business. Within a single generation the new corporate economy came of age as firms within a host of industries consolidated into ever larger companies. As a trickle of corporate mergers swelled into a flood, they revamped the basic structure of the American economy.

The years of corporate warfare between 1870 and 1890 had witnessed the spectacular growth of individual companies but only a dozen real giants, the combined capital of which did not reach $1 billion. However, as economist Ralph L. Nelson has shown, during the single decade between 1895 and 1904, there occurred 319 mergers with a total capitalization exceeding $6 billion. Of this amount, $2.4 billion or 40 percent involved only twenty-nine mergers; a single merger, the creation of United States Steel, accounted for 23 percent of the total or nearly $1.4 billion. Clearly a new era of giant enterprises had dawned, fed by a merger mania that saw an average of 301 companies swallowed each year by larger firms. In 1899 alone, 1,028 companies vanished in this manner. Once this pattern was established, however, further growth tended to involve the acquisition of independent companies rather than the merger of smaller firms into larger ones. According to Nelson, the former type accounted for only 16.5 percent of net firm disappearances between 1895 and 1904. Later, when the merger movement had lost its momentum, the figure rose to 47.5 percent for 1905–14 and 65.5 percent for 1915–20.

The emergence of so many giant enterprises stunned and alarmed contemporary observers. John Moody, editor of *Moody's Manual* and author of *The Truth about the Trusts* (1904), detailed in his book no fewer than 440 "trusts" that, he claimed, had an aggregate capital of $20.4 billion and controlled 8,664 industrial plants, transportation lines, and utility franchises. The seven largest industrial trusts were capitalized at $2.7 billion and operated 1,528 plants, while 298 "lesser industrial trusts," capitalized at $4 billion, operated 3,426 plants. The railroads, which still comprised the largest single industry in the nation, had by Moody's calculations consolidated into six gigantic alliances dominated by six interest groups that together controlled 709 railway companies with 164,586 miles of track and an aggregate capitalization exceeding $9 billion. Only about

250 lines with 39,500 miles of track remained outside the influence of the Big Six, which strongly influenced nearly a third of this mileage as well. As for the franchises, 103 gas, electric, and street railway companies operated 1,336 franchises with a combined capitalization of $3.7 billion while eight telephone and telegraph corporations owned 136 plants with a combined capitalization of $629 million.

By 1900 the pattern had become unmistakably clear: The age of enterprise had given birth to the age of organization. In a single generation the stray entrepreneurial seedlings that filled the economic hothouse had grown into towering rows of corporate giants, the size and complexity of which would have been unimaginable earlier. The restless energy of this greatest generation of entrepreneurs had wrought an organizational revolution that seemed to be dooming their breed to extinction. No one recognized the significance of this transformation better than John D. Rockefeller, who gave the era its most cogent epitaph:

> This movement was the origin of the whole modern economic administration. It has revolutionized the way of doing business all over the world. The time was ripe for it. It had to come, though all we saw at the moment was the need to save ourselves from wasteful competition.... The day of combination is here to stay. Individualism is gone, never to return.

He was only partly right. As managers came to dominate giant firms and whole industries, entrepreneurs began seeking other areas to exploit. A rising standard of living, coupled with leaps in productivity spurred by the growing use of electric power, galvanized a familiar but increasingly vibrant sector: the consumer economy. Giant firms went after national markets with brand-name products that could be advertised heavily. In the complex, rapidly shifting consumer economy that emerged after 1920 smaller firms could find niches from which to grow and flourish. Technological innovation, the backbone of industrial progress, quickened its pace, creating whole new industries dominated by new giant enterprises. It also spawned a host of new entrepreneurs who utilized the precedents and patterns established during the first phase of the organizational revolution.

6

Bargaining with Behemoths

I have seen America spread out from th' Atlantic to th' Pacific, with a branch office iv th' Standard Ile Comp'ny in ivry hamlet. I've seen the shackles dropped fr'm th' slave, so's he cud be lynched in Ohio... An' th' inventions... th' cotton-gin an' th' gin sour an th' bicycle an' th' flyin'-machine an' th' nickel-in-th'-slot machine an' th' Croker machine an' th' sody-fountain an' – crownin' wurruk iv our civilization – th' cash raygister.

        – Mr. Dooley (Finley Peter Dunne) 1897

THE METAPHOR OF THE ECONOMIC HOTHOUSE IS MISLEADING in at least one important respect. The image suggests a tidy, neatly ordered landscape when in fact the opposite proved to be the case. Rapid growth turned both the business world and society itself into tangled jungles. Bitter competition helped weed out the business environment and organize it around the triumphant giant enterprises that came to dominate it. Their power and focus contrasted sharply with the sprawling, unruly social institutions surrounding them. Gradually their influence and power compelled the rest of society to follow their example. In this way the organizational revolution did more than reshape the structure of American business. By influencing nearly every aspect of national life, it created the corporate society as well. As the organizational revolution spread beyond the economy to the social system, it transformed a society of individuals into one of organizations.

Americans had always placed economic development at the core of their civilization. The whole point to the free enterprise system was to enable individuals to pursue their own ambitions free of undue interference from government. Individualism emerged as the primary if largely mythic value of American culture along with the equally mythic ideal of the free market. Together they underwrote the American Dream, the holy grail of national myths that allowed and encouraged every man to go as far in life as his talents and energy took him. It was these beliefs writ into action that gave rise to the frenetic pace of industrialization.

However, individualism as expressed in the ideal of the open system had a dark side as well: It divorced economic power from social responsibility. The individual had few obligations to society beyond those imposed by his own conscience or the minimal and often ambiguous restraints of law. He could amass as much wealth and property as possible and do whatever he pleased with it without regard for the broader consequences of his actions. If a person succeeded in life (and success was nearly always defined in material terms), well and good. If he failed, he had no one to blame but himself. For every success story there might be a thousand failures, but their tales interested young men on the make far less than did sagas of success. Where political giants had served as role models in preindustrial America, business titans took their place after mid-century. Horatio Alger became the hero of the new American morality play.

Within this context the corporation evolved into the most powerful institution in the nation through a process steeped in irony. Created by individuals to serve their immediate needs, it outlasted them to become a creature in its own right. Born into a milieu that stressed the maximizing of individual freedom of action, it mutated into an entity that posed the greatest threat to individualism yet known. Conceived as an instrument of individual action, it amassed so much power and influence as to throw both the economic and social systems out of balance. The larger and more numerous corporations grew, the more people puzzled over their inner nature and external influence. Like Frankenstein's monster, they became an alien being far removed from their creator's intentions.

Speculators reveled in the opportunities provided by the complexity of corporate structures for gleaning profits by manipulating securities and other transactional schemes. Their depredations, especially those of insider manipulators, led later generations of writers to tar businessmen of this era with the generic label "robber barons." For the entrepreneurs who built great enterprises the label was inaccurate and unfortunate. They might be ruthless and hard charging, but whatever their faults they left behind major contributions to American economic development. The exploiters and wreckers were the true robber barons and did much to taint the reputation and public image of corporations. Apart from these predators, however, the corporations injected something very new into American life in the form of their hierarchical management structures and specialized departmental functions. They were harbingers of the age of bureaucracy.

In trying to grasp the nature of corporations, Americans resorted to their traditional habit of casting unfamiliar things in some familiar form. Rather than adjust their beliefs to accommodate this new entity, they tried at first to fit it into existing ideology. The Supreme Court took this approach in a series of cases beginning in 1873 by defining the corporation as an individual in the eyes of the law and therefore entitled to all the protection guaranteed individuals under the Fourteenth Amendment. In effect the Court wrote myth into law, yet to have done otherwise would have compelled the justices to redefine traditional concepts of property rights and the proper role of government in economic affairs. No court was willing to undertake that radical task, especially at a time when the prevailing mood was to maximize the range of individual action. Moreover, few people during the 1870s anticipated the role that corporations would come to play in American life. By the 1900s, however, the change had become painfully evident. "It is manifest," wrote Woodrow Wilson in 1907, "that we must adjust our legal and political principles to a new set of conditions which involve the whole moral and economic makeup of our economic life."

Corporate power developed swiftly within this framework of individualism. Like any private enterprise, the corporation could use its resources in any manner it chose with little or no concern for the broader consequences of its actions. The larger the company, the greater its effects upon society, but the difference went beyond scale. If, as was often said, the corporation lacked a body to kick or a soul to damn, it also lacked a conscience to prick or a lifespan to limit its influence. As an impersonal organization it was dedicated solely to making money. Individuals within the company might be sensitive to social needs or feel some twinge of social responsibility, and they might on occasion even formulate policies with these nobler goals in mind. More likely they channeled these feelings into private acts of charity. The business of the corporation, after all, was business. Any social benefits it might confer tended to be by-products of the quest for profits. Never before had so much power been tied to so narrow a focus.

Most Americans simply could not comprehend the size of these new giants. In 1893, for example, the federal government collected $386 million in revenue, spent $388 million, and had a national debt of $997 million. That same year the Pennsylvania Railroad alone earned $135 million, spent $96 million, and had a funded debt of $842 million. Taken together, the nation's railroads earned nearly $1.1 billion, spent $732 million in operating expenses alone, and owed $4.8 billion in funded debt. In 1891 the Pennsylvania Railroad employed about 110,000 people compared with 95,449 for the United States Post Office and 39,492 for the armed forces. In 1914 the federal government employed 212,973 people in the post offices and 165,919 in the armed forces while collecting $725 million in revenue. The Bell Telephone companies alone earned nearly $225 million and paid out more than $99 million in wages to their 142,527 workers.

By 1918 the nation had 318,000 corporations. The largest 5 percent of that number earned 79.6 percent of the total net income, while the smallest 75 percent of the group managed only 6 percent. A survey of industrial corporations in 1917 found twenty-seven rail systems with assets exceeding $200 million and 280 industrial companies with assets of at least $20 million. Four of the rail systems boasted assets exceeding $1 billion: the Pennsylvania ($2.7 billion), Southern Pacific ($1.79 billion), New York Central ($1.79 billion), and Union Pacific ($1.03 billion). Among the industrial firms United States Steel's assets stood at nearly $2.5 billion, by far the largest in the nation; Bethlehem Steel occupied third place with $382 million in assets, and Midvale Steel & Ordnance ranked sixth with $270 million. Standard Oil of New Jersey, which already had assets of $72 million in 1883, soared to $574 million to claim second place. The giant meat-packing firms, Armour & Company and Swift & Company, held fourth and fifth place with assets of $314 million and $306 million respectively. The remaining companies in the top ten included International Harvester ($265 million), E. I. du Pont de Nemours ($263 million), United States Rubber ($258 million), and Phelps Dodge ($232.3 million). General Electric barely missed the cut with $231.6 million in assets.

The emergence of corporate giants began in the 1880s and soon unbalanced the entire social system. Given its narrow purpose, the corporation could bring to bear all its resources on any specific action needed to achieve its goal, and it could do this for an indefinite length of time. No individual could do this, and no public institution had ever displayed the same drive or single-minded focus. Many Americans complained that in transcending human limitations the corporation had also transcended human restraints. Even some of the great entrepreneurs worried over what they had wrought. "A great business is really too big to be human," declared Henry Ford. "It grows so large as to supplant the personality of man. In a big business the employer, like the employee, is lost in the mass."

Especially did Americans worry that the growing legion of corporate behemoths might shut down the open system, which had always been regarded as the road to individual success. Had the economic hothouse sown the seeds of its own destruction? Part of the problem lay in the fact that the fabulous wealth produced by industrialization got distributed so unevenly. While the material lot of society as a whole improved steadily, the gaps between classes widened into chasms. Some men amassed huge personal fortunes that ensured their families generations of privilege. There had always been people of wealth in the United States but never so many of them with so incredibly much of it. The age of enterprise gave birth to both a powerful new moneyed aristocracy and an army of the poor. For every person who profited from the new industrial order, thousands more struggled to avoid being crushed by the wheels of progress.

The stark contrast between the rich and the poor shattered the cherished myth of America as a classless society. It also raised the specter of a society divided between a ruling plutocracy at one extreme and a demoralized working class at the other, both pressing hard against a growing but bewildered middle class. As early as 1879 Henry George sounded a warning that others soon echoed. "But just as ... a community realizes the conditions which all civilized communities are striving for, and advances in the scale of material progress ... so does poverty take a darker aspect," he wrote in *Progress and Poverty*. "It is as though an immense wedge were being forced, not underneath society, but through society. Those who are above the point of separation are elevated, but those who are below are crushed down. ... This association of poverty with progress is the great enigma of our times."

The emerging corporate economy was but one of many unsettling forces unleashed by industrialization. Americans had always welcomed change as a sign of progress, but during the late nineteenth century its momentum simply overwhelmed them. The population grew at an unprecedented rate. Between 1850 and 1900 it more than tripled from 23 million to 76 million; by 1920 it had increased another 39 percent to 106 million. It was also moving steadily from the country into cities and towns. In 1850 only about 15 percent of Americans lived in urban territory (defined as places with 2,500 or more people). By 1900 that figure had jumped to 40 percent and by 1920 to 51 percent. The United States had become a predominantly urban nation, thanks in large measure to industrialization and the enormous flow of immigrants into the country. Between 1850 and 1920 an astounding 31.7 million people migrated to the United States, nearly half of them after 1900.

This flood of immigrants presented Americans with a host of new challenges. Unlike earlier streams of newcomers, the vast majority of whom originated in England, Ireland, and Germany, much of this later wave came from Italy, Poland, Russia, and the Baltic states. They were truly foreign to Americans, bringing with them unfamiliar languages, customs, and ideas that did not assimilate easily into American culture. Their alien tongues and ideas confused and antagonized many Americans, some of whom regarded the newcomers as a menace to American ideals and institutions. A new and virulent strain of nativism soon expressed this rising fear of what were deemed unwanted intruders. A character in Henry Blake Fuller's novel *With the Procession* denounced the new breed of immigrants as "steerage-rats that have left their noisome holds to swarm into our houses, over them, through them, everywhere – between the floors, behind the wainscoting – everywhere."

Most of the new immigrants landed in the cities, where they were not the only strangers in town. The largest migration was internal as large numbers of rural folk left home to try their luck in some city or town where they not only collided with newcomers from abroad but felt as alien in their new surroundings as did the foreigners. In small town and city alike old-stock Americans resented this tidal wave of strangers who invaded their cherished domains and sometimes even threatened their dominance. The United States had always been a collection of ethnically, racially, culturally, and religiously diverse peoples, but the mix was fast becoming much larger, more complex, and more volatile as well as being more crowded together than ever before. The West was filling up with settlers, and the freed slaves, once confined to the South, began a trickle of outmigration that continued to swell. The face of America was changing and, nativists feared, so was its character.

These shifts in population and location profoundly changed the texture of American life. Among other things, they reflected striking changes in the work force and the ways people earned a living. More people than ever went to work, including women, whose presence in the labor force rose from 15 percent in 1870 to 21 percent in 1920, and children. In 1820 about 70 percent of the labor force worked in agricultural occupations; a century later the figure dwindled to 27 percent. An estimated 80 percent of Americans were self-employed in 1820; that figure dropped steadily until by 1940 it reached 20 percent. The rest of the work force exchanged their labor for wages or salary, which meant that their livelihood depended on people and forces entirely beyond their control. They had in effect become part of the industrial system in which economic opportunity lay not in going their own way but in finding a place within the existing scheme of things. The number of workers employed in manufacturing and hand trades, for example, soared from 2.3 million in 1870 to 10.9 million in 1920.

Within this welter of tumultuous change, the corporation alone cleaved to a clear path chiefly because of its narrow focus and its mastery of the principles of organization. Gradually its influence extended into the rest of society. Sector after sector of American life confronted the dislocations wrought by industrialization and came to the same conclusion: the solution to their difficulties lay in organization. The old reliance on rugged individualism and self-help proved inadequate in an age when men no longer controlled their economic destinies. In the corporate economy individual action exerted little influence on the course of events. What individuals could not do alone had to be done by combining into organizations with sufficient clout to be heeded. This realization set in motion the second phase of the organizational revolution: the creation of the corporate society.

The transformation did not come all at once and certainly not everywhere at once. For a time people in rural and much of small-town America clung comfortably to their old verities and customs. For them life went on pretty much as before with occasional glimpses of the storm of change raging beyond the horizon. In urban America, however, the maelstrom of change swirled violently in many directions at once because the pace of life was faster and all the primary forces behind change were centered there. The sense of homogeneity and community that characterized rural and small-town life found no roots in the city, the home of both the corporation and the immigrant. There, within a remarkably short time, a society of individuals mutated into one of organizations. As a result the emergence of the corporate society widened even farther the traditional divide between urban and rural America.

The very nature and demands of the corporate economy mandated changes in traditional American ways. The casual, free-wheeling style that had long characterized American life did not suit an emerging industrial order or the needs of a growing population thrown together in fast-growing cities and towns. The more specialized and complicated activities became, the more planning and cooperation they required to operate efficiently. Americans had elevated improvisation to an art form, but a complex industrial system demanded systemization and integration. New institutions had to be devised and old ones revamped to serve this new order of things.

The surge toward organization assumed several forms. Some groups organized to protect their private interests against the power wielded by corporations. These included labor unions, professional organizations, farm organizations, and some business organizations. Others formed organizations to advance some broad public interest or tackle some specific social problem. Within this category could be found reform groups, consumer leagues, charitable or philanthropic organizations, and groups formed to deal with some specific issue or problem such as alcoholism or child labor. A third cluster of organizations arose primarily for social, charitable, cultural, or recreational purposes. These ranged from lodges, clubs, YMCAs, and athletic teams to literary guilds, ladies' clubs, and symphony orchestras. In addition, existing institutions, most notably governments, churches, and schools, underwent profound changes in both their size and scope of activities.

Businessmen realized earlier than most the need for other types of organizations to protect and advance their interests. Firms within a given industry banded together in trade associations at the regional and national levels. By 1918 more than a thousand groups such as the National Metal Trades Association, the National Association of Wool Manufacturers, the American Brass Association, and the National Millers Association had come into existence. These organizations exchanged technical and other information and promoted the industry through newsletters and other channels. Sometimes they lobbied on behalf of the industry or went so far as to emulate pools by setting prices or production and sales quotas. In these roles the trade association endured as an important interest group.

Beyond the trade association, businessmen formed organizations to serve their interests at the national level. The National Civic Federation, National Association of Manufacturers, United States Chamber of Commerce, National Board of Trade, and National Council of Trade brought together both business leaders and firms from many sectors to promote common interests. Other groups such as the American Protective Tariff League, National Business League, American Manufacturers Export Association, and American Anti-Boycott Association sprang into existence to deal with specific issues. The Business League and Manufacturers Export Association, for example, worked to broaden overseas markets for American companies.

The rise of large enterprises also transformed the workplace. In small businesses the owner or boss had direct contact with his employees or was only one manager or superintendent removed from them. The corporation had no single owner but rather layers of salaried managers, superintendents, foremen, and inspectors who drew their authority from still other executives often located elsewhere. Instead of an actual person workers confronted a hierarchy of managers with whom they could neither bargain as equals nor plead their case. These new business bureaucracies existed not to accommodate human welfare but rather to maximize profits and efficiency. A new term, management-labor relations, arose to confirm this relationship in which labor was stripped of its social aspects and reduced to a commodity to be bought and sold.

In this new relationship workers had little choice but to accept the going wage or go elsewhere. They could do little to influence working conditions or bring a grievance to sympathetic ears. Real wages actually rose 10 to 20 percent during the 1870s and another 25 percent in the 1880s alone, but skilled workers reaped most of the gains and all workers put in long hours to earn them. In 1890 the work week usually consisted of six ten-hour days. Thirty years later skilled workers still toiled 50.4 hours and unskilled workers 53.7 hours every week. Moreover, the increased use of new technologies steadily reduced the skill level of workers. The large pool of available workers, fed by a steady stream of immigrants as well as women and children, helped keep wages down and enabled companies to impose long work hours in factories that were often dangerous and unhealthy hellholes.

Although accurate data on workplace accidents do not exist before 1920, one estimate claims that an average of 35,000 workers were killed and 536,000 injured every year between 1880 and 1900. Some 2,000 coal miners alone perished in work-related accidents every year between 1905 and 1920. The railroad industry took an especially grisly toll on its workers. Between 1890 and 1920 an appalling 89,039 railroaders were killed and 2,559,986 injured on the job. That averages out to 2,872 dead and 82,580 injured every year for 31 years. A serious accident might cost an employee not only a limb or some fingers but also his livelihood, plunging his family into poverty.

The relentless push to cut costs and increase output numbed workers with fatigue and boredom. Recurring cycles of depression and recession threw thousands of people out of work for indefinite lengths of time. Age, sickness, or the prejudice of a supervisor could also cost a person his job without warning. A survey by social reformer Robert Hunter in 1903 identified unemployment as the chief cause of poverty. Whole families worked long hours simply to survive. "I didn't live, I simply existed," said one weary woman to the New York State Factory Commission. "It took me months and months to save up money to buy a dress or a pair of shoes."

Working children bore the heaviest load and deepest scars in the new industrial order. The census of 1900 found more than 80,000 children under the age of sixteen working in textile factories. Southern mills had 30,000 workers under fourteen, 20,000 of them under twelve. One South Carolina mill posted this as one of its work rules: "All children, members of a family, above twelve years of age, shall work regularly in the mill and shall not be excused from services therein without the consent of the superintendent for good cause." Another 25,000 children under sixteen worked in mines, where some began as early as nine years old. The tobacco and cigar industries employed another 12,000 children under sixteen, and the glass industry 7,116. Many of them worked long hours in horrendous conditions. Observers were appalled at "the presence of three hundred children in the Chicago Stock Yards, scores of them standing ankle-deep in blood and refuse, as they do the work of butchers."

Helpless to effect changes on their own, many workers recognized that organization might accomplish what individuals could not achieve alone.

While the origins of unionism in the United States extend back into the preindustrial era, the character and scale of unions underwent a profound change during the 1880s, the same period that saw the rise of large corporations. Early unions tried to pursue a broad range of reforms to render industrial capitalism more humane. The most prominent of them, the Knights of Labor, hoped to enlist workers of all types during the 1880s. "Our order contemplates a radical change in the existing industrial system," it declared in 1884, but its fragile organization fell to pieces in 1886. In its place came the American Federation of Labor, which took a very different approach. Where reform unions like the Knights argued that the worker's lot could be bettered only by improving the social system itself, trade unions like the AF of L focused entirely on bread-and-butter issues directly affecting their members.

Although the right to collective bargaining was not formally legalized until 1935, many trade unions proved effective at dealing with employers. Through them labor became one more organized interest group in the corporate society. Although strikes still outraged employers and the public alike, labor leaders worked with enlightened corporate leaders to reform the workplace and smooth management-labor relations. By 1904 union membership exceeded two million and the unions came to resemble corporations with their hierarchy of leaders dressed in suits and occupying offices much like those of their business counterparts. To protect their members, they demanded from companies contracts that formalized work rules and procedures. Using the clout of large organizations, workers struck more often after 1900. The scale of stoppages increased, as did the amount of violence.

Professional people followed this same path toward organization, driven by the increased complexity and specialization of the industrial system. Preindustrial society had always valued the jack-of-all-trades, and even considered him the hallmark of true democracy. People moved easily from one occupation to another because none required extensive training and few had rigorous certification processes. Doctors might attend medical school; more frequently they apprenticed with another doctor or simply schooled themselves before hanging out a shingle. Lawyers apprenticed with another lawyer or, like Lincoln, studied on their own. A college degree was helpful but not necessary to teach school. Scientists learned their subjects on their own; the best of them were often gentleman scholars.

Engineers required more extensive training, but West Point had the only engineering program in the nation until the founding of Rensselaer Polytechnic Institute in 1824.

Industrialization, with its rapid expansion of technical knowledge and increased specialization, doomed this casual approach. The new order emphasized skills that could be acquired only through education and extensive training. Ironically, the professions grew more skilled and specialized just as new technologies deskilled workers and rendered many craftsmen extinct. The number of professional schools jumped from sixty in 1850 to 283 in 1900, and every profession formalized standards and/or codes of conduct for its field. This emphasis on standards had two advantages: It protected the public from charlatans, and it enabled many professions to establish their own criteria free of outside interference. The organization could thereby cloak its members with professional legitimacy and even curb competition among them by regulating the number of authorized practitioners.

From these efforts arose the American Medical Association, American Bar Association, and American Association of University Professors among others. Specialization led practitioners to form even more organizations. Medicine alone created ten such societies between 1864 and 1888. As early as 1883 the president of the AMA observed that "we have specialties for almost every part or region of the human body." Bankers gathered into the powerful American Bankers' Association, which rested on a base of forty-five state groups as well as numerous local clearinghouses. The American Association for the Advancement of Science, founded in 1848, saw its diverse members create specialized organizations for chemists (1876), chemical engineers (1880), foresters (1882), ornithologists (1883), climatologists (1884), electrical engineers (1885), geologists (1888), statisticians (1888), mathematicians (1888), and physicists (1888). Similarly, the American Social Science Association (1865) gave rise to specialized organizations for modern language scholars (1883), historians (1884), economists (1885), church historians (1885), political scientists (1889), and even folklorists (1888).

All these groups enabled their members to network with each other and exchange information. Most of them worked vigorously to protect and advance the interests of the profession. In broader terms they also helped confirm the identity of their members at a time when traditional sources of self-identity were eroding. To a greater degree than ever before, people in the corporate society defined themselves according to their economic function. As work grew more specialized, every profession acquired an aura of technical complexity unfathomable to laymen outside the field. The age of the specialist or "expert" had dawned, both as a fact of life and as a frame of mind. As a specialist in something, experts acquired a form of identification but along with it a narrower social and intellectual horizon. They became notorious as people who could seldom talk about their work with anyone except colleagues in their own field.

The organizational revolution brought with it a dramatic expansion of the middle class, which had earlier consisted largely of professional people and small businessmen. To its ranks came the welter of managers, technicians, clerks, sales people, and public service workers who filled the enormous number of jobs created by the rise of corporate and governmental bureaucracies. These new "white collar" workers – so called to distinguish them from "blue collar" factory workers – increased from 374,433 in 1870 to 3.2 million in 1910 and constituted more than a third of the entire middle class. During this same period the number of professional people soared 366 percent, partly because the number of professions grew almost as fast. The ranks of teachers and professors swelled from 128,265 to 614,905, reporters and editors from 5,375 to 34,382, designers and draftsmen from 1,291 to 47,449, artists from 4,120 to 34,094, and musicians from 16,170 to 139,310. Between 1870 and 1900 the number of trained nurses jumped 110 percent, technical engineers 60 percent, and veterinarians 80 percent.

A host of new fields emerged. Some people reached the middle class by providing some service that required a skill and then elevating its status by dignifying it as a profession. Undertakers joined together in a national association in 1884, adopted a code of ethics, and embraced the advice of their association president that the key to gaining respectability was to "get the public to *receive us as professional men.*" By the 1890s they were becoming known as "morticians" and courses in "mortuary science" began appearing in college curriculums. Plumbers sought the same respect. One of their number told the American Public Health Association in 1891 that "Plumbing is no longer merely a trade. Its importance and value in relation to health, and its requirements regarding scientific knowledge, have elevated it to a profession."

No one called themselves accountants in 1870. Bookkeepers performed those functions, but their tasks grew increasingly more complex and sophisticated. The American Association of Public Accountants, formed in 1887, still had only thirty-five members as late as 1892. In 1896, however, New York became the first state to certify public accountants. By 1905 a truly national association had emerged; five years later more than 39,000 people called themselves accountants. So fast did the profession grow that by 1914 no fewer than thirty-three states had enacted laws certifying public accountants, and already certain states, most notably Illinois and New York, heard charges that accountants unfairly restricted access to their ranks by imposing unreasonable admission standards. Nevertheless, the association continued to lobby for strict standards, stiff rules of conduct, and formal education for anyone seeking membership.

The proliferation of professions elevated the importance of education as well. Graduate and professional schools increased in number to train people for various vocations. A similar pattern emerged for most fields, whether law, public health, social work, urban planning, or teaching. Aspirants attended schools with similar curriculums, passed examinations based on national standards, read national journals, and joined national organizations. From this process sprang a cadre of middle-class urban professionals who recognized education as the doorway to success. As a Harvard student put it in the 1870s, "The degree of Harvard College is worth money to me in Chicago." Work beckoned to them in corporations, government, schools, libraries, laboratories, and a host of specialized businesses.

Managers and technicians formed the officer corps of the organizational revolution with its growing hierarchies and increased specialization. Critic Lewis Corey estimated that the number of managers mushroomed from 121,380 in 1870 to 893,867 in 1910, a rise of nearly 640 percent. About 65 percent of these worked in manufacturing, transportation, communication, mining, and construction, 5 percent in trade, and 6 percent in banking. By 1910 the field could be subdivided into upper and lower management, the latter including 61 percent of the total. The 8,118 technicians of 1870 swelled by 1910 to 109,198, of whom some 81 percent were engineers of various specialized types. Chemists, assayers, metallurgists, and laboratory technicians of all kinds were among the others. Their presence reflected the growing sophistication of technology that could no longer be entrusted to people not trained for the work.

Professions arose where none had existed before. The founding in 1904 of the Advertising Federation of America signaled the rise of what soon became a major profession. The fledgling advertising industry needed not only writers but artists as well to design illustrations, posters, and other visual material. Some new technologies, such as the telephone, camera, phonograph, and motion picture, created whole new industries and a host of new occupations to service them. The rapidly developing electrical industry, for example, generated not only thousands of manufacturing, clerical, and sales jobs but also an army of technicians ranging from engineers to linemen. The advent of the automobile spawned a flood of new occupations in the fields of design, construction, sales, and service.

Professionalism invaded sports and the arts as well. As the economy grew in size and wealth, more of its resources went into the arts, leisure, and recreation. Sports at every level grew more formalized and turned into businesses. Baseball had been a growing national craze even before the Civil War; afterward it turned into a national mania. The *New York Times* estimated that over a thousand clubs were active in 1869. The first professional baseball team, the Cincinnati Reds, appeared that same year and the first professional league in 1876. By 1903 the baseball business had stabilized into two major leagues who agreed to meet each other in what became the first World Series. Football did not create professional teams until the 1920s, but it became an immensely popular college sport after its rules were formalized in the 1870s. The first All-America team was named in 1889, and four years later Harvard hired its first paid athletic director. Already major universities realized that the craze for football brought huge crowds to games and with them handsome revenues for the school. The taint of quasi-professionalism – players especially recruited and sometimes paid under the table – began to infect football as it had amateur baseball teams.

Apart from professionals, an enormous number of people edged their way into the middle class by serving as the foot soldiers of the corporate economy in jobs that required less education or training. Working-class people seeking escape from the drudgery of the factory eagerly took jobs as clerks, secretaries, typists, sales people, drummers, telephone operators, bookkeepers, and sales agents among others. They accepted meager pay and long hours in return for a more pleasant work environment, the dignity of being a white collar worker, less exhausting toil, a bit more security, and the hope of advancement.

Politics too underwent a seismic shift. In response to the growing power of the private sector, governments had little choice but to fight size with size. Most problems surfaced first at the state and local levels. Dealing with them usually meant expanding the powers of government and range of its services. However, a growing sense of outrage over abuses of power by state governments led to a movement between 1870 and 1900 to curb their powers. State authorities found themselves besieged by a welter of contradictory pressures. Citizens demanded both increased services and lower taxes while special interests lobbied incessantly for favors. Politicians regarded office as a source of power and profit even as reformers railed against corruption and launched wholesale attacks on a wide range of social evils. State indebtedness actually dropped 26 percent during the 1880s, which benefited state budgets at the expense of social services that were reduced even as the demand for them grew.

Many cities and states expanded their activities despite the hail of criticism heaped on them for waste, corruption, and graft. To cite one example, New York in 1901 passed the nation's first major regulatory act dealing with tenement conditions. It called into existence a new agency, the New York Tenement House Commission, which in a dozen years employed 165 inspectors and 200 other people to handle the paperwork involved in fielding over 500,000 violation complaints. Between 1901 and 1913, then, a single agency in one city added some 365 new white-collar workers to deal with just one problem. Several states formed railroad commissions in an effort to curb what they deemed overly high rates, discriminatory pricing, and other unsavory business practices.

A pattern of osmosis characterized the handling of many social issues. When the dimensions of a problem overwhelmed municipal authorities, they sought help from the state legislature, where much of the power for governing cities rested anyway. State governments responded by creating new boards, commissions, and departments, but matters such as the regulation of railroads and other large corporations, factory conditions, social welfare issues, children and women's labor, the purity of foods and drugs, and countless others simply transcended state boundaries. The reform impulse seeped ever upward toward Washington, but not before new agencies had been created at nearly every level.

Traditionally, the federal government had tried to maximize individual liberty while intruding into American life as little as possible. Despite the periodic onset of recessions or depressions, Washington seldom intervened directly in the nation's economic life. As late as 1893, on the cusp of a major depression that would last four years, President Grover Cleveland felt compelled to remind Americans that "The lessons of paternalism ought to be unlearned and the better lesson taught that while the people should patriotically and cheerfully support their government, its functions do not include the support of the people." As the problems wrought by industrialization mounted, however, this attitude slowly melted away. The emergence of large, powerful corporations created so great an imbalance as to raise a growing clamor for government to intervene.

From this clamor arose a rainbow of reform movements that after 1900 coalesced into the Progressive movement, which was less an organized movement than a mosaic of discrete, often piecemeal and overlapping efforts to solve a catalog of problems generated by the growth of the industrial system. Like some earlier reform impulses, Progressivism originated at the local level and climbed the governmental ladder when attempted reforms at a lower rung proved inadequate. Unlike the earlier Populist movement, which had its roots in rural America, the Progressive impulse began in the cities and small towns. Its advocates were not the downtrodden but rather an assortment of middle- and upper-class citizens eager to cure the social ills that seemed suddenly to have infested American life.

The most obvious targets were the giant corporations that had come to dominate the economy and unleashed a torrent of change in American life. To many critics they seemed to embody a fatal irony. The open system had enabled talented individuals to erect giant organizations that, once in place, threatened to shut down the open system itself. Much of the rhetoric of Progressivism struck the same note of alarm: that huge corporations were burying the little man. Take away the open system with the opportunities it offered ambitious individuals, it warned, and the whole scaffolding of democracy might collapse.

The result was a burst of growth that started the federal government down the road toward bureaucratic giantism and a more active role in areas of American life seldom touched by it in the past. Between 1880 and 1914 the federal government created its first regulatory commission, added three new cabinet departments, and formed several new boards and commissions along with countless special commissions to study particular problems. At the same time, existing agencies grew by taking on new responsibilities. The number of federal civilian employees increased from 100,200 in 1881 to 401,887 in 1914 while federal expenditures jumped from $268 million in 1880 to $726 million in 1914. Like the corporations themselves, the federal government began a gradual transformation from a small enterprise to a mammoth organization.

By 1900 two principles had become clear to most Americans. First, in an industrial society all roads led to organization. Like it or not, the individual had become less a prime mover and more a part of some greater whole, where true power resided. Second, since organization was itself an instrument of power, the groups that organized most effectively did better than those that did not or could not. As a rule, the tighter the organization, the narrower its aims, and the greater the resources it could command, the more likely it was to succeed in its goals. Corporations, lobbies, and political machines used their superior organizations and clear sense of purpose to gain power at the expense of consumers, workers, and reformers who lacked these advantages. Skilled workers organized far more effectively than unskilled ones; doctors and lawyers advanced their interests far better than teachers. Government could command huge resources but lacked any unity of purpose or direction. Too often it became the tool of those private interests powerful enough to get what they wanted from it.

Above all, the corporate society remained a private society despite the growth of government. The holy grail of a balanced system hovered ever out of reach as real power remained firmly in the hands of private interest groups reluctant to accept or even acknowledge responsibility for the broader social consequences of their actions. Two sensational public investigations reinforced the image of an economy and society firmly in the clutches of business titans. In New York state the Armstrong investigation of 1905 uncovered abuses within the life insurance industry, while the congressional Pujo Committee hearings of 1912–13 exposed similar problems in the banking industry and drew a chilling portrait of the "Money Trust" – an interlocking web of connections in which a relatively few men sat astride many if not most of the nation's giant firms.

The regulation of business remained a peculiarly thorny problem. A series of Supreme Court cases between 1886 and 1890 had extended the mantle of protection offered corporations by the Fourteenth and Fifteenth amendments. By 1890 some twenty-one states and territories had provisions against restraints of trade, but few made serious efforts to enforce them. The federal government had no coherent body of law dealing with monopoly or restraint of trade until passage of the Sherman Antitrust Act in 1890. Three years earlier Congress had taken its first tentative step toward regulating business by passing the Interstate Commerce Act to deal with the nation's largest industry, the railroads. From this act came the first federal regulatory agency, the Interstate Commerce Commission (ICC), which did little more than gather valuable data on railroads until the 1910s. State railroad commissions, which had been around since the 1870s, often proved more effective but varied widely in their powers and effectiveness from state to state.

However, the ICC set an important precedent in the attempt by states and the federal government to regulate corporations. Later new federal agencies were created to deal with such industries as electric power, telephone, and other forms of transportation and public services. Regulation produced mixed and often frustrating results, prompting some reformers to improve upon the first federal effort to outlaw restraint of trade. The Sherman Act, weakened by loopholes, did nothing to slow the consolidation of big business; indeed, the first great wave of mergers between 1895 and 1904 took place after the Sherman Act became law. The act was used as much or more against labor unions than corporations. President Theodore Roosevelt used the Sherman Act for the first time against railroads in what became the Northern Securities case (1904), and his successor, William Howard Taft, invoked it to break up Standard Oil and American Tobacco in 1911 and the Union Pacific–Southern Pacific combination in 1912 among other efforts.

In the long run these cases proved straws in the wind. The railroads broken up by the Northern Securities case came back together in 1970, and the Union Pacific Railroad reacquired the Southern Pacific system in 1996. In the short run, as biographer Ron Chernow showed, the breakup of Standard Oil provided a supreme if unintentional irony. Rockefeller owned about 25 percent of Standard Oil's shares when the Supreme Court decision spun off thirty-three subsidiary companies from the parent firm. As a result Rockefeller owned a quarter of every one of the new independent companies as well. His estimated net worth, which hovered around $300 million in 1911, mushroomed to nearly $1 billion as the assets of the new companies quintupled in value over the next decade. Rockefeller made more money without lifting a finger than he had at hard work for so many years, and Standard Oil of New Jersey still remained the nation's second largest corporation and the world's largest oil company.

The mounting crusade against big business reached its crescendo in the election of 1912, which pitted Taft against his former patron Roosevelt and Woodrow Wilson. As early as 1901, shortly after becoming president, Roosevelt declared to Congress that "Corporations, and especially combinations of corporations, should be managed under public regulation. Experience has shown that under our system of government the necessary supervision can not be obtained by State action. It must therefore be achieved by national action." But, he added, "We can do nothing of good in the way of regulating and supervising these corporations until we fix clearly in our minds that we are not attacking the corporations, but endeavoring to do away with any evil in them."

Wilson's approach differed less from that of Roosevelt than has generally been regarded. As historian Martin Sklar observed, Wilson made a clear distinction between large corporations and trusts. The former were, he acknowledged, "the combinations necessarily effected for the transaction of modern business" and "grew just as naturally as an oak grows." By comparison, the trust "grew just as naturally as a weed grows . . . they have been put together not by natural processes, but by the will, the deliberate planning will, of men who . . . wished to make their power secure against competition." He regarded the corporation itself as a positive force in the modern economy and conceded that *"The old time of individual competition is probably gone by."* His remedy was not to break up a corporation but to find and punish the officers who *"used that corporation for something that was illegal"* (Wilson's emphasis).

Once elected in 1912, Wilson managed to enact a program that followed his preference for a policy of regulating business through a blend of commission rule and judicial enforcement of antitrust law. Three key pieces of legislation embodied this approach. The Clayton Antitrust Act (1914) and the Federal Trade Commission Act (1914) became the basis for future national antitrust policy and effectively removed the issue from politics until the 1930s. The Federal Reserve Act (1913) brought effective organization to the nation's long chaotic banking system by creating at least the basic structure for the regulation of credit and capital markets.

As the infrastructure of modern life gradually emerged, it evoked a mixed response in most Americans. On one hand they applauded the unmistakable signs of progress reflected above all by a rising standard of living. On the other, they worried about the epidemic of "bigness" that seemed to be infecting more and more areas of daily life. A people who had always admired bigness were fast coming to view it as too much of a good thing. Corporations had become too large, cities had grown so large and unruly as to be ungovernable except by shadowy political machines, once simple rituals of life had become more formal and elaborate, and change itself had become less a novelty than a way of life. For many Americans, this growing uneasiness over where things were heading evolved into what amounted to a revolt against modernism, and no institution embodied modernism more than the large corporation. Increasingly they resented the forces that were transforming the very fabric of American life. From that resentment would spring a century of cultural clashes.

7

The Collision of City and Country

A government is nothing but a business, and you can't do business with a lot of officials, who check and cross one another and who come and go, there this year, out the next. A business man wants to do business with one man, and one who is always there to remember and carry out the – business.

        – Richard Croker, Tammany Hall boss

TENSIONS HAD LONG EXISTED BETWEEN RURAL AND URBAN America. The nation had been overwhelmingly rural for most of its existence, but as industrialization shifted the demographic balance toward urban areas, society grew more fragmented. As new technologies quickened the pace of change in American life, the gap between urban and rural folk widened into a chasm. Change came slowest to rural and small-town America, what historian Robert Wiebe aptly called "island communities" dominated by local elites, where people clung to familiar customs and life went on much as before with occasional but growing intrusions from the storm of change engulfing the distant cities. From this ever widening clash of values arose the cultural wars that exploded after 1880.

    Urban America emerged as the heart of a powerful new ethos that defined progress in material terms. The corporations made their headquarters there and new technologies first flourished there. Cities were home to the big department stores, an incredible array of shops and goods, amusements of every kind from the opera to the dance hall, a smorgasbord of restaurants offering cuisines of all kinds, an endless parade of fads and fashions, trappings of wealth beyond the wildest imaginations of rural folk, hordes of carriages filling the streets, and crowds of people scurrying along sidewalks. The city was a place of constant motion, its air heavy with a cacophony of noises and odors. It radiated energy, pulsated with action, and bristled with the ambitions of countless thousands to go somewhere, be someone, and do something. Novelists best captured its restless energy and endless contradictions. Frank Norris, in his novel *The Pit* (1903), described the gravitational pull of booming Chicago this way:

> The Great Grey City, brooking no rivals, imposed its dominion upon a reach of country larger than many a kingdom of the Old World. For thousands of miles beyond its confines was its influence felt. Out, far out, far away in the snow and shadow of Northern Wisconsin forests, axes and saws bit the bark of century-old trees, stimulated by this city's energy. Just as far to the southward pick and drill leaped to the assault of veins of anthracite, moved by her central power. Her force turned the wheels of harvester and seeder a thousand miles distant in Iowa and Kansas. Her force spun the screws and propellers of innumerable squadrons of lake steamers crowding the Sault Sainte Marie. For her and because of her the Central States, all the Great Northwest roared with traffic and industry; sawmills screamed; factories, their smoke blackening the sky, clashed and flamed; wheels turned, pistons leaped in their cylinders; cog gripped cog; beltings clasped the drums of mammoth wheels; and converters of forges belched into the clouded sky their tempest breath of molten steel.

Sheer growth gradually severed a town from most of its traditions as a community, made it more impersonal, its population more diverse and mobile, its range of social contacts narrower, its institutions more specialized, and its variety of opportunities greater until older residents no longer recognized it as the place they had once known. The city emerged as the ultimate marketplace where anything and everything could be bought or sold, and where every relationship, economic and noneconomic, became a transaction. People came to the city to seek a career, improve their lives, find adventure, but first and foremost to make money. In the market economy money was king. It served as the yardstick of success and therefore the fuel of ambition. "What men respect in this town," said a character in Robert Herrick's novel *The Common Lot* (1904), "is money – first, last, and all the time."

Wealth held an irresistible appeal for Americans. Many if not most of them equated success and social standing with making money. While the cash nexus had always intoxicated Americans, it became a national obsession in the industrial era when fortunes piled up at an astounding rate to unheard-of sizes. Some wanted what money could buy, others simply the challenge of accumulating it. "I do not love the money," admitted meat magnate Philip D. Armour. "What I do love is the getting of it. . . . What other interest can you suggest to me? I do not read. I do not take part in politics. What can I do?" Moralists warned sternly against the corrupting influence of money. "The love of money is the besetting sin of commercial peoples," wrote Reverend Josiah Strong. "Our soil is peculiarly favorable to the growth of this 'root of all evil.' . . . In other lands the aristocracy is one of birth; in ours it is one of wealth."

Some of the richest entrepreneurs shared this concern over the corrupting influence of money. At age twenty-eight Andrew Carnegie, who began life dirt poor, cried, "I'm rich; I'm rich." Five years later, however, he wrote a memo to himself saying that "the amassing of wealth is one of the worse species of idolatry. No idol more debasing than the worship of money." John D. Rockefeller agreed. "The impression was gaining ground with me," he recalled, "that it was a good thing to let the money be my slave and not make myself a slave to money." But for farm boys or immigrants new to the city, making money became of necessity a first priority. Theodore Vail, who turned American Telephone & Telegraph Company into a giant enterprise, said as a young man, "I have had all of the dam' farm I want. I am going where I can make some money." Thousands of young men echoed his sentiments, and all of them knew where to go to make it.

But cities were no Eden or safe haven for newcomers. Frenetic growth and the lack of effective government made most cities the perpetual problem children of American democracy. "There is no denying that the government of cities is the one conspicuous failure of the United States," wrote Lord James Bryce, a keen observer of American life. "The faults of the State governments," he added, "are insignificant compared with the extravagance, corruption, and mismanagement which mark the administration of most of the great cities."

The industrial economy made the city a place of fabulous wealth and material prosperity. In the process it also generated huge social overhead costs ranging from environmental damage, health hazards, and brutal working conditions to social disorders such as slums, corruption, and rising crime rates to psychological tolls exacted by poverty, social dislocation, and the stress wrought by constant change. A curious paradox arose: The more integrated the corporate economy became, the more alienated the corporate society grew. The more organized and formal American life became, the more volatile and fragmented it grew. The social unrest unleashed by economic progress gave rise to the political upheavals that historians have lumped together under the rubric of the Progressive movement without knowing exactly what that meant. At its heart lay a fear of bigness and unbridled change.

This fear of bigness was in part a revolt against modernism, a reaction to the forces that were ripping apart the familiar fabric of American life. The new industrial city embodied all the elements underlying this fear. It directly challenged traditional American values while at the same time offering the allure of a life filled with material possessions and promising ever more pleasure, comfort, convenience, and ease. In this manner cities became a perverse magnet, alternately attracting rural folks with their novelties and excitement and repelling them with its vices and corrupting influence. Many succumbed to the lure and came to the city in search of adventure, opportunity, and escape from the numbing monotony of the farm. Others clung to their traditional values and denounced cities as sinks of corruption that seduced young people from their homes and values. The intensity of this clash of cultures has scarcely lessened over the course of the past century.

Industrialization created a new American landscape as urban places gobbled up large chunks of open land. New villages and towns dotted rural areas, especially in areas penetrated by the railroad. Some cities expanded their borders into the surrounding countryside while others found themselves hedged in by new suburbs that often incorporated to avoid being swallowed up by the city. The building of a new plant or mill often gave birth to a new town. Gary, Indiana, came into existence to house workers for a giant United States Steel mill. The pattern itself was familiar; mill towns and villages could be found throughout New England. Sometimes one or more such villages were embedded within a town. In Rhode Island, for example, the textile mill village of Peace Dale was but one of fifteen villages within the town of South Kingstown. One early observer noted that "In 1840 it would have been difficult to find 50 out of 479 townships in Southern New England which did not have at least one manufacturing village clustered around a cotton or a woolen mill, an iron furnace, a chair factory, or a carriage shop."

As towns grew into cities and cities into metropolitan areas, a common pattern of land use developed. Traditional policy assumed an abundance of land, but in cities far more than elsewhere location became even more important than quantity. In most industrial urban centers the general rule was that the nearer the land to the center of town, the more valuable it was. Distance from the center meant increased time and expense for travel, delays in transportation and communication, and other complications. In this way urban land took on a peculiar kind of scarcity in that there might be plenty of land but only a limited amount in the right places. This meant that every city could possess only a given quantity of prime land, and competition for it was likely to be intense. From this fact flowed a complex string of consequences.

Growth intensified the demand for prime downtown real estate, driving up prices until only the largest interests could afford it. Smaller proprietors and residents moved to cheaper land around the core. Gradually the downtown area evolved into specialized business districts dominated by offices, banks, hotels, restaurants, theaters, and retail establishments. Beyond this core lay increasingly uniform districts of industrial, factory, warehouse, and smaller retail sectors along with clusters of residential neighborhoods ranging from inner-city ghettos and lower-class tenements to lower-middle-class homes, tidy middle-class houses, and spacious upperclass manors. This so-called sector and ring pattern evolved not by design but by the play of the market, yet it imprinted urban landscapes with both a structure and a dynamic as surely as if it had come from some master plan.

Growing cities and towns required facilities and services. Higher taxes paid the bills if public agencies provided them, or higher service charges if they came from private companies. In either case higher costs drove land values upward, which in turn led owners to seek methods of exploiting their parcels more intensively. The most obvious way to produce a greater return on investment was to erect larger and taller buildings capable of housing more people or activities. From this inexorable logic came the profusion of skyscrapers, apartment buildings, and tenements – the latter often consisting of carving once proud family residences into several apartments, each of them housing too many people because a single family could not afford the rent. As the rings spread outward, the cycle repeated itself. Residences gave way to commercial or industrial buildings, single-family dwellings turned into multifamily units or warehouses or retail establishments, and once fashionable neighborhoods deteriorated into slums.

This pattern of land use reinforced the image of the city as a place of business where everything became a business. Most Americans were slow to grasp the social costs that resulted. The most obvious one was a pattern of rigid urban segregation. The rise of zoning laws after 1900 did much to preserve the patterns already created. Conceived as an instrument for preventing unscrupulous real estate operators from destroying the integrity of a neighborhood by acquiring a parcel and using it for whatever function brought the greatest profit, zoning also became a tool for keeping "undesirables" out. In the process, however, zoning confirmed existing patterns of segregation and uniformity for generations to come. At the same time, a change in zoning could be used as a wedge for transforming the nature of a neighborhood.

The grid pattern that characterized so many American cities and towns also reinforced their patterns of land use. Established in 1785, the federal survey system defined townships as square plots of land six miles long on each side and subdivided into thirty-six-square-mile lots or sections of 640 acres each. From this tidy system emerged the grid pattern that to a surveyor seemed logical but to the eye produced an unbroken landscape of squares and rectangles that made one town indistinguishable from another. Their dull uniformity led Lord Bryce to complain that "their monotony haunts one like a nightmare." But the grid influence did not stop there. As towns grew into cities and the demand for land soared, it became standard practice to partition the sections into regular-sized units that were easy to sell or resell. From this logic emerged the standard-sized lot that usually measured 20 or 25 feet wide by 100 feet deep.

The standard-sized lot clearly imposed limitations on what could be built. Within every city block after block filled up with endless rows of stores, offices, businesses, residences, and tenements, most of them constructed from uniform designs on standard lots. "With five or six exceptions," wrote Bryce, "American cities differ from one another only herein that some of them are built more with brick than with wood, and others more with wood than with brick. In all else they are alike, great and small." Buildings or houses lined straight, narrow streets leavened only rarely by an open space, park, playground, or even a curved street pattern. Amenities came slowly to most cities, largely because they brought no income.

European cities took pride in their fountains, which most American cities lacked. "Why go on building miles of stone thoroughfares in our great towns," asked a *Scribner's Magazine* editorial in 1901, "without so much as a spray of water, in any part of them, to make rainbows in the sun, and to cause our spirits to take wings a little at the sight?"

In cities and smaller communities throughout the nation rapid growth caused older residents and newcomers alike to feel increasingly like strangers in a strange land. Between 1860 and 1920 the urban population grew at a rate of 48 percent each decade or twice that of the population as a whole. The number of cities with 50,000 or more people mushroomed from sixteen to 144. Most of them harbored a patchwork quilt of ethnic neighborhoods where the newcomers, native and foreign, huddled together in once proud neighborhoods that had deteriorated into slums. The worst of these crammed people together in almost unimaginable numbers. One Lower East Side ghetto in New York City somehow housed 30,000 people in a five- or six-block area. Its thirty-two acres averaged 986 persons per acre, far higher than the 485 people per acre in Prague, the worst slum in Europe, or even the 706 in Bombay, the most crowded slum in the world outside of New York City.

The need for parks became painfully obvious to larger cities as their populations soared and crowded together. Parks came to be viewed as the city's lungs, but attempts to set aside land for them inevitably aroused opposition from real estate operators and other interests who wanted it for other purposes. New York had wisely created its vast Central Park in the 1850s, when the land lay far from downtown and was still essentially rural in character. Kansas City managed to fashion an elaborate network embracing 2,100 acres of parkland and forty-five miles of avenues at a cost of $10 million, all of it paid through assessments on adjoining property. This approach worked because nearby residents realized that the open space increased their property values. "It was found," explained the city's landscape architect, "that wherever parks and boulevards were established, the character of the neighborhoods at once improved." But too few cities adopted the Kansas City formula.

Urban life took a psychic as well as a physical toll. For businessmen the city became an arena that rang with their clashes. Where their forebears had fought nature or Indians or sometimes one another, in business they often competed fiercely against unknown and unseen rivals in contests that seemed as much a struggle for survival as for success. The rise of corporate power added new dimensions to business clashes, and competition within organizations was no less intense than that between them. "It's dog eat dog in our business as all over nowadays," sighed a character in Robert Herrick's novel *The Memoirs of an American Citizen* (1905). "There's a change coming over business, and you feel it the same as you feel a shift in the wind. It's harder fighting to live now than ever before, and it can't go on like this forever. The big dog will eat up the rest."

The contests pitted raw power against power, cunning against cunning, whether the stakes involved shares of stock or whole business empires. Men struggled not only against each other but against that vast impersonal nexus of economic forces and relations called the market, some combination of which might at any moment crush an individual scheme or punish a brash interloper. The business arena did not long suffer the timid or the squeamish; its demands left both victor and vanquished equally exhausted. A character in *The Pit* recoiled from the spectacle, murmuring that "There is something terrible about it . . . something insensate. In a way, it doesn't seem human. It's like a great tidal wave. It's all very well for the individual just as long as he can keep afloat, but once fallen, how horribly quick it would crush him, annihilate him, how horribly quick, and with such horrible indifference!"

The demands of business led men to divide their lives into distinct spheres, elevating work above all other activities. The devotion to what was called "practical affairs" became obsessive as businessmen developed their own code about business and life. Instead of making life their business, many men made business their life and became prisoners of their careers. So it was with David Marshall in Henry Blake Fuller's novel *With the Procession* (1895):

> Why did he go to bed at half-past nine? In order that he might be at the store by half-past seven. Why must he be at the store by half-past seven? Because a very large area to the west and northwest of the town looked to him for supplies of teas, coffees, spices, flour, sugar, baking-powder; because he had always been accustomed to furnish these supplies; because it was the only thing he wanted to do; because it was the only thing he could do; because it was the only thing he was pleased and proud to do; because it was the sole thing which enabled him to look upon himself as a useful, stable, honored member of society.

Where once work had been simply part of people's lives, it came to subsume other areas of activity. Family life revolved around the work schedule. Religion increasingly took a back seat to secular affairs and was confined to churchgoing or neglected entirely. Culture was shunted into the hands of women or a meager band of artists and professional aesthetes who struggled to bring the arts to the attention of an indifferent public too busy with "practical" affairs.

This growing schism between work and the rest of life had profound moral implications. The ethical standards and code of conduct in the business world contrasted sharply with those outside it. Businessmen large and small passed off behavior that might be regarded as unethical or "sharp" in the larger society with the explanation that such things were "a matter of business." Railroad titan E. H. Harriman once betrayed a confidence from his most trusted advisor. When the latter protested, Harriman replied, "Of course, I can't respect a confidence that ties my hands in a matter of momentous consequence to the operations in which I am engaged. I must be the judge of what is right and wrong in these things." If business was a world unto itself, everything else could be – and was – reduced to mere weapons in commercial warfare.

In this sense critics regarded business as corrupting, not only for its pursuit of wealth but for the jungle ethic it spawned. Many painted an overly romantic comparison between the virtues of the simple, honest life of the country farmer and those of the ruthless urban businessman. Few writers drew a more unsparing moral from the success saga than William Dean Howells in his novel *A Hazard of New Fortunes* (1890). The story revolves around a simple farmer who discovers natural gas on his farm and becomes a millionaire but not a happy one:

> His moral decay began with his perception of the opportunity of making money quickly and abundantly, which offered itself to him after he sold his farm. He awoke to it slowly, from a desolation in which he tasted the last bitter of homesickness, the utter misery of idleness and listlessness. When he broke down and cried for the hard-working wholesome life he had lost, he was near the end of his season of despair, but he was also near the end of what was best in himself.

In pursuing this theme of lost innocence and character, Howells and a host of other writers gave literary expression to what was fast becoming the great American morality play in which the pursuit of riches and success drove good men to do evil things, twisted their characters, wore them out, blighted their sense of values, and left them spiritually bankrupt within the prison of their earthly treasures. Here was the flip side of the classic Horatio Alger success story in which the poor boy makes good without being corrupted by the process. The ordeal of business etched its toll into the features as well as the soul of many of its practitioners. "No impression so promptly assaults the arriving visitor of the United States," wrote Henry James, "as that of the overwhelming preponderance . . . of the unmitigated 'business man' face, ranging through its various possibilities, its extraordinary actualities, of intensity."

Small wonder that country folk tended to view the city with a mixture of hostility and envy, suspicion and desire. Farm families could not prevent their children from running off to the city in search of better prospects; nor could they change the wicked ways of the city. But they could and did exert a powerful political influence over cities. Most municipalities were corporations chartered by the state legislature, and rural representatives dominated most state legislatures. Municipal charters were, like all statutes, subject to revision by the legislature, which could amend, repeal, or create charters in any manner it chose and even force incorporation on the people of a locality against their wishes. Most charters severely limited the city's powers to govern, and court decisions underscored the legislature's authority by declaring that cities possessed only those powers enumerated in their charters. As late as 1923 the Supreme Court in *Trenton v. New Jersey* ruled that cities were a subdivision of the state, and that the state could grant or withhold powers and privileges however it saw fit. "Municipalities," the court decreed, "have no inherent right of self-government which is beyond the legislative control of the state."

Prior to 1850 state legislatures seldom interfered in municipal affairs. However, the rapid growth of cities in both size and number strained their ability to provide even basic services for their swelling population. Services that once were voluntary, such as firefighting and even policing, had to be professionalized, but most municipal charters severely limited the taxing as well as other powers. To make matters worse, a movement arose during the 1850s to incorporate the principles of the federal Constitution into the constitutions of the states. After 1850 legislatures in turn began foisting on cities a system of governance based on boards or departments independent of the mayor or city council that took charge of particular functions such as education, police, water, utilities, and maintenance. This separation of powers decentralized city governments at a time when rapid growth kept piling new responsibilities on them. The mayor was left with few powers ranging from the veto to the appointive.

Legislators wielded power over everything from the city's taxing power to services such as transportation and utilities. In a dispute they did not hesitate to strip local officials of their authority. The Pennsylvania legislature in 1901 removed the mayor of Pittsburgh from office and directed the governor to appoint his successor for the next two years. It also saddled Philadelphia with a hugely expensive city hall denounced by one critic as "projected upon a scale of magnificence better suited for the capitol of an empire than the municipal building of a debt-burdened city," and then forced the city to pick up the tab. State party leaders routinely expanded their patronage base by adding new jobs to the city's payrolls, and retiring party politicos often treated themselves to lucrative positions on specially created city boards or commissions. In 1886 the New York legislature passed a total of 681 bills, 280 of which concerned "the affairs of some particular county, city, village, or town, specifically and expressly named."

City dwellers could not control their own taxation rates or how their money was spent. Neither could they determine their election procedures, educational system, public works priorities, or other basic functions. Cleveland discovered in 1911 that it could not do such things as isolate tuberculosis patients, provide public lectures or entertainments, banish dogs, chickens, or other noise-making animals from the city, or manufacture ice for charitable distribution. Every new action required a special enabling act from the legislature. A city could not borrow money or raise taxes or feed beggars without applying to the legislature. In effect, city hall served as little more than an agent for the state. The practical result was to create a vacuum of power in urban government just at the time when expanding cities urgently needed effective management.

Between 1870 and 1900 many cities launched campaigns to gain "home rule." Some, like New York and Philadelphia, tried to strengthen the mayor's hand by giving him absolute power to appoint and remove most higher municipal officials. Others worked to loosen the chains of legislative control by seeking for cities above a certain size the right to frame their own charters. Missouri was the first state to adopt this plan through a constitutional amendment in 1875, but by 1912 only eight other states had followed suit. Despite these and other efforts, municipal government remained a blight on American democracy. Lord Bryce pointed out that "Not only has each State its own system of laws for the government of cities, but within a State there is . . . little uniformity in municipal arrangements. Larger cities are often governed differently from the smaller ones, and one large city is differently organized from another."

However, the business of the city was business, and in most respects the city was all business. This dictum applied to politics no less than to other fields. Here, as elsewhere, a new breed of entrepreneurs arose to provide the services and organization so glaringly lacking in municipal government. Like entrepreneurs in other fields, they possessed a talent for bringing order out of chaos and for creating a coherent system of management that satisfied the needs if not always the scruples of their clients. In the urban marketplace they erected profit-making organizations that were no less disciplined than the great corporations. What the trust and holding company were to the industrial economy, the political machine became to municipal government.

Like the big corporations, the machines arose in response to an environment characterized by disorder and instability. Their ascendance can be understood only within the context of the wholesale failure of municipal government. The degree of political disorder within most cities can hardly be exaggerated. In 1891 a committee of the New York state senate described this confusion in unsparing terms:

> It is frequently impossible for the legislature, municipal officers, or even for the courts to tell what the law means . . . impossible for any one, either in private life or public office, to tell what the exact business condition of any city is . . . municipal officers can escape responsibility to the public on account of the unintelligibility of the laws and the insufficient publicity of the facts . . . the conflict of authority is sometimes so great as to result in a complete or partial paralysis of the service . . . These are conditions which . . . produce waste and mismanagement such as is now the distinguishing feature of municipal business as compared with that of private corporations.

The machines flourished because they got things done when no one else could. The thousands of newcomers flocking to the city needed jobs, food, shelter, clothing, water, heat, transportation, medical care, legal assistance, and other services. Their presence offended many of the old genteel class that had long dominated city life until it grew too large, varied, and unruly for them to control. In the larger cities the established classes lost power to shrewd political bosses who created well-organized political organizations anchored solidly in the immigrant vote. A few even extended their influence into county and state government, while others were content to strike agreements with their state colleagues for an orderly division of markets.

With impressive skill the bosses managed to forge efficient organizations by appealing to the dispossessed of society. Their method was simple but effective: Provide some level of social services for the people most in need of them and ask only for their vote in return. No one else paid attention to the immigrants and downtrodden except as a collective labor pool or teeming source of crime, disease, and alien ideas and customs. Thus did the political boss fashion urban politics into a profitable business. "A political machine is a business organization in a particular field – getting votes and winning elections," observed political scientists Edward C. Banfield and James Q. Wilson.

Journalist Lincoln Steffens, who probably knew more bosses personally than any other American, saw the connection clearly. "Politics is business," he grumbled. "That's what's the matter with it. That's what's the matter with everything, – art, literature, religion, journalism, law, medicine, – they're all business." Few bosses disagreed with him, and the more candid among them took pride in their role. "Like a businessman in business," said Richard Croker, a Tammany Hall boss in New York City, "I work for my own pocket all the time." George Washington Plunkitt, a Tammany henchman best known for his phrase "I seen my opportunities and I took 'em," recalled his start in politics in terms that echoed a Horatio Alger hero:

> After goin' through the apprenticeship of the business while I was a boy by workin' around the district headquarters and hustlin' about the polls on election day, I set out when I cast my first vote to win fame and money in New York City politics. . . . What I did was to get some marketable goods. . . . I had a cousin . . . who didn't take any particular interest in politics, I went to him and said: "Tommy, I'm goin' to be a politician, and I want to get a followin'; can I count on you? He said: "Sure, George." That's how I started in business. I got a marketable commodity – one

vote. . . . Before long I had sixty men back of me and formed the George
Washington Plunkitt Association. . . . I had marketable goods and there
was bids for them from all sides, and I was a risin' man in politics.

Like other businessmen, the boss displayed a talent for satisfying a wide
range of clients from the poor who needed jobs or coal for heat in winter
to businessmen who needed licenses, shortcuts through red tape, or other
special favors and were willing to pay for them. To get this done, the boss
devised a new mechanism (the machine) to organize his raw materials
(voters), production equipment (political offices), and the marketplace.
Usually machines arose at the local (district or ward) level, and many
confined their business there amid keen competition from political rivals.
The more ambitious leaders defeated their rivals, absorbed competitors,
and forged alliances until they put together an organization capable of
dominating an entire city. A few managed to utilize an existing social or
party organization, such as New York's Tammany Hall, in gaining control
of a city.

In carrying out this program, the boss organized his troops into a disciplined army. Although no two machines were alike, nearly all of them followed a similar pattern of organization. The base of their political pyramid
extended beyond the party to social clubs, athletic teams, fire companies,
and various lodges, all of which served political as well as social roles.
Through these groups and a network of loyal lieutenants – the district
captains, "heelers," runners, and block captains – the boss got out the
vote for his slate of candidates in local elections. If reformers or rival
politicos posed a threat, he might resort to other methods. The party faithful would vote early and often, taking the identity of someone long dead
or departed. Ward bosses might recruit hordes of drifters as temporary
residents until election time. Gangs of bully boys and friendly policemen
chased off supporters of the opposition or detained them until the polls
closed.

The ties that bound this political army together included not only obvious material rewards but loyalty, personal ambition, and tradition. The
machine was above all an instrument of personal politics that served basic
human needs. At its heart lay a network of close personal ties among people who had few other options for personal advancement. To those who
inhabited the cold netherworld of the city, the machine offered a beacon of

warmth and hope. For newcomers of all kinds, this combination of material gain and personal attention proved irresistible. Jobs and the possibility of advancement especially attracted them. The boss commanded a wide range of patronage positions. Every city needed police and firemen, water workers, garbage collectors, and a host of laborers; every office could use clerks, assistants, and other staff and maintenance people. Leaders and their lieutenants bestowed upon themselves various posts with honorific titles, generous salaries, and modest duties. Places were found for relatives as well. Lawyers were kept on retainer or given positions; some were elevated to judgeships to serve the machine from the bench.

Every boss regarded the police as his prized foot-soldiers. For Irish and other immigrants, few jobs rivaled that of policeman. The police in turn remained loyal to the machine and served it well. "Machine rule in American politics," wrote historian Alexander B. Callow, "has been made possible only through control of the police." During the 1890s the Lexow Committee in New York City uncovered a well-organized police graft system that raked in $7 million a year from saloons, bawdyhouses, and gambling dens. Of this take, 20 percent went to the patrolmen who served as collectors, another 35 to 50 percent to the precinct commanders, and the rest to the inspector. Testimony also revealed that policemen paid anywhere from $300 to $15,000 for the privilege of being hired or promoted. Similar operations existed in Chicago, Boston, Philadelphia, Kansas City, and many other cities. Minneapolis boss Albert "Doc" Ames first purged the police force of honest officers and then ordered his appointees to organize the city's vice on a paying basis. Everyone from burglars to prostitutes to gamblers worked with the police under what amounted to a kind of licensing system.

Through its network of patronage the machine rewarded its faithful and received from them not only loyalty but kickbacks as well. As a business organization the machine sold its product (political influence) to a wide variety of customers and drew income from three broad categories of activity: salaries, supplies, and services. When appointing its friends to real or imagined posts in city government, the machine exacted a tithe from their salaries. Some positions, notably judgeships and police posts, were sold for a flat fee and an understanding that the recipient would do the machine's bidding and contribute to its campaign fund. Supplies offered another choice revenue stream. On everything the city bought, from soap to stationary to horses, eager buyers gave the machine a flat fee or percentage of the contract. Services provided an especially lucrative source of income. The machine was, after all, a service organization by nature, and it charged handsomely for two broad types of work: protection and privilege.

Protection involved winking at illegal activities in return for a flat fee or percentage of the take. Brothels, freelance prostitutes, gambling joints, saloons, and vice establishments of every kind paid the machine to let them operate outside the law on a regular basis. This arrangement actually offered two civic advantages rarely appreciated by reformers: It restricted vice establishments to one section of town – the so-called river wards or red light districts – and it stabilized urban crime by normalizing relations between criminals and the police. In New York, for example, the detective bureau permitted a certain number of each type of criminal to operate so long as they kept their practice within reasonable bounds. Each of these groups – pickpockets, for example – in turn divided the city among themselves, giving each member an area to monopolize. Few legitimate business pools worked more effectively. If outsiders intruded, police and criminals worked together to nail them. If a criminal inadvertently robbed someone with pull or privilege, the loot was promptly returned and the police were showered with praise for their efficient work.

Privilege covered a wide assortment of activities. Every city had franchises to sell, streets to pave, buildings to construct, sewers to lay, bond issues to market, and a host of other services. Anyone seeking these contracts paid handsomely for them. Individuals and small business owners who needed a license or permit, low tax assessment, favorable zoning ruling, waiver of some regulation, or any similar favor could obtain it for a price. In some cases the machine allowed banks to hold municipal funds interest free in return for whatever services it might need from the bank apart from contributions to the party. From these sources the machine earned impressive sums that enabled it to reward its workers and enhance its power. Steffens blamed these evils not on the machine but on the businessmen who offered the bribes. Tom Johnson, a former traction magnate turned reform mayor of Cleveland, set him straight:

> First, you thought it was bad politicians, who turned out to be pretty good fellows. Then you blamed the bad business men who bribed the

good fellows, till you discovered that not all business men bribed and that those who did were pretty good business men. . . . Hell! Can't you see that its privileged business that does it? . . . It's those who seek privileges who corrupt, it's those who possess privilege that defend our corrupt politics. . . . It is privilege that causes evil in the world, not wickedness and not men.

Frederic C. Howe, another reformer, came to a similar conclusion from his years of experience:

An examination of the conditions in city after city discloses one sleepless influence that is common to them all . . . the privileges of the street railways, the gas, the water, the telephone, and electric lighting companies. The connection of these industries with politics explains most of the corruption; it explains the power of the boss and the machine; it suggests the explanation of the indifference of the "best" citizen and his hostility to democratic reform.

Bosses served as the crucial intermediaries in the chain of corruption. "The boss came in through political apathy," Howe added. "He has grown rich through privilege. . . . He is the link which unites the criminal rich with the criminal poor." This same reasoning led even a conservative reformer for good government like Mayor William J. Gaynor of New York to blast the "so-called 'leading' citizens" because they "get a million dollars out of the city dishonestly while the 'boss' gets a thousand."

Despite their unsavory reputation, political bosses performed vital functions for every city. Although critics liked to portray the political boss as a dictator, he was more a broker who ruled not by force but by satisfying his customers. His power depended on his ability to satisfy clients both within and without the machine. Within his own organization he allocated offices and other "gravy," enforced discipline, and resolved conflicts among the ranks. To outsiders he acted as an agent for those seeking services or favors ranging from franchises to waivers of the law. In both roles he handled transactions, mediated disputes, and collected fees for his work, whether a percentage, a flat sum, or simply the intangible capital of favors to be collected later. To the boss political power was a commodity that he bought as cheaply as possible and sold at the highest price. To say that some bosses relished power for its own sake is only to say that they enjoyed their work.

"I've been called a boss," said Jim Pendergast of Kansas City. "All there is to it is having friends, doing things for people, and then later on they'll do things for you. . . . You can't coerce people into doing things for you – you can't make them vote for you. I never coerced anybody in my life. Wherever you see a man bulldozing anybody he don't last long."

Writer Harold Zink, in a study of twenty municipal bosses, all but one of whom operated between 1860 and 1920, found too much variety among them to create any profile of a typical boss. However, they did share some characteristics. Most of them came from humble origins, got little education, became self-reliant at an early age, went into politics by joining some organization, and worked their way gradually to the top as one might do in any major enterprise. In short, they fit not only the Horatio Alger model but also that of any ambitious young man with enough talent and grit to become successful in business. And for all their rapacity, they provided genuine services to both the city and its residents. To many people, including some who strongly disapproved of him, the boss was the man who got things done for people who had nowhere else to turn.

Reformers railed against the bosses as engines of corruption and occasionally drove them from office for a time, but they failed to provide a viable alternative. The boss endured in large part because the machine was the only effective social services agency the city possessed. "There's got to be in every ward somebody that any bloke can come to – no matter what he's done – and get help," declared Martin Lomasney, a Boston boss. "Help, you understand; none of your law and justice, but help." Ward and district leaders, aldermen, and other local party officials were usually the actual dispensers of charity, the "somebody" in every ward. Although their motives were mixed and their own rewards handsome, they provided important services. Others might have done the job better and more cheaply, but there were no others willing or able to perform the variety of services the machine did. As long as the city shirked from providing these services, the machine and its flock remained unassailable.

Urban reformers created a host of organizations seeking to oust the bosses and restore "good government" to the cities. Between 1880 and 1920 American cities became hotbeds of reform pushed by a motley blend of staid businessmen, righteous clergy, utopian visionaries, career do-gooders, journalists, social workers, ordinary citizens outraged by corruption or other evils, and politicians who had sniffed the winds of change. No plan or program united them; they tackled a mosaic of problems and seldom agreed on the best approach to any of them. According to historian Melvin G. Holli, they resorted to two basic strategies. Structural reformers confined themselves to "charter tinkering, elaborate audit procedures, and the drive to impose businesslike efficiency upon city governments." By contrast social reformers looked to democratize municipal government and broaden its base of social services. Between 1880 and 1920 it was the structuralists who dominated the crusades to purify urban politics.

Structural reformers agreed with the bosses on one key point: They viewed the city as a business organization that should be run according to sound business principles. They disagreed over who should run it, what kinds of business should be transacted, and who should benefit. Reformers wanted the city run as an efficient and economical public corporation for the benefit of the public interest. Their notion of the public, however, was limited to the "good people" who paid taxes, did honest work, and were sober, upright citizens. Structural reformers concluded that the machine lay at the heart of the problem and must therefore be destroyed. Displaying only contempt for the lower-class voters who sustained the machine, they sought an administration run by businessmen and trained experts who knew what was best for the city. Once in office, they cut spending to the bone, ignored the plight of the poor, and oversaw expenditures by wrapping the purchasing process in rolls of red tape. In most cases these policies led an exasperated electorate to drive them from power and opened the door for the return of the machine.

The quest of the structural reformers for scientific efficiency did produce two new approaches to municipal government: the city commission and the city manager systems. The commission arose in the wake of a hurricane that devastated Galveston, Texas, in 1900. It embodied a concept advanced in 1896 by John H. Patterson, founder of the National Cash Register Company, who argued that "a city is a great business enterprise whose stockholders are the people." Ultimately it vested power in the hands of a mayor and four commissioners elected by all the city's voters, a process that in one stroke abolished the old tradition of ward politics. As historian James H. Weinstein noted, the commissioners were "vested with combined powers of mayor and board of aldermen. Each commission headed a city department and functioned as legislator and administrator," with the mayor exercising "general coordinating influence over all." Put another way, the city was to be run not by politicians but by a board of directors.

So popular did the commission model become that by 1912 more than 200 cities had adopted some version of it. At first businessmen, chambers of commerce, boards of trade, and other civic groups gave it glowing endorsements, but the plan soon revealed some major weaknesses. Critics noted that concentrating power in the hands of a few administrators actually made it easier for corrupt interests to gain control. If the system attracted more good men to office, it did not eliminate either incompetence or free municipal affairs from political logrolling. Commissioners tended to trade favors or sought to build a power base around the department they oversaw, which resulted in what one critic called "five separate governments," each one centered around a commissioner.

To remedy these defects, H. S. Gilbertson created a refined version of the commission that became the genesis for the city manager plan. Under it the commissioners retained their legislative powers but surrendered all administrative functions to an appointed city manager, who presided over the city's day-to-day affairs and hopefully removed them from direct political pressure. This approach refined the business model: The city manager served as president of the company charged with implementing the policies formed by the commissioners as his board of directors. It proved appealing enough for 242 cities to adopt it between 1913 and 1923, and it remains in use to this day in smaller cities and towns. Where successful, it transformed the basis of urban politics by eliminating the mechanism through which working men, immigrants, and other minorities had entered politics at the neighborhood level.

The new approaches also brought to power well-meaning people who were indifferent if not hostile to the social services provided by the old system. Where the machine had provided assistance to the poor and opportunity to ambitious young men, the commission and city manager plans offered instead efficiency, honesty, and good government. Where reformers and "decent" citizens preached the virtues of democracy and civic responsibility to the city's underclass, the machine offered jobs and other favors. This bloodless approach ignored the larger social needs of the

city. Young Walter Lippmann, an ardent reformer himself, understood this
dilemma better than most and spelled it out in *A Preface to Politics* (1914):

> You cannot beat the bosses with the reformer's taboo. You will not get
> far on the Bowery with the cost unit system and low taxes. . . . I am aware
> of the contract-grafts, the franchise-steals, the dirty streets, the bribing
> and the blackmail, the vice-and-crime partnership, the Big Business
> alliances of Tammany Hall. And yet it seems to me that Tammany Hall
> has a better perception of human need and comes nearer to being what
> a government should be, than any scheme yet proposed by a group of
> "uptown good government" enthusiasts.

These approaches seldom worked in larger cities with their widely
diverse constituencies and more complex political mixes. By contrast the
social reformers tended to view the city less as a business than as a servant to its people. One of them, Brand Whitlock, thought that "The word
'reformer' like the word 'politician' had degenerated, and, in the mind of
the common man, come to connote something very disagreeable. In four
terms as mayor [of Toledo] I came to know both species pretty well, and,
in the later connotations of the term, I prefer politician. He, at least, is
human."

While small and medium-sized cities transformed their political struc-
tures, the larger ones continued to grapple with what critic Van Wyck
Brooks called "the old endless unfruitful seesaw of corruption and reform."
A handful of urban reformers took a more radical tack of social reform.
They included Tom Johnson and Newton D. Baker in Cleveland, Samuel
M. "Golden Rule" Jones and Whitlock in Toledo, Hazen S. Pingree in
Detroit, and Mark Fagan in Jersey City. All shared Pingree's credo that "I
have come to lean upon the common people as the real foundation upon
which good government must rest."

Unlike most structural reformers, who tended to be a drab, colorless
lot, the social reformers exuded warmth, personal magnetism, and deep
humanitarian impulses. They became champions of the urban underdogs,
defending the rights of the "people" against the vested interests of both
the corporation and the machine. Most were political pragmatists who
tackled important issues that affected the entire citizenry, including transit
fares, utility rates, municipal ownership of utilities, schools, free lunch

programs, parks, playgrounds, public health, social welfare programs, and that old favorite, political corruption. Their efforts inevitably aroused fierce opposition from entrenched interests and prompted them to resort to unorthodox tactics.

Johnson, Jones, and Pingree had all risen from modest origins to become successful and wealthy businessmen. Yet they all embraced radical reform programs that infuriated the business interests who were often the targets of their policies. Johnson especially understood the business mentality and proved an expert technician in government. Like Pingree and Jones, he responded to the need for parks, playgrounds, public baths, and other social welfare programs, but he also pushed for municipal control of utilities and services. One admirer described his handling of Cleveland's garbage problem:

> When Mr. Johnson became mayor the city was disposing of its garbage under the contract plan at an annual cost of $69,000. When the contract expired the city bought the plant, and the very first year under municipal ownership and operation, reduced 10,000 more tons of garbage than under the contract method, and at a cost of $10,000 less and this, notwithstanding a reduction in the hours of employees and an increase of their wages.

A municipal electric plant instituted by Johnson cut the city's electric bill by more than one-third. He saved money for 90 percent of the people who used city water by installing meters, pushed through a model building code, established meat and dairy inspection, paved hundreds of miles of road, and implemented new street-cleaning operations. Against savage opposition he won a three-cent fare for streetcars but lost a long and bitter struggle to acquire the lines for the city. After eight years as mayor, he lost both his fortune and his health but not his faith in the people and his belief that privilege lay at the core of urban corruption. The social reformers pushed urban government into new realms of possibilities, but their imprint depended almost entirely on their personalities. The legacy of the structural reformers proved more enduring, but urban reform never found a viable middle ground between the two approaches.

What Melvin Holli called the "conservative revolution in city government" proved a Pyrrhic victory because it never touched the basic social needs of urban America. The crusades of the structuralists undermined the one significant institution that took heed of the immigrant's presence and helped assimilate him into their new surroundings. Blinded by the belief that they had got to the heart of the urban dilemma, the structuralists remained little more than moral plumbers forever tinkering with and adjusting the pipes of the political system. Despite occasional advances, managing cities remained the black hole of American government. At the same time, cities revealed in vivid detail just how much of American life had become a business, and how much business had become the core of American life.

8

The Mastery of Mass Markets

Our thinkers, whether in the field of morals or in the field of economics, have before them nothing less than the task of translating law and morals into terms of modern business.

— Woodrow Wilson

HOW SUCCESSFUL WAS THE ECONOMIC HOTHOUSE? A FEW FIG-ures can at least suggest what it did for productivity. During the 1870s American gross national product, measured in 1958 dollars, averaged about $23 billion a year. That figure reached $52.7 billion in 1890, $76.7 billion in 1900, and $125.6 billion in 1914. In per capita terms the amount jumped from $531 in the 1870s to $1,267 in 1914. Between 1839 and 1899 total commodity output rose at a rate of 50 percent every decade. The population also soared but only at about half this rate; as a result, the output per capita in 1899 increased by 250 percent of that of half a century earlier. Nonfarm output per man-hour rose 28 percent during the 1890s despite the depression and jumped another 49 percent by 1919. The number of business concerns went from 427,000 in 1870 to nearly 1.2 million in 1900 and more than 1.8 million in 1920.

Disposable income increased for workers at all levels, driven by earnings that rose while prices fell. Disposable personal income, which averaged $14.1 billion around the turn of the century, reached $33.3 billion by the eve of World War I and soared to $71.5 billion by 1920, thanks in part to wartime inflation. Using 1914 dollars as a measure, the average annual earnings of nonfarm employees went from $375 in 1870 to $573 in 1900. During these same years, the consumer price index (1914 = 100) fell from 124.9 to 84.3. Between 1900 and 1914 real earnings for all employees rose from $496 to $639 while the consumer price index moved from 84.3 to 100. These figures do not take into account income lost through unemployment, including layoffs. By one estimate, the average annual loss in earnings from unemployment increased from $51 in 1900 to $84 in 1914.

Although unions were neither legal nor very strong throughout this period, they managed to win gains for some workers. A union worker in manufacturing toiled an average of 53 hours a week in 1900 for 34.1 cents an hour or $18.07 a week compared to $8.83 a week for lower-skilled workers. By 1914 the union work week dropped to 48.8 hours a week and pay rose to 43.8 cents an hour or $21.37 a week, while lower-skilled workers averaged $10.78. Despite the relative disadvantage of unions in the bargaining process, organizers exerted enough clout to generate a large number of work stoppages. Between 1886 and 1900 companies endured an average of 1,411 stoppages involving an average of 625,000 workers every year. Most involved protests over wages and hours, but a large number of walkouts centered around the right of workers to organize themselves.

Figures, of course, never tell the whole story. Once the depression of 1893–7 finally lifted, life for Americans got better, at least in material terms. As the components driving the process of industrialization matured, they began changing almost every aspect of daily life. Production increased at a spectacular rate, bringing with it an explosion of new goods. New technologies, most notably the automobile, camera, telephone, motion picture, and phonograph, introduced Americans to unexpected pleasures and possibilities. Thus began the pattern by which today's novelty or luxury became tomorrow's necessity. The expansion of electric power opened the door to a new world of products, services, and conveniences.

For many fortunate people the home itself underwent dramatic changes. New tools and techniques expedited construction, making once luxury features available to more owners. Early versions of prefabricated houses appeared before 1900, and it was even possible to order one through a catalog. Inside the home central heating, which used radiators or pipes to circulate steam heat throughout the house, replaced stoves and fireplaces. Indoor plumbing provided not only running water but a space new to most homes, the bathroom, which became a technological showcase as a whole new industry arose to manufacture sinks, bathtubs, and toilets made of porcelain. Electric lights made rooms brighter, cleaner, fresher, and less dangerous. Electric receptacles enabled the use of a wide variety of appliances that reduced the monotony of many household chores.

Although these and other changes came at a different pace for different people, they involved nothing less than the recasting of American life at its foundation, and with it a revamping of American values. Both became firmly rooted in the idea of material progress as the defining element of a great civilization. As the material quality of their lives improved, Americans came to believe ever more that things were getting better and would continue to do so, thanks to technology, productivity, and American know-how. Tomorrow would always bring a sensation – be it a product, technology, or innovation – that would make today's marvel seem quaint by comparison. The economic hothouse had worked its wonders to an extent that amazed even its cultivators. No one could have predicted the depth to which the changes it wrought would penetrate American life and values.

One of the most fundamental changes involved the gradual emergence of what became the consumer economy and society. The growth of cities did much to speed this process; urban dwellers usually lacked the time, materials, or inclination to make what they needed, and nearly everything could be found in the city's shops, stores, and marketplaces. The goods were there in ever proliferating variety. As historian William Leach noted, "By the late 1890s so many goods, in fact, were flowing out of factories and into stores that businessmen feared overproduction, glut, panic, and depression."

This surge in output burst onto American life within a remarkably short time. The rapid growth of the electric utility industry after 1890 created a major industrial sector where none had existed before while also providing a vital new source of power for manufacturing and other companies. By 1892 two giant firms, General Electric and Westinghouse, dominated the manufacture of electrical equipment. In other fields the combination of organizational innovation and new technologies enabled corporations to produce more goods with fewer workers in ways never before possible. Scale of operation often proved less important than efficiency of production. As Alfred D. Chandler, Jr. stressed, "Increases in productivity and decreases in unit costs . . . resulted far more from the increases in volume and velocity of throughput than from a growth in the size of the factory or plant."

No product exemplified these trends more spectacularly than the automobile. During its early years the motor car remained a plaything of the wealthy. For a time hundreds of different carmakers vied for the public's attention with vehicles powered by steam, electricity, and the newfangled internal combustion engine, which ultimately prevailed. From this crowded field one man and one car emerged far above the rest. Henry Ford developed a vision – some would say obsession – to produce a simple, reliable, durable automobile "so low in price that no man making a good salary will be unable to own one – and enjoy with his family the blessing of hours of pleasure in God's great open space." After forming his own company in 1903 Ford tinkered with various designs before unveiling his masterpiece in 1908. The Model T, considered one of the most perfect machines ever created, cost $850, far less than nearly any other car. By 1927, its final production year, the price had dropped to $263.

Americans fell in love with the Model T. As management expert Peter Drucker declared, the car "could be totally mass-produced, largely by semi-skilled labor, and . . . driven by the owner and repaired by him." These factors mattered at a time when the nation had no paved road system, no dealer network, and no support system of garages, gas stations, and other facilities. The car had only four basic constructional units: the power plant, frame, front axle, and rear axle. When Ford formed his company in 1903, the total number of cars sold in the country amounted to only 11,235. Ford and his men designed not only a revolutionary new vehicle but also an advanced system for building it. "The way to make automobiles," he insisted, "is . . . to make them all alike . . . just like one pin is like another pin when it comes from a pin factory." This belief drove him to pioneer an advanced version of mass production: the assembly line.

Ford's plant at Highland Park, just north of Detroit, became the prototype for this type of innovation with its moving assembling line, interchangeable parts, and unprecedented wage of five dollars a day. Ford extolled his high wages as one factor enabling his workers to afford their own Model T, but he had to pay them for another reason. Assembly-line work with its endlessly repetitive motions proved so boring that even with good pay labor turnover in the plant reached unprecedented figures; in 1913, the year before Ford introduced the five-dollar day, it soared to 380 percent. By 1916 the price of the Model T had fallen to $360, and that year Ford sold 577,036 cars. During the next decade he eclipsed even the impressive Highland Park operation by gradually phasing in what became the most spectacular manufacturing plant in the nation if not the world: the River Rouge complex situated just south of Detroit.

A work in progress from 1917 to 1928, the Rouge dwarfed anything that had come before. The sprawling complex was a mile long and a mile and a half wide. It contained ninety-three buildings along with ore docks, steel and glass furnaces, coke ovens, and even a soybean conversion plant for turning soybeans into plastic automobile parts. A huge power plant produced enough electricity to light the city of Detroit. The transportation system featured a hundred miles of railroad track with sixteen locomotives, a bus network, and fifteen miles of paved roads. At its peak the Rouge employed more than 100,000 workers and had its own fire, police, and medical facilities. The gigantic plant housed 120 miles of conveyors to keep the production process moving along. Raw materials entered its huge maw at one end and finished Model T's emerged from the other at the rate of one new car every forty-nine seconds. By 1926 Ford had produced more than half the cars made in the United States and more than twice the output of his nearest rival, General Motors.

In less than a generation Ford advanced the automobile from a luxury to a necessity in American life. The rapid spread of automobiles transformed the American landscape as a vast infrastructure of roads, facilities, and satellite businesses sprang up everywhere. Ford himself became a national folk hero, although later his reputation would be tarnished by numerous blemishes including unsavory labor practices and unvarnished anti-Semitism. Nevertheless, Ford shoved the country into a new era by making it a nation on wheels. During the 1920s the automobile industry became one of the main pillars of the American economy. After 1926 General Motors, with its broader line of cars, more effective organization, and superior marketing, moved past Ford in sales, but Henry Ford remained the founding father of the automobile industry.

New technologies also helped other industries increase their output. During the 1880s Proctor & Gamble employed a mechanical crusher to produce its Ivory soap in enormous quantities. Henry P. Crowell devised an integrated mill based on new machines to produce his Quaker Oats in astounding quantities. Other manufacturers, most notably Borden, H. J. Heinz, Campbell Soup, and Libby, used continuous-process canning techniques to create food products that changed American cooking and eating habits. Armour, Swift, Wilson, Morris, and Cudahy turned the production of meat and animal by-products into a highly integrated process. American Sugar Refining Company, American Cotton Oil Company, and Corn Products Refining Company did likewise for their products. National Biscuit Company, created by the merger of three companies in 1897, proudly traced the path it had followed in its annual report for 1901:

> When the company started, it was an aggregation of plants. It is now an organized company.... [A] radical change has been wrought into our business. In the past, the managers of large industrial corporations have thought it necessary, for success, to control or limit competition. So, when this company started, it was believed that we must control competition or buy it. The first meant a ruinous war of prices and great loss of profits; the second, constantly increasing capitalization. Experience soon proved to us that... either of these courses, if persevered in, must bring disaster.... We turned our attention... to improving the internal management of our own business, to getting the full benefit from purchasing our raw materials in large quantities, to economizing the expense of manufacture, to systematizing and rendering more effective our selling department, and above all... to improving the quality of our goods and the condition in which they should reach the consumer.

For businessmen and manufacturers the new productivity created another kind of problem: how to dispose of the huge flow of goods pouring forth from their plants. As small companies mutated into major corporations with giant plants or large numbers of factories, the amount of capital investment at stake demanded that production remain constant if not growing. Any slackening of output meant a decline in income even though rent, interest, utilities, and other costs still had to be met. Put another way, the dramatic increase in scale of operation compelled corporations to keep the goods flowing or suffer heavy losses. Andrew Carnegie understood the formula before most other businessmen. "Run our works full," he decreed, "we must run them at any price.... Cut the prices; scoop the market; run the mills full."

Not surprisingly, then, the attention of businessmen shifted increasingly from production to marketing. The problem was not only how to get more people to buy more goods; it was how to enable them to buy more goods even when they did not actually need them or could not afford them. For many companies the marketing challenge involved finding new techniques and tactics for selling goods. Two tools proved indispensable for many consumer items: brand names and advertising. Both depended on the development of regional and national markets that enabled manufacturers to reach huge numbers of potential customers. As the ability to reach these markets increased after 1880, more and more companies came to recognize the symbiotic relationship between brand names and advertising. From this recognition emerged the consumer economy, a revolution wrought by the transformation of the traditional customer into a consumer.

Historian Susan Strasser has detailed this transformation in her incisive *Satisfaction Guaranteed: The Making of the American Mass Market*. For generations the small stores that had served urban and rural communities alike dominated retailing by offering customers advice, friendly service, local gossip, some employment for young people, and especially credit for families who lived from payday to payday. Wholesalers provided local merchants with a wide variety of goods, few of which carried brand names. When customers asked for some item, the merchant selected it for them. Merchants balked at selling most branded goods because of the lower profit margin on them; instead they steered their customers to substitute items. Their direct contact with customers gave them an advantage over distant manufacturers known only by a brand name. Customers relied on them for advice and usually did not have the option of going to a shelf or counter and choosing the item they wanted.

However, the variety and quantity of branded goods flowing from factories continued to increase. "It is wonderful to note the volume of package trading in food products, groceries, and patent medicines," noted Artemas Ward, an early copywriter and editor, in 1900. "Sugar, molasses, vinegar, flour, cheese, dried apples – a hundred and one things once regarded as staples to be sold only in bulk now come within the package field." So too with toothpaste, breakfast cereal, chewing gum, safety razors, shoe polish, baking soda, and countless other products, leading Ward to exclaim that "There has been a revolution in the methods of American trade within the past twenty years." At mid-century a few companies, notably Singer and McCormick had pioneered in creating their own distribution system as well as brand name. The pattern they established spread to other products, thanks in part to advances in packaging.

Packaging was crucial to the branding process in that it gave the product a distinctive appearance and set it apart from items sold in bulk such as crackers, flour, and pickles. Francis Wolles patented the first machine to make paper bags in 1852; later he formed the Union Paper Bag Machine Company, which came to control 90 percent of the nation's paper-bag business. The square-bottomed bag appeared in the late 1860s and the folding cardboard carton for products like crackers and cereals in the early 1880s. Bottle making became fully automatic after 1903. Aluminum foil became available after 1910 and cellophane in 1913. The ability to wrap and package goods, especially food items, enhanced not only branding but also claims for sanitation and quality as well. Design became ever more important as manufacturers sought a distinctive look for every product. In the catch phrase of a later generation, the medium became the message.

Once branding became established, manufacturers realized that any named item could be heavily advertised and promoted on a national level. Newspapers and magazines became the venue for newly crafted campaigns not only to sell an item but to plant its brand name firmly in the buyer's mind as well. In 1900 National Biscuit (Nabisco) called one of its cartons "In-Er-Seal" and used it for no fewer than forty-four different branded products. The company spent more on advertising than any other corporation except American Tobacco and Royal Baking Powder. Although, as Strasser notes, National Biscuit still did 75 percent of its business in bulk goods as late as 1923, it pioneered in impressing on consumers the habit of brand recognition. Long-delayed legislation in 1905 finally put trademarks on firm legal ground and protected them from infringement. Within a year of the new law 10,000 new trademarks were registered. Unlike patents or copyrights, they never expired.

The Scott Paper Company illustrates this transition nicely. For three decades it manufactured some 300 different private-label paper products and sold them to wholesalers. In 1909 it stopped making these items and began producing only five articles under its own label. Even more, Scott did not sell its new line of goods through wholesalers but created its own sales force backed by a vigorous advertising campaign. H. J. Heinz built a giant organization to distribute his line of food products; by 1922 it included fifty-eight branch offices and seventy foreign agencies. During the 1900s more and more companies, including Nabisco, Colgate, Proctor & Gamble, Gillette, and Sherwin-Williams, began selling directly to retailers. The objective was not only to eliminate wholesalers but also to control distribution and handling of the product at the retail level. To be successful, manufacturers had to get retailers to feature their products over those of competitors. One way to accomplish this was to take the decision out of the hands of the merchant and put it in the hands of the buyer. Advertising played a crucial role in effecting this change.

During the 1880s four consumer items pioneered in national advertising. Three were soaps; the fourth was Royal Baking Powder. As early as 1905 *Printer's Ink* pronounced it "a golden age in trademarks." By the 1920s hundreds of brand names flooded every available media with appeals that grew increasingly sophisticated. The need to promote brands did much to transform advertising from a practice to a full-blown industry ever in search of more elaborate techniques. Where once advertising men simply sold space, increasingly they began to conceive of the approach and to write copy for their clients. N. W. Ayer & Son, one of the first full-service advertising agencies, conducted the first marketing survey as early as 1879. During the next two decades it came increasingly to deal with national corporations rather than local businesses, yet the firm did not hire its first copywriter until 1892. "In the 1880s," noted William Leach, "there were only two copyrighters of any consequence in the country; by the late 1890s there were hundreds, by 1915 thousands."

The quest for learning what the consumer wanted led inevitably to the still young field of psychology. As early as 1903 Walter Dill Scott began publishing the articles that five years later became his influential *The Psychology of Advertising*. How many advertisers, he asked, "describe a piano so vividly that the reader can hear it? How many food products are so described that the reader can taste the food?" Earnest Elmo Calkins, who formed in 1902 what he claimed to be "the first full-service agency," brought a bold new sensibility to advertising. Discarding the stodgy, traditional approach, his firm gained renown for its clever jingles and appealing characters. "Advertising was so poor in those days," he recalled, "that anything done to it was an improvement." Some firms, most notably the department stores, recognized early their dependence on advertising. "The time to advertise," said John Wanamaker, "is all the time." They also realized that the copy had to be livelier, and that copy by itself was no longer enough. During the 1890s the visual image, once regarded as mere hucksterism, began to transform advertising as well as the broader culture.

"Pictures are first principles," argued one advocate. "You may forget what you read – if you read at all. But what you see, you know instantly." Wanamaker, who had long shown a genius for promoting and advertising his department store, observed that "Pictures are the lesson books of the uneducated." Images came in the form of lavish posters and illustrations, some of them drawn by well-known artists such as Maxwell Parrish, and in photographs. For department stores they also came in the form of tableaux displayed in large public windows glowing with light and color. As Leach has shown, the art of window dressing emerged during these years, thanks in part to newer, cheaper, stronger types of plate glass. The display window became a crossroad of art and commerce, seeking to entice the viewer and bring the "goods out in a blaze of glory."

The man who wrote the book on window dressing knew a good deal about fantasy. L. Frank Baum started his monthly journal *The Show Window* in 1897 and the following year organized the National Association of Window Trimmers. His message was clear: Use the most artful means to "arouse in the observer the cupidity and longing to possess the goods." Baum himself left retailing in 1900 to earn his fame in another field; that year his *The Wonderful Wizard of Oz* first delighted the public and prompted a parade of sequels. He left behind a legacy of commercial art filled with color and light to create mood and atmosphere. The spectacle of store windows dazzled some viewers and unsettled others who resented the allures offered by cleverly staged displays. "It is a work of art that window," protested novelist Edna Ferber of a Chicago display in the winter of 1911, "a breeder of anarchism, a destroyer of contentment. . . . It boasts peaches, downy and golden, when peaches have no right to be, strawberries glow therein when shortcake is a last summer's memory."

Advertising also began to inflict itself more insistently on people in other public spaces. Billboards and posters multiplied as the ability to print quality color reproductions grew cheaper and more efficient. After 1900 a new sign of the times emerged in the form of electric displays that pressed their message on even the most resistant passerby. O. J. Gude, who later coined the phrase "The Great White Way" to describe the spectacle of electric signs that illuminated Times Square in New York, pioneered in arranging and brokering electric displays. "Sign boards are so placed," he argued, "that everybody must read them, and absorb them, and absorb the advertisement's lesson willingly or unwillingly. The constant reading of 'Buy Blank's Biscuits' makes the name part of one's sub-conscious knowledge." H. J. Heinz bought one prominent space and filled it with a forty-five-foot-long pickle in green lights. Below it other bulbs spelled out the "57 Varieties," each of them in a different color. By 1910 more than twenty blocks on Broadway glowed with electric advertisements, including a huge portrayal of a Roman chariot race that measured seventy-two feet high and ninety feet wide. Already some advertising men had come to appreciate the value of overkill.

Advertising men followed the usual pattern by forming in 1899 the Association of American Advertisers. As more firms advertised more extensively in more venues, the industry mushroomed in size. Ayer put together the first million-dollar campaign in 1899 for Nabisco's Uneeda Biscuits. W. K. Kellogg placed the first ads for his corn flakes in six Midwestern newspapers in 1906; by 1915 he was spending more than $1 million annually on advertising. Asa Griggs Candler registered the Coca-Cola trademark in 1893 and relied heavily on advertising to earn $9.4 million in sales and $2.4 million in profits by 1914. As historian Richard Tedlow observed, "Coca-Cola was advertising incarnate." In 1912 the Advertising Club of America named it the best-advertised product in the nation; that year it spent $1.2 million on advertising, more than its total sales had been in 1904. Other companies followed suit. Where advertisers had spent an estimated $200 million in 1880, they poured out more than $1.3 billion in 1914.

The more creative advertising men came up with campaigns that seem strikingly modern even today. Strasser recounts the landmark strategy used by Proctor & Gamble (P&G) in 1912 to introduce Crisco to the American public. It began with magazine ads touting "An Absolutely New Product, A Discovery Which Will Affect Every Kitchen in America." In fact the company had devoted five years of secret research to creating in the laboratory a viable all-vegetable solid fat to replace the use of lard. The result was a new branded product intended to replace a traditional one if Americans could be persuaded to try it.

For nearly a year the company engaged in product testing with a limited number of customers to refine the product. In December 1911, a month before opening its national campaign, it sent between three and six cans of Crisco to every grocer in the United States with a letter describing the advertising blitz soon to follow. The magazine ads urged readers to get Crisco from their local grocer. "If your own grocer does not keep it," some added, "you probably will find it in one of the other stores in your neighborhood." For four years P&G hammered away at the Crisco promotion, enlisting grocer support, publishing pamphlets filled with recipes, and even sending six demonstrators around the country to conduct cooking schools. To lure the railroad dining-car trade, P&G created a special ten-pound container; another special package intended for Jewish neighborhoods bore the assurance of two rabbis that the contents were kosher. Marketers today still utilize some version of every one of these practices.

Quaker Oats boasted that it had "the largest sale of any Cereal Food in the World." In the summer of 1891 the company invaded a new market by sending a fifteen-car freight train to Portland, Oregon, to promote its cereal and hand out samples. Earlier it had put half-ounce packages of the cereal in every Portland mailbox and sent an advance man to generate news stories and buy space in local papers. Razor manufacturer King Gillette used ads to speak directly to consumers, urging them to use his new "safety razor" that needed neither honing nor stropping as did a straight razor. Early in the game Gillette came to understand that large profits lay not merely in selling razors but even more in the repeat sale of double-edged blades for them. To that end he ran ads teaching men how to shave themselves with quick, easy strokes. In 1911 Woodbury Soap introduced sex appeal to the mass market with an ad in *Ladies Home Journal* featuring the slogan, "The skin you love to touch."

Still other manufacturers resorted to creating images of cute or sentimental characters to promote their product. Jell-O had its Kewpies (Strasser called them "the Smurfs of their day"), Campbell Soups its Campbell Kids, a pancake company its Aunt Jemima, and a cereal named H-O Force an elderly gent named Sunny Jim. Grandmothers abounded in ads, as did adorable children. Heinz portrayed the purity of its products with the image of an idealized worker, "The Girl in the White Cap." The stream of visitors who toured the Heinz factory actually saw young women wearing uniforms and white caps on the production line. Clever slogans also served to entice buyers. George Eastman, who transformed the photography business, came up with the name "Kodak" for his revolutionary new camera. In ads portraying three generations of a family, he urged readers to "Make Kodak your family historian." Eastman also came up with one of the best slogans ever devised: "You press the button, we do the rest." Ivory soap hit early on the slogans it would use for decades: "99$^{44}/_{100}$% Pure" and "It Floats."

Advertisements did more than entice people to buy; they offered the promise of a better life through consumer goods. New products had not only to win customer confidence but also to teach buyers new habits and convince them of better ways to do things. As the pace of American life grew faster, old customs and traditions fell by the wayside. Eastman capitalized on that tendency by creating a product that enabled ordinary people to record their past cheaply and easily. In democratizing photography he institutionalized the preservation of memories and moved Americans down a course that would dominate the next century: the substitution of visual for verbal communication. Food manufacturers sold the convenience of premade and easily served products such as cereals, bread, and canned soups to people accustomed to making their own. Gillette freed shavers from a trip to the barber and the tyranny of the straight razor. Coca-Cola offered a beverage that all classes of people could afford and enjoy.

In their advertising campaigns manufacturers had an even more ambitious goal: to steer customers away from merchant influence toward their own branded products by persuading them to tell the merchant exactly what they wanted. Branding worked only when the customer asked specifically for the product, and it worked even better if the customer could fetch it directly off the shelf rather than rely on a clerk. Self-service scarcely existed even in chain stores before 1912, but it offered several advantages to stores seeking a mass market. It greatly reduced labor costs, streamlined operations by allowing customers to roam at will before checking out, enabled the customer to choose his or her own products without interference, and eliminated delivery.

A&P, the nation's largest food chain, opened its "Economy Stores" in 1913 that featured several innovations but stopped short of self-service. Clarence Saunders seems to have been the first to put the concept into full use. He opened his first Piggly Wiggly grocery store in Memphis, Tennessee, in 1916 and patented his design the following year. Instead of using clerks, Saunders created a system of aisles that allowed customers to reach every piece of merchandise. Customers entered through a turnstile, carried baskets for their selections, and paid a cashier on leaving. On this premise Saunders forged an empire of 1,200 stores by 1922 only to be financially ruined by a stock-market corner in 1923. The Piggly Wiggly chain lived on and more than doubled in size.

When self-service became the rule rather than the exception, the customer became a consumer. Until then, manufacturers used the two-edged strategy of inducements to win merchants to their product or advertising and promotions to win the customer. In effect the manufacturer succeeded in reversing the law of supply and demand by creating a demand that had not existed before. Here was Chandler's "Visible Hand" writ large. His thesis declared that "In many sectors of the economy the visible hand of management replaced what Adam Smith referred to as the invisible hand of market forces." The world of Adam Smith (which happened also to be that of the founding of the United States and the writing of its Constitution) never envisioned the creation of an enormous, highly integrated industrialized economy or the implications posed by its ability to pour forth a seemingly unending flow of goods of infinite variety. Nor could it have imagined the role that would come to be played by advertising and promotion in the marketing of these goods.

Transforming the customer into a consumer created an entirely new relationship between the manufacturer and those who bought his products, one that was direct but unbalanced in favor of the former. The customer knew the merchant personally; the consumer had no contact with the manufacturer and knew little about the company beyond what ads revealed. Distant manufacturers offered no clear assurance about the quality of their goods. "We buy everything, and have no idea of the processes by which articles are produced," complained Ellen Richards, an early consumer advocate, "and have no means of knowing beforehand what the quality may be." The rise of packaged foods, which promised but did not always deliver purity and sanitation, accelerated the lengthy fight over the quality of food and drugs. Attempts to prevent adulterated food had been made at the state and local levels, but not until 1906 did Congress finally pass the Pure Food and Drug Act, which marked the entrance of the federal government into the regulation of such goods.

In the emerging consumer economy the marketplace became the arena in which people and products met and mingled. Increasingly consumers bought what they found on the shelf and asked for whatever appealed to them in some advertisement. Over time this process helped improve the quality and variety of goods since people would not buy again a product they found wanting, let alone recommend it to friends. As the variety of goods increased and filled a greater part of daily life, they set in motion forces that became dominant during the 1920s. The traditional savings ethic gave way to a spending ethic, spurred in part by the rise of installment buying that made it possible for people to enjoy goods before they could actually pay for them. Advertising insinuated itself into ever more corners of American life, laying the foundation for a culture in which it would be impossible to escape its cloying presence.

Consumer products performed another important function. As American society became more diverse and mobile, cutting loose from its roots in older, more distinct cultural heritages, people came increasingly to define themselves less by who they were than by what they did. Status and success came to be measured by one's job or profession as well as by the possessions one owned. Gradually after 1900 the consumer economy moved to the center of the culture, providing a semblance of unity or at least connection for a complex, multicultural nation. For a people devoted to the ideal of material progress, it was the logical and in many respects only integrating force. The lavish output of goods demonstrated that the system worked even if the distribution of its largesse was badly skewed. In the increasingly fragmented and segmented corporate society it served as a unifying thread by standardizing tastes through consumer products, magazines, sports, music, and other cultural meeting points.

Businessmen did more than provide goods or services; they furnished the glue that bound together a diverse people divided by a host of cultural conflicts. For better or worse, the economic hothouse had done much to create a nation much too large, diverse, and increasingly connected to rely on the small-town habits and customs that had long formed its core value system. The galloping pace of technological innovation ensured that the future belonged more to change than to stability. The belief that tomorrow would be better than today, and that more goods of higher quality defined what was meant by "better," emerged as the national mantra by the 1920s. In this context the consumer economy gave Americans a common national vocabulary that soon became their standard language.

World War I, far from disrupting this pattern, set the stage for its rapid development much as the Civil War had prepared the ground for the economic hothouse. The ravages of this bloody, exhausting war left the United States as the globe's economic giant by default. Even in 1914 it led the world in manufacturing with 56 percent of total output compared with only 16 percent for Germany and 14 percent for Great Britain. However, the war turned the United States from a debtor nation owing $3.8 billion to other countries into a creditor owed $12.5 billion by others, thereby converting what had been debt service into income. The war also organized, standardized, and centralized American life as never before. The draft required every male between 18 and 45 to register, and the 4.7 million summoned to service learned firsthand about regimentation. A Division of Planning and Statistics introduced Americans to the realm not only of statistics but of government planning as well.

The demands of war gave businessmen a golden opportunity to refurbish reputations blackened by the scandals and revelations of muckrakers that had thrown them into disrepute since 1900. The unprecedented controls placed on American industry required experienced businessmen to manage them through new centralizing agencies such as the War Industries Board headed by Bernard Baruch. The WIB exerted authority over manufacturing, priorities, conversion of facilities, price fixing, and other areas. Two other agencies, the National War Labor Board and the War Labor Policies Board, handled labor matters while the Food Administration organized that sector under the capable leadership of Herbert Hoover. The War Finance Corporation, which took charge of financing war industries, was one of several government-owned corporations created to handle specific problems. This first extensive use of such corporations became an important precedent in later years.

The most dramatic use of this device came in December 1917 when President Woodrow Wilson nationalized the nation's gridlocked railroads and placed them under the control of a new agency, the United States Railroad Administration. For the rest of the war USRA ran the railroads as an integrated national system rather than separate companies. The Committee on Public Information was formed to produce propaganda in support of the war effort and manage war news. In the process it also trained a generation of bright young minds in techniques of persuasion that were later applied to everything from politics to advertising. One of these bright young men, Edward Bernays, used his experience to create a new profession that would become known as public relations.

In organizing the nation's economy, the new boards imposed drastic measures. Many items were rigidly standardized to make production more efficient. The variety of automobile tires was slashed from 287 to 9, steel plows from 312 to 76, and buggy wheels from 232 to 4. Expenditures for new manufacturing plants and equipment soared from $600 million in 1915 to $2.5 billion in 1918. Valuable German patents, especially in dyes and chemicals, were confiscated and became sources of huge profits to American firms, some of which emerged as giants during the conflict. Wartime inflation, along with insatiable wartime demand, proved a bonanza for American farmers, who saw the price of wheat and cotton nearly triple between 1913 and 1919. In response farmers eagerly bought more land on credit and planted record crops, setting the stage for renewed miseries after 1920. To raise money for the war, the federal government resorted to five high-powered bond drives that not only fetched huge sums but also gave some 22 million Americans their first lesson about owning securities and their desirability as a form of wealth. After the war they became the broader market that Wall Street had long sought but never realized.

By 1920, despite the inevitable postwar economic slump that produced a sharp but brief recession, the American economy stood poised at the threshold of a golden era – what social critic Frederick Lewis Allen called "the seven fat years" – that in many respects mark the beginning of the modern era of business. That year saw the election of a new Republican president, Warren G. Harding, who declared that "The business of America is the business of everybody in America. . . . This is essentially a business country. . . . We must get back to the methods of business." His successor, the taciturn Calvin Coolidge, put the same sentiment more succinctly when he said in 1925, "The chief business of the American people is business." Time has proved them more right than they ever imagined.

Epilogue

THE BOUNDARIES OF BIG BUSINESS

I do not find foreign countries foreign.

> – Alfred M. Zeien, Chairman, Gillette Company

I N ONE RESPECT AT LEAST THE ECONOMIC HOTHOUSE SUC-ceeded all too well. It laid the foundation not only for the domination of American life by business but also for the rise of a culture with an amazing, irresistible tendency to transform every single aspect of American life first into a business and then into a larger business. No institution, activity, or value has escaped this relentless organizing into some form of commerce. Some of the most obvious examples include the arts, politics, religion, education, sports, sex, media, entertainment, the family, childhood, and, of course, history. Commercialization rolled like a tsunami into every corner of American life, propelled largely by the continued pressure exerted by the forces discussed earlier: organization, technological innovation, advertising, and the relentless energy of entrepreneurs. The scale and scope of enterprises grow ever larger and now embrace the globe as easily as once they did regional markets.

In the economy produced by the economic hothouse, it was only natural for companies to seek new markets in every corner of the world. As the competitive arena expanded from national to global realms, firms found themselves dealing on a level that transcended their old loyalties and identities. The rise of multinational corporations signaled the emergence of a new economic order grounded in markets that defied older strictures and limitations. Modern giant corporations know no boundaries or national loyalties, and in many respects they exert more influence worldwide than nations or their diplomats. Both manufacturing and services are routinely outsourced to other nations. Products routinely have mixed backgrounds in their design, manufacture, and composition. What nationality is a Toyota that is designed in California and built in Kentucky? A Chevrolet built in Mexico or a Ford built in Germany? Designer clothes made in China or the Philippines?

If there is a truism that characterizes the modern age, it is that the more things change, the more they become big business. Advertising, propelled by new media – most notably television – has spread its influence into every corner of American life until it managed to reduce every facet of human activity into a product. The culture of consumption now occupies center stage both at home and in many places abroad. Today's bitter culture wars trace their origins to this transformation of life at home and abroad. At bottom they are clashes between the homogenizing forces of commercial culture and those who resent modernism in all its forms and cling to traditional cultural values and patterns. Clashes over religion and ethnic differences take center stage in this struggle because they are strongholds of traditional society. Modern marketing undermines these influences by striving to make all the world a market and all its people merely consumers.

Advertising has gone global in a huge way. Worldwide advertising outlays reached an estimated $256 billion in 1990. Planet Hollywood hoped to make its name a reality, and Reebok underwrote an ad campaign around the theme of "Planet Reebok," which had "no boundaries." Brand names that waged their first competitive wars in local stores have now invaded nations throughout the world, carrying with them not only products but cultural values as well. It is now possible to have a Big Mac or KFC with a Coke or a Pepsi almost anywhere on earth. The saturation bombing of the senses by advertising has among other things carried images of American culture to the far reaches of the globe. Some people embrace them; others react violently to them, denouncing their influence even as they wear Nike sneakers or Gap sweatshirts.

The broader effects of this permeation have yet to be fully reckoned. What is clear is that it has changed American life and business to an extent that can scarcely be measured, and that its influence shows no signs of slowing down. As the cultural cleavages grow deeper, the influence of business grows stronger. The complex chain of developments beginning with the economic hothouse has succeeded in creating a nation largely in its own image, and one increasingly devoted to images. By the 1920s the emerging consumer economy became the glue that held an increasingly diverse society together. The overriding question today is whether it can extend that same influence to the even more diverse peoples of the world faster than opposition to it tears whole societies apart. Business, after all, seeks only to conquer the world, not actually run it.

Sources and Suggested Readings

Many of the sources used for this book make excellent follow-up reading as well. The list given below offers suggestions for pursuing the subjects taken up in each chapter.

General Histories

Chandler, Alfred D., Jr. *The Visible Hand: The Managerial Revolution in American Business* (Cambridge, Mass., 1977).

Cochran, Thomas C. *Business in American Life: A History* (New York, 1972).

Klein, Maury. *The Flowering of the Third America* (Chicago, 1993).

Porter, Glenn. *The Rise of Big Business, 1860–1910* (New York, 1973).

Prologue

Bruchey, Stuart, *Cotton and the Growth of the American Economy: 1890–1860* (New York, 1967).

Bruchey, Stuart. *The Roots of American Economic Growth, 1607–1861* (New York, 1965).

Green, Constance. *Eli Whitney and the Birth of American Technology* (Boston, 1956).

Hounshell, David A. *From the American System to Mass Production, 1800–1932* (Baltimore, 1984).

Hurst, J. Willard. *Law and the Conditions of Freedom in the Nineteenth Century United States* (Madison, Wis., 1956).

Kennedy, Roger G. *Mr. Jefferson's Lost Cause: Land, Farmers, Slavery, and the Louisiana Purchase* (New York, 2003).

Kukla, Jon. *A Wilderness So Immense: The Louisiana Purchase and the Destiny of America* (New York, 2003).

Malone, Dumas. *Jefferson the President: First Term, 1801–1805* (Boston, 1970).

Potter, David M. *People of Plenty: Economic Abundance and the American Character* (Chicago, 1954).

Sheldon, Garrett Ward. *The Political Philosophy of Thomas Jefferson* (Baltimore, 1991).

Tocqueville, Alexis de. *Democracy in America* (New York, 1945), 2 vols.

Woodman, Harold D. *Slavery and the Southern Economy* (New York, 1966).

Chapter 1

Byrn, Edward W. *The Progress of Invention in the Nineteenth Century* (New York, 1900).

Cowan, Ruth Schwarz. *A Social History of American Technology* (New York, 1997).

Drucker, Peter F. *Innovation and Entrepreneurship* (New York, 1985).

Haber, Samuel. *Efficiency and Uplift* (Chicago, 1964).

Hindle, Brook. *Emulation and Invention* (New York, 1982).

Hughes, Jonathan R. T. *The Vital Few: The Entrepreneur & American Economic Progress* (New York, 1986).

Hughes, Thomas P. *American Genesis* (New York, 1989).

Klein, Maury. *The Change Makers* (New York, 2003).

Klein, Maury. *The Life and Legend of Jay Gould* (Baltimore, 1986).

Livesay, Harold C. *American Made: The Men Who Shaped the American Economy* (Boston, 1979).

Noble, David F. *America by Design* (New York, 1977).

Rosenberg, Nathan. *Technology and American Economic Growth* (New York, 1972).

Schumpeter, Joseph A. *Capitalism, Socialism, and Democracy* (New York, 1950).

Schumpeter, Joseph A. *The Theory of Economic Development* (New York, 1969).

Tedlow, Richard S. *Giants of Enterprise: Seven Business Innovators and the Empires They Built* (New York, 2001).

Chapter 2

Billington, Ray Allen. *The Far Western Frontier* (New York, 1974).

Clark, John G. *The Grain Trade in the Old Northwest* (Urbana, Ill., 1966).

Danbom, David B. *Born in the Country: A History of Rural America* (Baltimore, 1995).

Gates, Paul W. *The Farmer's Age: Agriculture, 1815–1860* (New York, 1960).

Klein, Maury, and Harvey A. Kantor. *Prisoners of Progress: American Industrial Cities, 1850–1920* (New York, 1976).

Schlebecker, John T. *Whereby We Thrive: A History of American Farming, 1607–1972* (Ames, Ia., 1975).

Shannon, Fred A. *The Farmer's Last Frontier: Agriculture, 1860–1897* (New York, 1945).

Chapter 3

Bernstein, Peter L. *Wedding of the Waters: The Erie Canal and the Making of a Great Nation* (New York, 2005).

Hunter, Louis C. *Steamboats on the Western Rivers* (New York, 1969).

Israel, Paul. *Edison: A Life of Invention* (New York, 1998).

Klein, Maury. *The Great Richmond Terminal: A Study in Businessmen and Business Strategy* (Charlottesville, Va., 1970).

Klein, Maury. *The Life and Legend of E. H. Harriman* (Chapel Hill, N.C., 2000).

Klein, Maury. *Unfinished Business: Railroads and American Life* (Hanover, N.H., 2004).

Lane, Wheaton J. *Commodore Vanderbilt: An Epic of the Steam Age* (New York, 1942).

Larson, John Lauritz. *Internal Improvement: National Public Works and the Promise of Popular Government in the Early United States* (Chapel Hill, N.C., 2001).

Silverman, Kenneth. *Lightning Man: The Accursed Life of Samuel F. B. Morse* (New York, 2003).

Stover, John F. *American Railroads* (Chicago, 1961).

Taylor, George Rogers. *The Transportation Revolution, 1815–1860* (New York, 1951).

Thompson, Robert L. *Wiring the Continent* (Princeton, 1947).

Chapter 4

Bathe, Greville and Dorothy. *Oliver Evans: A Chronicle of Early American Engineering* (Philadelphia, 1935).

Bordeau, Sanford P. *Volts to Hertz: The Rise of Electricity* (Minneapolis, 1982).

Carlson, W. Bernard. *Innovation as a Social Process: Elihu Thomson and the Rise of General Electric* (New York, 1991).

Childs, Marquis. *The Farmer Takes a Hand: The Electric Power Revolution in Rural America* (New York, 1952).

Friedel, Robert D., and Paul Israel. *Edison's Electric Light: Biography of an Invention* (New Brunswick, N.J., 1995).

Hills, Richard L. *Power from Steam: A History of the Stationary Steam Engine* (Cambridge, 1989).

Hughes, Thomas P. *Networks of Power: Electrification in Western Society, 1880–1930* (Baltimore, 1983).

Jonnes, Jill. *Empires of Light: Edison, Tesla, Westinghouse and the Race to Electrify the World* (New York, 2003).

McDonald, Forrest. *Insull* (Chicago, 1962).

Nye, David E. *Electrifying America: Social Meanings of a New Technology* (Cambridge, Mass., 1992).

Passer, Harold C. *The Electrical Manufacturers, 1875–1900* (Cambridge, Mass., 1953).

Philip, Cynthia Owen. *Robert Fulton: A Biography* (New York, 1985).

Seifer, Marc J. *Wizard: The Life and Times of Nikola Tesla* (Secaucus, N.J., 1996).

Sharlin, Harold I. *The Making of the Electrical Age* (New York, 1963).

Chapter 5

Appel, Joseph H. *The Business Biography of John Wanamaker: Founder and Builder* (New York, 1930).

Chandler, Alfred D. Jr. *Strategy and Structure* (Cambridge, Mass., 1962).

Chernow, Ron. *Titan: The Life of John D. Rockefeller, Sr.* (New York, 1998).

Dewing, Arthur S. *The Financial Policy of Corporations* (New York, 1953), 2 vols.

Durden, Robert F. *The Dukes of Durham, 1865–1929* (Durham, N.C., 1975).

Emmet, Boris, and John E. Jeuck. *Catalogues and Counters: A History of Sears, Roebuck and Company* (Chicago, 1950).

Gibbons, Herbert A. *John Wanamaker* (New York, 1926), 2 vols.

Lamoreaux, Naomi R. *The Great Merger Movement in American Business, 1895–1904* (New York, 1985).

Livesay, Harold C. *Andrew Carnegie and the Rise of Big Business* (Boston, 1975).

Nelson, Ralph L. *Merger Movements in American Industry, 1895–1956* (Princeton, 1959).

Paine, Albert Bigelow. *Theodore M. Vail: A Biography* (New York, 1929).

Penney, James Cash. *Fifty Years with the Golden Rule* (New York, 1950).

Strouse, Jean. *Morgan: American Financier* (New York, 1999).

Wall, Joseph Frazier. *Andrew Carnegie* (New York, 1970).

Winkler, John K. *Five and Ten: The Fabulous Life of F. W. Woolworth* (Freeport, N.Y., 1970).

Chapter 6

Bledstein, Burton J. *The Culture of Professionalism* (New York, 1976).

Blumin, Stuart M. *The Emergence of the Middle Class* (New York, 1989).

Daniels, Roger. *Coming to America* (New York, 1990).

Dubofsky, Melvin. *Industrialism and the American Worker, 1865–1920* (Arlington Heights, Ill., 1985).

Gutman, Herbert G. *Work, Culture, and Society in Industrializing America* (New York, 1976).

Higham, John. *Strangers in the Land* (New Brunswick, N.J., 1955).

Hoogenboom, Ari, and Olive Hoogenboom. *A History of the ICC: From Panacea to Palliative* (New York, 1976).

Keller, Morton. *Affairs of State: Public Life in Late Nineteenth Century America* (Cambridge, Mass., 1977).

Klein, Maury, and Harvey A. Kantor. *Prisoners of Progress: American Industrial Cities, 1850–1920* (New York, 1976).

Mills, C. Wright. *White Collar* (New York, 1951).

Montgomery, David. *The Fall of the House of Labor* (New York, 1987).

Rayback, Joseph. *A History of American Labor* (New York, 1966).

Taylor, Philip. *The Distant Magnet* (New York, 1971).

Weinstein, James. *The Corporate Ideal in the Liberal State, 1900–1916* (Boston, 1968).

Wittke, Carl. *We Who Built America* (New York, 1939).

Zeff, Stephen A. (ed.). *The U.S. Accounting Profession in the 1890s and Early 1900s* (New York, 1988).

Zunz, Olivier. *Making America Corporate* (Chicago, 1990).

Chapter 7

Bryce, James. *The American Commonwealth* (New York, 1888), 2 vols.

Callow, Alexander B. *The City Boss in America: An Interpretive Reader* (New York, 1976).

Howe, Frederic C. *The Confessions of a Reformer* (New York, 1925).

Klein, Maury, and Harvey A. Kantor. *Prisoners of Progress: American Industrial Cities, 1850–1920* (New York, 1976).

McKelvey, Blake. *The Urbanization of America, 1860–1915* (New Brunswick, N.J., 1963).

Riordan, William L. *Plunkitt of Tammany Hall* (New York, 1995).

Steffens, Lincoln. *The Autobiography of Lincoln Steffens* (New York, 1931).

Steffens, Lincoln. *Shame of the Cities* (New York, 1957).

Warner, Sam Bass, Jr. *The Urban Wilderness* (New York, 1972).

Wiebe, Robert. *Businessmen and Reform* (Chicago, 1968).

Wiebe, Robert. *The Search for Order, 1877–1920* (New York, 1967).

Zink, Harold. *City Bosses in the United States: A Study of Twenty Municipal Bosses* (Durham, N.C., 1930).

Chapter 8

Bronner, Simon J. (ed.) *Consuming Visions: Accumulation and Display of Goods in America, 1880–1920* (New York, 1989).

Horowitz, Daniel. *The Morality of Spending: Attitudes toward the Consumer Society in America, 1875–1940* (Baltimore, 1985).

Lacey, Robert. *Ford: The Men and the Machine* (Boston, 1986).

Leach, William. *Land of Desire: Merchants, Power, and the Rise of a New American Culture* (New York, 1993).

Lears, Jackson. *Fables of Abundance: A Cultural History of Advertising in America* (New York, 1994).

Lewis, David L. *The Public Image of Henry Ford* (Detroit, 1976).

Strasser, Susan. *Satisfaction Guaranteed: The Making of the American Mass Market* (New York, 1989).

Sward, Keith. *The Legend of Henry Ford* (New York, 1972).

Tedlow, Richard. *New and Improved: The Story of Mass Marketing in America* (New York, 1990).

Young, James Harvey. *Pure Food: Securing the Federal Food and Drugs Act of 1906* (Princeton, 1989).

Young, James Harvey. *The Toadstool Millionaires: A Social History of Patent Medicines before Federal Regulation* (Princeton, 1961).

Epilogue

Barber, Benjamin R. *Jihad vs. McWorld: How Globalism and Tribalism Are Reshaping the World* (New York, 1995).

Hunter, James Davison. *Culture Wars: The Struggle to Define America* (New York, 1991).

Marchand, Roland. *Advertising the American Dream: Making Way for Modernity, 1920–1940* (Berkeley, Calif., 1985).

Marchand, Roland. *Creating the Corporate Soul: The Rise of Public Relations and Corporate Imagery in American Big Business* (Berkeley, Calif., 1998).

Twitchell, James B. *AdCult USA: The Triumph of Advertising in American Culture* (New York, 1996).

Index